Touchstones of Tradition

Touchstones of Tradition:

Insights from the Material Culture of

Miccosukee and Seminole People

Editor

William H. Marquardt

2023

Published by Southern Yellow Pine (SYP) Publishing

4351 Natural Bridge Rd.

Tallahassee, FL 32305

This book commemorates a century of cooperation and consultation between the Florida Museum of Natural History, the University of Florida, and the Miccosukee and Seminole people of South Florida, 1923-2023. All chapters were inspired by objects in the ethnographic collections of the Florida Museum. The contents, opinions, and interpretations expressed in this book are those of the individual authors and editor and do not necessarily reflect the views and opinions of the Florida Museum of Natural History, the University of Florida, or Southern Yellow Pine Publishing nor does the mention of brands or trade names constitute endorsement. This book is not a publication of the Florida Museum of Natural History, and no University of Florida funds were involved in its manufacture.

ISBN-13: 978-1-59616-128-3

Library of Congress Control Number: 2023939641

Printed in the United States of America

First Edition May 2023

Contents

Editor's Preface

This book is inspired by objects, specifically certain objects in the Florida Ethnographic Collection within the Anthropology division of the Florida Museum of Natural History and, to an extent, similar objects in other museums and private collections around the world. What is ethnography? Let us characterize it as the accumulation and conservation of information about ethnic groups and define an ethnic group as a cluster of people who share beliefs and practices and who recognize among themselves a shared ancestry or lived history.

Today, two Native American tribes in South Florida are federally recognized. A smaller population of independent or "traditional" Indian people choose to belong to neither tribe. The government-recognized entities are the Seminole Tribe of Florida (founded 1957) and the Miccosukee Tribe of Indians of Florida (founded 1962). Two different languages are spoken. Most members of the Seminole Tribe speak the Mikasuki language, or *i:laponki*. The Mikasuki-speakers (*i:laponathli*) make up some seventy percent of the two recognized tribes. The other language spoken among South Florida Indian people is Muscogee, or Creek. The Muscogee-speakers (*ci:saponathli*) live mainly at the Brighton Reservation, northwest of Lake Okeechobee. Many South Florida natives also speak English.

This is not a book about the complex history of South Florida Indian people. Much has been written about that subject, and the interested reader is invited to consult references to this topic in the individual chapters as well as the respective websites of the Miccosukee and Seminole tribes. This book is instead about material culture and the insights we can gain by studying it. By material culture we mean objects made or used by people. The material culture of the Seminole and Miccosukee is unique and widely recognized. It carries elements of tradition dating directly back to the people who thrived in the southeastern United States before the arrival of Europeans, yet it endures today, evolving and changing among twenty-first century Indian people.

Items made and used by Seminole/Miccosukee people are included in museum collections throughout the world, as well as in the museums of Native people themselves. One of the largest and most comprehensive museum collections of Seminole/Miccosukee objects is the Florida Museum's Florida Ethnographic Collection (FEC). The Florida Museum is the official natural history museum of Florida. The collection and care of objects from Florida's Native Americans is specifically mandated in its enabling legislation. Specifically, the Museum is required by law to

collect and maintain a depository of biological, archaeological, and *ethnographic* specimens and materials in sufficient numbers and quantities to provide within the state and region a base for research on the variety, evolution, and conservation of wild species; the composition, distribution, importance, and functioning of natural ecosystems; and the distribution of prehistoric and historic archaeological sites and *an understanding of the aboriginal and early European cultures that occupied them.* (Florida Statutes 1004.56, emphasis added)

Museums are valued sources of information on Native culture and history. When appropriate, some objects curated in museum collections are included in exhibits and other educational programs. Curated collections are visited and studied by scholars, including Native Americans. Until my retirement in 2018, it was my privilege to care for and enhance the FEC in my role as Curator of South Florida Archaeology and Ethnography.

One of the most comprehensive and historically significant private collections of North American Indian art was accumulated by Keith and Sara Reeves, residents of Winter Park, Florida. Keith is retired architect. Both he and his wife Sara were intensely interested in Native American culture and in fact Sara was adopted into the Hopi tribe. Between 2008 and 2019, they generously donated Native American objects to the Museum's collections, including a number from Florida. In 2018 the Reeves proposed to subsidize the research of five scholars, one each year for five years, to study some aspect of the FEC. They asked me to choose and invite the scholars, coordinate their efforts, and edit the findings at the conclusion of the five-year period. This book is the result. Unfortunately, Sara Reeves died of cancer in April 2022. She was a passionate supporter of this work. The five scholars and I respectfully dedicate this book to her memory.

A diversity of research topics awaits the reader. In Chapter 1, Sandra Starr contributes a history of turban-wearing among Natives of South, Middle, and North America, culminating in the practice among eighteenth, nineteenth, and twentieth-century Creeks, Seminoles, and Miccosukees. In Chapter 2, Brent Weisman presents a detailed study of the clothing worn by a Seminole warrior in 1857 during the Third Seminole War. In Chapter 3, Stacey Huber describes and compares two rare Seminole "long coats" from the 1820s-1840s, then places them in context with similar garments in the collections of other museums. In Chapter 4, Patsy West describes and contextualizes the development of Seminole/Miccosukee arts through the craft guild operated by Edith Boehmer and the Glade Cross Mission directed by Deaconess Harriet Bedell. In Chapter 5, Austin Bell provides historical background and a classification of the iconic and beloved Seminole/Miccosukee dolls that were first made to supplement income at "tourist camps" operated by Mikasuki-speaking Seminoles in the early twentieth century. Chapter 6 serves as an epilogue, in which I highlight 100 years of collaboration between the Florida Museum of Natural History and the Native American tribes of South Florida. The statements and interpretations in this book are those of the individual authors and do not necessarily reflect the views of the University of Florida.

In addition to my sincere appreciation of Keith and Sara's support of this project, I offer my thanks to Gina Bliss Smith for her book design and layout; to Kristen Grace, Florida Museum photographer, for excellent production of images from the collection; and to South Florida Collections Manager Jennifer Green and her predecessor Karen Walker for assistance with object research. Karen also kindly proofread the entire book and offered valuable suggestions. It was a pleasure working with all five scholars whose chapters appear in this book, and I hope readers will find their contributions as fascinating as I do. Finally, I thank the many Miccosukee and Seminole tribal members I have spoken with over the years for their patience with my questions, their willingness to help me understand their world, and their genuine good will. For those I had the pleasure of getting to know well, thank you for your friendship.

Gainesville, Florida, March 31, 2023

Contributors

Austin Bell holds degrees in Anthropology (B.A.) and Museology (M.A.) from the University of Florida. He is also a graduate of the Smithsonian's Summer Institute in Museum Anthropology. He serves as Curator of Collections at the Marco Island Historical Society and holds an appointment as a Consulting Scholar to the Penn Museum. He is the author of *Marco Island* and *The Nine Lives of Florida's Famous Key Marco Cat.*

Stacey Huber is a 2015 graduate of the University of Nebraska-Lincoln, History of Textiles and Quilt Studies Master of Arts program. For her M.A. thesis project, she curated the exhibit "#Nativemade: Seminole and Miccosukee Patchwork" at the International Quilt Study Center in Lincoln, Nebraska. The exhibit focused on how social media is influencing the way Seminole and Miccosukee tribal members share their native patchwork craft traditions. After graduating, Stacey worked for 6 years as an assistant collections manager for the Florida Ethnographic Collection at the Florida Museum of Natural History.

William Marquardt is Curator Emeritus of South Florida Archaeology and Ethnography at the Florida Museum of Natural History. He holds the Ph.D. degree in anthropology from Washington University, St. Louis. Before his retirement in 2018, he undertook archaeological fieldwork in New Mexico, Kentucky, South Carolina, Georgia, Florida, and Burgundy (France). He co-founded the Randell Research Center at Pineland and was the curator of the Florida Museum's Hall of South Florida People and Environments.

Sandra Starr received an M.A. degree in Museum Studies from the University of Florida. Her studies were focused on the material culture of the precolumbian indigenous people of the Western Hemisphere. She curated an exhibition for the Florida Museum of Natural History of items drawn from the 3600 objects within the Pearsall collection of American Indian art, on display from 2003 through 2007. Following this she served for 11 years in the Department of Research at the Smithsonian Institution's National Museum of the American Indian.

Brent Weisman earned his Ph.D. at the University of Florida. He worked as a state lands archaeologist for the Florida Division of Historical Resources before moving to the University of South Florida in 1995. His research and teaching focused on North American Indian histories, cultures, and archaeologies, historical archaeology, museum practice, Florida archaeology, and public archaeology. Brent's publications include two books on Florida Seminole and Miccosukee topics and, most recently, the co-edited volume *We Come for Good: Archaeology and Tribal Historic Preservation at the Seminole Tribe of Florida.* He retired in 2015 and is now Professor Emeritus of Anthropology.

Patsy West was curator, Historical Association of Southern Florida, Miami. She holds the B.A. degree from Florida State University and is the creator and director of the Seminole/Miccosukee Archive. She has been involved in independent projects with both the Seminole and Miccosukee tribes; created a History Series for the *Seminole Tribune;* taught K-12 at the Tribe's charter school; and aided in opening Ah-Tah-Thi-Ki Museum. In 1989, she organized the "Patchwork and Palmettos Symposium" at the Fort Lauderdale Museum of Art. She is the author of two books with the University Press of Florida and two photographic books with Arcadia Press.

1

Turbans and Tradition: Southeastern Indians in New World Negotiations

Sandra L. Starr

The Florida Museum of Natural History holds in its collections contemporary examples of Seminole/Miccosukee male headwear referred to as turbans (Figures 1a, 1b). The turban shown in Figure 1a once belonged to medicine leader Doctor Tiger (Abiagee) (ca.1853-1947) and is at least eighty years old. At first glance, it appears to be a simply made device of colored cotton fabric wrapped around a cardboard form.

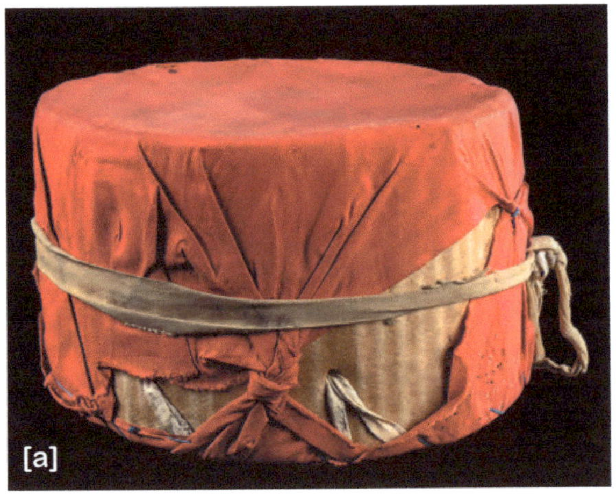

Now well-worn and faded, it may once have been encircled by a metal band serving as a crown-like decoration. A small hole in the edge of the crown suggests that it was once adorned with a feather. The turban in Figure 1b was made and worn by tribal cultural and spiritual leader Jimmie O'Toole Osceola, Panther Clan (1925-2005), whose creation of patchwork-style designs gives personal meaning to his use of the "fire" pattern with particular bird plumes indicating the power of his office.

But these contemporary turbans do not themselves inform us of the depth of historic and even precolumbian turban traditions. In fact, the turban as indigenous headwear in the Western Hemisphere

can be found across 3000 years as a signifier of group identity, social status, a protection from weather, a carrying device, as well as an indicator of leadership, with feather color or origin carefully selected to reflect the attributes of a particular bird (Krech 2009:201), and among the Creek as a signal for an intention of war or peace (Krech

[a]

[b]

Figure 1. *(a) Turban belonging to Doctor Tiger, Miccosukee. Collected by John Goggin from Deaconess Bedell, 1950s. Florida Museum of Natural History, cat. no. 92901. (b) Turban created in 1996 by Jimmie O'Toole Osceola, Panther Clan (1925-2005), with "fire design" patchwork and ostrich feathers. Gift of I. S. K. Reeves V and Sara W. Reeves. Florida Museum of Natural History, cat. no. 2019-19-1.*

2009:122-123). The evolution of contemporary Florida Seminole/Miccosukee turbans such as these brings a story of long-distance migration, the establishment of thriving precolumbian southeastern U.S. chiefdoms, the advent of the European invasion onto the soil of today's North America, subjugation and deception, and forced removal from established homelands.

According to Creek tribal elders, the Muscogee Creek originally migrated north out of an area of Northern Mexico known today as Texas, crossed the Red River, and traveled eastward to become founders of Mississippian-era mound-building chiefdoms (Muscogee Creek Nation 2018; Justin Giles, personal communication, 2018). The significance of Seminole/Miccosukee/Creek turbans as headwear continued throughout the time of the unification of the Muscogee as a confederacy as they confronted increasing threats from a land-seeking colonial federal government in North America, and as a signal of leadership during twentieth-century military negotiations. They remain a sign of tribal identity into the twenty-first century.

Documenting Evidence of Ancient Turbans

The cultural value of indigenous objects in the Western Hemisphere is difficult to discern because ritualistic and ceremonial meanings of cultural material were not written down but rather spoken from adult to child as sacred gifts passed along as correctly and precisely as first heard. Without the use of alphabets for writing,

origin stories and accounts of daily life, attire, and ceremony were illustrated on walls, ceramics, metals, stone, and wood, as well as woven within the fibers of baskets and textiles to be left for today's researchers to decipher.

Fortunately, efforts were made by European explorers and curiosity-seekers to document the cultures of the Indians of the Western Hemisphere through diaries, illustrations, and map details. These people included land-planning engineers, naturalists, ethnologists, and – later – photographers. These documents, both written and visual, indicate that turban-wearing was common, even if not fully understood. Because of further efforts by archaeologists, evidence of the turban as a prestigious object within the ancient coastal peoples of Chile and Peru, as an indicator of hereditary kingship within the precolumbian Maya of Central America and the Yucatán, and as headgear for commoner and elite alike throughout precolumbian Mexico can be substantiated.

Earliest Turbans Served as Group and Individual Identity

Andean Turbans as Group and Individual Identity

The Atacama Desert covers the entire far northern area of Chile up to the border of today's Peru. In their exhibit catalog *Chile before Chile,* The Museo Chileno de Arte Precolombino discusses the turban customs of the ancient Atacama Desert peoples. In a section titled "Talking through your

Hat," anthropologist and curator José Berenguer Rodríguez concludes that

"Tell me what you wear on your head and I will tell you who you are," seems to have been the motto of the Far North region, where for more than 3000 years turbans, caps, helmets, and hoods that protected their wearers from the harsh desert climate also indicated their social status or membership in a particular ethnic group. Based on their presence in ancient tombs, these head coverings also accompanied their owners on their journey to the great beyond. (Rodríguez 2013:36) (Figure 2)

Studies show a direct correlation between the rise of Northern Andean textile skills and the addition of camelid (llama) hair and human hair to turbans

Figure 2. *Turban attributed to sites of the fishing societies of Camarones in the Arica region of northern coastal Chile, ca. 2000 BC with coastal bird feathers, human hair, and wool skeins. Photograph courtesy of David Bernstein, David Bernstein Pre-Columbian Art Gallery, NY, object 91283B.*

Figure 3. *Wool skein turban with accessories, Faldas del Morro, Chile ca. 900-400 BC. From the permanent exhibition, "Chile before Chile" at the Chilean Museum of Precolumbian Art, Santiago, 2014, mchap/dscy 1980.*

Figure 4. *Turban, Paracas, Peru, ca. 100 BC-AD 200. Photograph by Daniel Giannoni, National Museum of the Archaeology, Anthropology, and History of Peru, Lima (Ministerio de Cultura del Perú. Museo Nacional de Arqueología, Antropología e Historia del Perú), 01.000376.00.*

on the coast as an act of conspicuous display of social status and sophistication. "[I]t seems clear that 'hair' (human and animal), was, as a privileged substance, symbolically and socially manipulated" (Gallardo 1993:13). The stunning turban in Figure 3 was created between 900 and 400 BC by the ancient Faldas del Morro people in the Arica Region of northern Chile. Another Chilean example (not shown) is found at the Museo Arqueológico San Miguel de Azapa in Northern Chile, created in the same style of fiber cordage but adorned with pelican feathers, an example of "3500 years of yarn skein 'turban' headdresses," ones created from the "gatherings of hand-knotted skeins of dyed wool crowned with important feathers" (Peters 2004).

Clark and Rodman note in their paper, "Ancient Andean Headgear: Medium and Measure of Cultural Identity," that "the elaboration of headgear probably is, and always has been, the most universal means of visually communicating individual and group identity. While headgear may function basically as head protection, style, tradition, and social context determine the forms of headgear that evolve." The authors also note that at the time of the Conquest, Spanish chroniclers "repeatedly commented upon the diversity of headdresses worn by different groups subsumed under the Inca Empire, which made it easy to distinguish one group from another" (Clark and Rodman 1994:293-295, 298). The Chilean Museum of Pre-Columbian Art (2018) notes that the most notable and characteristic of the burial attire of an elite male member of Paracas society of coastal Peru at 300 BC-AD 100 was "the turban, which was made from thick skeins of camelid wool… A long band of cloth wound around the head like a turban (Figure 4) and sometimes decorated with a plume of feathers." The addition of significant feathers to turbans would endure into the twenty-first century in North America.

Turbans and Power in the Maya Empire at AD 776

Far north of Paracas, Peru, at the southernmost part of the Maya Empire in Honduras, the ancient archaeological site of Copán held its sacred places within an impenetrable rainforest. An elite meeting place for the gathering of the royal hierarchy at AD 776 reveals a carved-relief altar (Figures 5a, 5b) depicting an entire genealogy of sixteen kings, all of them of a single dynastic family, and lids of incense burners holding ceramic images of these magistrates (Figure 6). Four generations of rulers were documented by the significance of their turbans. "The turban worn by these figures marks them as royal personages, as is the case for all of the rulers depicted on Altar Q" (Bell et al. 2004:109). "They wear turbans (the exclusive headdress of the Copánecs)" (Baudez 2015:26) and "…at Nim Li Punit … the kings wear the Copán turban headdress" (von Schwerin 2011:277, citing Martin and Grube 2000 and Schele and Mathews 1998). "Unlike Palenque and other sites, when rulers of Copán received the headband, … [they were referring] to the distinctive woven cloth turbans that were a marker of Copánec identity" (Schele and Newsome 1991:5). "Although the specific style of the turban may be unique to Copán, its function was identical to the headbands and headdresses of other polities. It could act as both an indicator of Copánec identity and a device to identify individuals…" (Wright 2011:179) (Figure 7).

There is some indication that the turbans were made of cotton gauze and their shape maintained

Figure 5. (a) (detail) Four turbaned rulers depicted at Altar Q (west side), Copán, Honduras, illustrating the passing of the royal scepter to the next in succession of 16 dynastic rulers, Copán AD 446 to ca. 882. (b) (detail) Four more turbaned rulers of 16 represented at Altar Q, Copán, Honduras. Photo by Adalberto Vega from Copán Ruinas, Honduras Flickr, Creative Commons.

Figure 6. Incensario (incense burner) lids. Museum of Archaeology, Copán, Honduras. Mayaruins.com, Copán Village, Creative Commons.

with the fluid of the yucca plant leaf. "The use of [yucca] starch by the Maya is attested to by numerous representations of persons wearing what appear to be starched netting or gauze headdresses" (Urban and Schortman 1986:307). This observation agrees with those of both Christopher Columbus in the Caribbean and Hernando de Soto in today's state of Alabama, both places where yucca flourishes, comparing the turbans they saw there to the turbans of the Moors whom they had witnessed being driven out of Spain. Yucca also flourishes in Florida, where the twentieth-century Seminole would later wear a similar tightly wrapped turban of concen-tric circles of cloth as to have it seem to extend out as a sun hat (Figures 8 and 9).

The Flamboyant Kingly Court of Bonampak at AD 790

Looking toward the north into the state of Chiapas located at the Guatemala/Southern Mexico border, a place known for extensive early trade networks, there stands an archaeological site known as Bonampak, holding murals created ca. AD 790. They reveal "scenes of kingly accession and celebration, brutal warfare, and acts of self-sacrifice" (Smithsonian National Museum of the American Indian 2012) and provide clear insight into the regalia of the Maya court and nobles, all adorned with flamboyant turbans (Figure 10).

Teotihuacan-Era Mexico and Turban-Wearing

Scholars surmise that the glorious imperial trade and ceremonial center of Teotihuacan (ca. 200 BC-AD 900) may have been developed by the Maya, Zapotec, and Mixtec peoples, who would have transported their traditional turbans there on their heads. Turbans are found in the daily life of the men of the state of Nayarit in Western Mexico while engaged in a ballgame during the period 300 BC-AD 250 (Figures 11a, 11b). Evidence of turban headwear in ceramic figurines of this period in Mexico has also been documented by archaeologist James A. Ford, who attests that "The Early Classic Santa Cruz Phase examples (AD 200-600)

Figure 7. *Stone sculpture of the twelfth Maya ruler of Copán, Chan Imix K'awiil, "Smoke Jaguar" (AD 628-695). He wears a turban typical of Copán royalty rather than a ceremonial costume and headdress. Photo by Dennis Jarvis from Halifax, Canada – Honduras-0430, Wikipedia Commons.*

Figures 8 and 9. *(detail) Seminole men (Loxahatchee Seminole) at Jupiter Lighthouse in the 1880s. Photographs by Melvin Spencer, Lighthouse Keeper. Archaeological and Historical Conservancy, Inc., courtesy Robert Carr.*

wore turban headdresses" (Ford 1969:80). A funerary urn for a revered ancestor shows evidence of an elaborate turban (ca. AD 700) (Figure 12). Most impressive is a turban image in relief on stone said to be of one of two competing rulers confronting one another, feathers flying, on Stela 3 at the Olmec site of La Venta (AD 400-900) (Figure 13).

Figurines capturing every detail of the dress and accouterments of those deceased have been delicately rendered, including the graciousness and sophistication of dignitaries' turbans (Figure 14).

Turbans in Mississippian-Period North America

Contact of both benign and ill-willed foreign observers from fifteenth and sixteenth-century Europe with the Western Hemisphere enabled written and illustrated documentation of the ancient indigenous peoples of the Americas. The Late Woodland and Mississippian cultures in the southeastern part of North America from AD 800 to 1600 were part of the era of undocumented societies, but their art and architecture continued to carry their histories and they hold some keys to identifying the ancient traditions of turban headwear.

In observing the turban's leap from ancient Mexico and the Maya Yucatán, it appears that the mound-building societies may have also designated the cacique, chief priest, or headman as the person chosen for the most ornamentally elaborate turban. Evidence of this inference is seen in present-day Georgia in the artifacts of the Etowah mound site, populated from about AD 950 to 1450. The word Etowah is a word transliterated from the Mvskoke *"etvlwv"* or *"etalwa"* (Martin and Mauldin 2000:41). The Muscogee (Creek) people themselves believe they "are descendants of a remarkable culture that, before 1500 AD, spanned the entire region known today as the Southeastern United States.

Figure 10. (detail) Maya murals at archaeological site Bonampak, Southern Chiapas, Mexico, illustrating the story of the last ruling family of Bonampak under Chan Muwan and his wife Lady Rabbit, AD 790-792. Photographs by Ryanacandee Flickr, Creative Commons; Steve Silverman Flickr, Creative Commons, and MayaRuinas.blog.

The Jaina Island Royal Burials: AD 800-1200

Contemporaneous with the Late Woodland-Early Mississippian cultures of North America, Maya elite male and female nobles were being buried at Jaina Island off the northern coast of Campeche, Yucatán, during the Late Classic period, AD 800-1200.

[a]

[b]

Figure 11. (a) Nayarit, West Mexico, ball-court model, ca. 200 BC-AD 500. Courtesy Los Angeles County Museum of Art, The Proctor Stafford Collection, purchased with funds provided by Mr. and Mrs. Allan C. Balch, M.86.296.34, www.lacma.org. (b) Nayarit ballplayer, West Mexico, polychrome ceramic (terracotta) figure, Western Mexico, ca. 300 BC-AD 200. Courtesy Minneapolis Institute of Art, The John R. Van Derlip Fund 47.2, Public Domain.

Early ancestors of the Muscogee constructed magnificent earthen pyramids along the rivers of this region as part of their elaborate ceremonial complexes" (Muscogee Creek Nation 2018). The Florida Seminole and Miccosukee tribes are derivatives of the Muscogee Creek and it is likely that their traditional use of turbans can be traced to this ancestral connection. A human effigy found at the Etowah site, dated to about AD 1250-1375, is wearing a simple turban-like head wrap.

During the 1500s, Indian people of the Americas were perceived variously by Europeans as novelties, spectacles, and possible sources of labor while in pursuit of grander things: gold and land. A player in the devastation of the last of the grand mound-building peoples was Hernando de Soto in his search for gold along the Coosa, Tallapoosa, and Alabama rivers in 1540. Hoping that the "savages" who lived there would show him the way, Soto came upon the town of Athahachi, where he encountered the tall and imposing Tascaluza, overseer of the province of Mabila (Lewis 2013:18). A diary entry by Soto's private secretary, Rodrigo

Rangel, reveals what may be the first written reference to a turban in the New World:

On Sunday, the tenth of October, the Governor entered in the town of Tuscalusa, which was called Athahachi, a new town; and the cacique was on a balcony that was made on a mound to one side of the plaza, about his head a certain headdress like an almaizar, worn like a Moor, which gave him an appearance of authority, and a blanket of feathers down to his feet, very authoritative, seated upon some high cushions, and many principals of his Indians with him. He was of as tall a stature as that of Antonico of the guard of the Emperor our lord, and of very good proportions, a very well built and noble man. (Clayton et al. 1995; translation by John E. Worth; see Figure 15)

When referring to the "almaizar," Rangel was likening it to those turbans they had witnessed being worn by the Moors recently ousted from Spain in 1492. An almaizar is translated from Spanish as "the turban or toque that the Arabs use to cover, protect or adorn the head," but with deeper study the word alludes to a gauze-like cloth of linen (flax) worn by the Moors, an interesting incident of eastern meeting western turban traditions.

Hernando de Soto's observation may *not* have been the first turban-sighting in the New World because Christopher Columbus, upon encountering the indigenous people of Trinidad in 1498, wrote in his diary, "...y traian la cabeza atada con

Figure 12. *(detail) Urn, State of Oaxaca, southwest coastal Mexico, ca. 700 BC-AD 1560. Courtesy of The British Museum, Am.1946.19.7, Creative Commons.*

Figure 13. *(detail) Olmec relief sculpture, La Venta, Mexico, archaeological site, Stela 3, Tabasco. Olmec peoples inhabited the coast of Veracruz and Western Tabasco on the Gulf of Mexico ca. 1200–400 BC, Creative Commons.*

un panuelo de algodon tejido a labores y colores, el cual creia yo que era almaizar" ("Their heads were bound round with cotton scarves elaborately worked with colours, which resembled the Moorish head-dresses") (Major 1847:116). Thus, Christopher Columbus also made note of the likeness of the turbans he encountered on the heads of the indigenous people of Trinidad to those of the Moors. Ironically, three hundred years later in the early 1800s, representatives of the southeastern Indians of North America would actually have occasion themselves to be face-to-face at Federal negotiating tables with turbaned representatives of the Ottoman Turkish Moors of Tunis.

End-of-Era Mound Builders Retain Their Turban Tradition

John Lawson was an English naturalist and writer who explored the Blue Ridge foothills in 1711. His description of the Keowee people of that region matches the description of the Kiawa/Okonee people written by the chroniclers of Hernando de Soto 170 years before, stating that they were extremely tall, and that they wore turbans. A link to the Muscogee/Creek/Seminole turban tradition can be inferred here according to Oconee history because original Kiawa town names can be translated by modern Creek dictionaries. Also, their province originally included Etalwa (Etowah). Both the Oconee and the Kiawa had claim to be the descendants of the people who built Etalwa, that is, the ancestors of the Muscogee Creeks.

Earliest visual documentation of turbans that connect the mound-builders to the Muscogee Creek is seen in a ca. 1720-1728 drawing by French naturalist and historian Antoine-Simon Le Page du Pratz (1718). His illustration titled "Le Transport du Grand Soleil" (Figure 16) shows

Figure 14. *Whistle in the form of a seated female dignitary, Mexico, Campeche, Jaina Island, Late Classic Maya, 600-900 AD, earthenware - De Young Museum - DSC00678.JPG by Daderot, Creative Commons.*

Figure 15. *Bronze door panel of Montgomery, Alabama, Department of Archives and History, depicting an encounter between conquistador Hernando de Soto and Mississippian Chief Tuscaloosa (Tascaluza). The George F. Landegger Collection of Alabama Photographs in Carol M. Highsmith's America. Library of Congress, Prints and Photographs Division.*

the Great Sun, ruler of the Natchez society in Mississippi, being carried in a litter by his servants to the Great Corn festival. The litter-bearers wear a simple wrapped headgear while the Great Sun wears the ornate turban. Some scholars believe that Le Page du Pratz may have misperceived the total power of the Natchez cacique in that the Natchez were simply part of a larger confederacy of tribes. According to today's Natchez Nation (Barnett 2018), "the ancient Natchez were a precursor and confederator of the 'original' Muscogee (Creek) Confederacy." "The French

observed the Great Sun, a Natchez chief, in his role as ceremonial leader and assumed that he was the ruler of the Natchez nation. In fact, however, political power in the Natchez confederacy was distributed among the chiefs of five villages or settlement districts" (Barnett 2018).

European Gift-Giving Fosters Turban Transformation

The first European visitors, both curious and destructive, came prepared to cajole the New World people by offering them gifts. De Soto's mission was gold, not land, but the later Dutch, English, French, and Spanish had other long-term settlement plans in mind. In 1609, Henry Hudson, commissioned by the Dutch East India Company, sailed his ship *Half Moon* into Chesapeake Bay

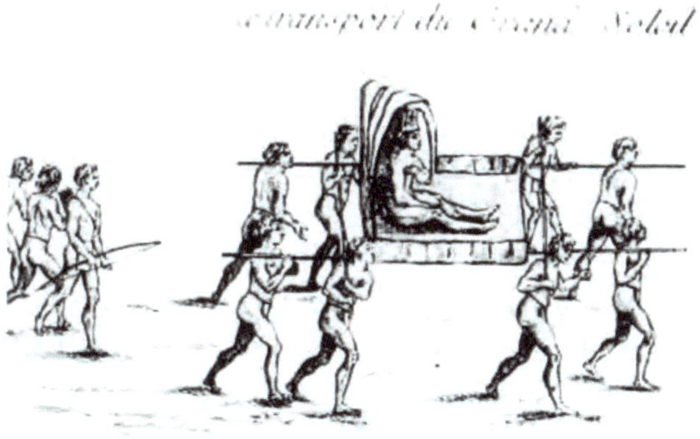

Figure 16. *(detail) Le Transport du Grand Soleil [The Great Sun]. Both holy man and king, he is carried to a corn harvest festival in his litter wearing his royal turban. Mississippian Natchez culture, AD 700-1730s. Sketch by Antoine Le Page du Pratz for his eyewitness 1785 account, The History of Louisiana. Library of Congress Rare Book and Special Collections Division, Washington, DC. Control No. 2001695747.*

Figure 17. *(detail) Penn's Treaty with the Indians, 1662, by Benjamin West, 1771. Pennsylvania Academy of the Fine Arts, Philadelphia. Public Domain, Wikipedia Commons.*

and up the river later to be named after him trading steel knives, hatchets, and beads for Native corn, bread, oysters, and fur pelts (Englar 2008:4). He was followed by William Penn, who in 1682 traded "guns, clothing, pipes and tobacco, tools, glasses, needles, blankets, and bells" (Leiser 2005) for land, and all of Indian country felt the impact.

In Figure 17, William Penn's associates offer the Native people a bolt of plain muslin as the major gift, and a promise in their treaty that it be sent to them "forever," a promise still kept today. The new source of ready-made cloth presaged a total life-style change for indigenous Americans, and ever-more-sophisticated fabrics to come fed into their desire for more encultured turbans as signs of leadership in an increasingly complicated society,

reminiscent of that same desire in ancient precolumbian Chile and Peru.

In the South, the Cherokee welcomed the English in 1673 to Echota, the eastern Tennessee center of the Cherokee people, to establish trade relations. American Indians would now step into the power game by playing one contending European trading nation against another for what they had become accustomed to: weapons and items of prestige. "In one of his final letters as governor of Louisiana, Vaudreuil (Pierre de Riguad, Marquis de Vaudreuil, governor of French Louisiana) summarized the ways in which the material component of Choctaw

expressions of martial masculinity influenced French policy. Having confronted some headmen about why a number of their brethren continued to seek out the English, the Choctaw explained to him the importance of access to guns, ammunitions, paint, and *cloth* to their identities as true men" (Sparacio 2018:255; emphasis added). At 1752, Vaudreuil again wrote to Antoine Louis Rouillé, commissioner to the French East India Trading Company about the vanity of the Choctaw:

Being able to perform the masculine tasks of conspicuous display, hunting, and raiding would prove difficult in the absence of these

Figure 18. *Linen and cotton checked, sample book, 1767, New York City, Fair Use.*

trade goods, and since the French had "no means of gratifying" their demands, the Choctaws searched for alternative sources. (Sparacio 2018:255 quoting Vaudreuil to Rouillé, 28 January 1752)

Part of the "conspicuous display" was owning increasingly elaborate turbans made of European plaid wools, striped silks, and colorful, flowery calico scarfs, shawls, and sashes embellished with rare regional feathers, suitable for even-footing in New World negotiations (Figure 18).

Turbans at the New World Bargaining Table

The Southeast seemed open-for-the-taking by Europeans and Euro-Americans, who were in need of expansion and mindful of cross-Atlantic trade for commodities that their new Native friends could provide in kind. By the end of the eighteenth century, major land bargains would be negotiated between the U.S. President and Native envoys received by him from southeastern Indian confederacies. Increased non-Native interest in who these Native negotiators were and what they looked like produced important images drawn and painted for use as map detail illustrations, on broadsides, and in newspapers circulated both in America and across the Atlantic. This new image of the New World savage, one in full regalia with stylish turbans of East Indian, Turkish, French, and English fabrics, squarely positioned tribal elite at the negotiating table, although not for long.

As early as 1710, members of the Creek Confederacy began to be treated by Europeans as well as Colonial American powers as trading nations with the long-range goal of sealing the allegiance of the Indians in wars against trade competitors and against other Indian nations, as well as securing their particular commitment to be suppliers of Indian furs, hides, and pelts. British, Spanish, French, and colonial Americans all scrambled to curry their favor. European monarchs now expressed their eagerness to "civilize" their Indian "children" by bringing their state of undress into the stylish eighteenth century and invited them to London to make the point and encourage a treaty of dependence. In 1730, when Montoy of the Cherokee agreed to accept King George II as their protector, seven of the headmen were invited to visit the king at Windsor Castle, and the September 12, 1730 *London Daily Journal* reported that the Cherokee attested to the fact that the King "had put fine cloaths on their backs (pointing to the cloaths), and that they should never forget such kind dealings, but should declare the same to their countrymen; and thereupon the Prince laid the feather [likely a white bald eagle feather] with a bit of skin upon the table, saying, 'It should be as good as the Bible to bind the contract with King George'" (Norton 2002:1). This same report soon appeared in the December 8, 1730, issue of the *Pennsylvania Gazette*, further carrying the notion that the southern Indians were worldly and worthy negotiators.

In 1733, British General James Oglethorpe was dispatched by King George II to convince interlocutors of the Lower Creeks to allow the British to establish a colony to be named Savannah (Figure 19). The *Treaty of Savannah Articles of Friendship and Commerce* was precise. Among the articles was the agreement that the Creeks would trade only with them at the rates of payment in pelts that were carefully listed. Also, the Creeks would give the British all the lands for which "they have no use." And lastly, that the

Figure 19. *Oglethorpe with the Creek Indians in Georgia, 1733. Hargrett Rare Book and Manuscript Library, University of Georgia Libraries, Athens.*

Creeks would "give no encouragement to any other White People but themselves (the British) to settle among us (the Creeks), and that we will not have any correspondence with the Spaniards or French." Whether yearning for peace among the intruders, or a desire to advance their civilization in "dressing for success" in future politics, the Creek signatories to the 1733 Treaty of Savannah were willing to trade their deerskins from the hunt for European materials, among them new materials for stylish turbans:

> three yards of cadiz [the cheapest undyed striped checked or blue fabric imported to Britain from India and made or paid for in Cadiz, Spain], two yards strouds [a coarse woolen trade cloth], one yard plains [a sturdy wool textile also called negro cloth]"
> (Georgia Historical Quarterly 1920:15).

By 1762, another group of Upper Cherokee leaders had visited King George III in London, securing for the southern Indians a firm position within their respective towns concerning both international dealings and exotic couture. Keeping a flow of exotic European-manufactured silk, chintz, and calico textiles coming across the Atlantic ensured the fulfillment of the European demand back home for furs, hides, skins, and pelts. This grand scheme, one that was exacerbated by George Washington himself through his creation in the 1760s of an American factory system and the establishment of trading posts to deter foreign monopoly on business with the Indians, was fated to deplete the forests of Native food sources,

drive the Indians into debt, and eventually corner them into settling their debts with land (Nichols 2016:12-34). The advent of European gifts and trade goods changed the futures of the indigenous people forever. The tracking of this paradigm shift in the Southeast can clearly be seen by following the ever-more-"civilized" clothing styles of the Native peoples, especially their traditional turban styles and materials, as well as the endurance of the traditional significance of turbans as emblems of leadership in the Western Hemisphere.

Panton, Leslie and Company and Creek Trade Monopoly

The British-Scottish trading firm of Panton, Leslie and Company in Florida led the way to cornering the Creek trade by locating trading houses at both Pensacola and St. Augustine by 1776. By 1783 when Spain began to control Florida, Panton, Leslie and Company was given total control of the Indian trade in the area (Upchurch 1969:117-119). With important Creek connections working directly with the Creek towns, an enormous trade monopoly took hold within the Southeast. A new method of international commerce was devised through the use of mixed-blood Creeks as trading agents, such as Tustunnuggee Hutkee/ White Warrior (William McIntosh) (Figure 20). Son of a Creek mother and Tory-officer father; Red Eagle (William Weatherford) of Creek, French, and Scottish ancestry; and Alexander McGillivray, Hoboi-Hili-Miko (Good Child King), the son of an accomplished Scottish fur-trader father and Wind Clan French-Creek mother. The portrait of William McIntosh in British-Americanized

Figure 20. *(detail) William McIntosh (also known as Tustunnuggee Hutkee), a Creek chief, 1836-1844, by Thomas Loraine and James Hall, Public Domain.*

Figure 21. *(detail) A Boy in a Cape and Turban (Portrait of Prince Rupert of the Palatinate), grandson of James I, England), by Jan Lievens, Netherlands, 1631. www.theleidencollection. com/archive/; accessed August 26, 2019. The Leiden Collection, 1626.30, Inventory No. JL-104.*

Figure 22. *(detail) Portrait of Gentleman in Levantine [Turkish] Dress, Orientalist, after Giovanni Battista Lampi, late eighteenth century. Source: Darnley Fine Art 2022.*

Figure 23. *Seated Persian, red chalk drawing, Museum of Fine Arts, Boston, 65.2612. Copied after Antoine Watteau (French, 1684–1721), undated. Bequest of Forsyth Wickes— The Forsyth Wickes Collection, public domain. Louis XIV received Mohammad Reza Beg, an ambassador from Persia into the Hall of Mirrors at Versailles during the "Turquerie" fashion period.*

attire using European goods, and the incorporation of same concerning their traditional turbans with the addition of silver ornaments and headbands, clearly represents their new standing as international leaders throughout the late 1700s, creating a rising issue of power contention falling at the feet of George Washington nearing 1790.

Trade, Treaties, Turquerie, and Turbans

Contemporaneously, while the traditional southeastern indigenous turban headdress was being revolutionized through access to exotic trade cloth imports, British, French, and American leaders and diplomats as well as the socialites around them were falling under another turban fashion spell

known as "Turquerie" and "Orientalism" as a result of European trade alliances sought with Persia, Turkey, and the Ottoman Empire (Metropolitan Museum of Art 1968:223-239). Stories and souvenirs brought back by ambassadors and traders introduced the exotic art and culture of the "Turks" (Figures 21-25). Even while in the throes of impending war, women of a newly established social class in the American Colonies, formerly British subjects, continued to look to

Figure 24. *(detail) Portrait of Lady Elizabeth Howard (1701-1739), eldest daughter of Charles Howard, Third Earl of Carlisle, in Turkish costume, by George Knapton, ca. 1730. Pinterest. www.Gogmsite.Net/GrandLadies, Fair Use.*

Figure 25. *(detail) Lady Charlotte Susan Maria Bury, an English novelist whose publications included Self-indulgence: A Tale of the Nineteenth Century, 1812, reflective of the political and social times. Image 1802 or ca. 1810-1812 by Archibald Skirving. Source: Wikidata, open for downloading.*

Figure 26. *George III, artist unknown, late eighteenth century. National Portrait Gallery, London, D8005. Given by Henry Witte Martin, 186, Creative Commons.*

Figure 27. *"The Queen of Hearts Cover'd with Diamonds," Queen Charlotte, Consort of George III, 1786. Artist unknown. Library of Congress Control Number 2006689307.*

the British for high-society fashion trends. They quickly adopted the accouterments of Turquerie, and King George was the ultimate devotee (Figures 26-27). John Singleton Copley, artist to American presidents, encouraged the trend in his pre-Revolutionary War portraits of wealthy Colonial women where his sitters wore turbans, including the wife of General Thomas Gage (Figure 28). This cross-cultural fascination and imitation was visually documented by other acclaimed artists who moved among the indigenous societies as well as those of Philadelphia and Washington. In the final decade of this eventful

century, the divergent types of high-level turban-wearers, American, American Indian, European, and Ottoman Tunisian, would meet on an occasion of international intrigue and diplomacy, making for a profound mélange of "conspicuous display."

After the Revolution, George Washington was even more anxious to get the Creeks to agree to a land deal, so anxious that in 1790 he invited 24 representative leaders of the Upper, Middle, and Lower Creek Confederacy to come to New York City, which served as the Capital until one could be established in Philadelphia in 1792. Five were

Figure 28. *(detail) Margaret Kemble Gage, wife of General Thomas Gage, dressed in the Turquerie style, by John Singleton Copley, ca. 1771. Putnam Foundation, Timken Museum of Art, Public Domain.*

invited to dinner including the Muscogee Creek Alexander McGillivray, their chief negotiator, and four other headmen: Tuskatche Mico (Birdtail King), Hopothle Mico (Tallasee King), Stimafutchkee (Good Humor), and Hysac (The Woman's Man) (Figures 29-32). Popular portrait artist John Trumbull was at Washington's home to work on a large portrait of the first President. Not to disturb the discussion, Trumbull sat aside and sketched the only extant portraits documenting this occasion. Alexander McGillivray was not then or thereafter portrayed, although his signature (Figure 33) speaks for him and his presence as a highly educated figure worthy of representing the Creeks in negotiating with Washington (Starr 2012). The importance of Trumbull's sketches in preserving the detailed appearance of their turbans is invaluable (Brown and Cohen 2016).

The 1790 Treaty of New York (Appleton 2011) included a clause indicating the mood of the Federal government in dealing with the "Indian problem," a clause to enforce their "plan of civilization," including the learning of the skills of agriculture as an alternative to hunting, thus opening up their territories to new non-Native homesteading. Federal Indian Agent Benjamin Hawkins was sent to teach the Creeks (Figure 34) and he lived among them for twenty years. In the 1805 painting "Benjamin Hawkins and the Creek Indians" by an unknown artist, Hawkins speaks directly to an unnamed man dressed in an

Figure 29. *(detail) Stimafutchkee, or Good Humor, of the Coosades (Koasati) by John Trumbull, 1790. Source: The Indians of the Southeastern United States by John Reed Swanton, Smithsonian Bureau of American Ethnology, Bulletin 137, 1946, p. 1025.*

Figure 30. *(detail) Tuskatche Mico, or the Birdtail King of the Cusitahs by John Trumbull, 1790. New York Public Library Digital Collections. The Miriam and Ira D. Wallach Division of Art, Prints and Photographs, Public Domain.*

Figure 31. *(detail) Woman's Man, Hysac (Isaac) by John Trumbull, 1790. Source: The Indians of the Southeastern United States by John Reed Swanton, Smithsonian Bureau of American Ethnology, Bulletin 137, 1946, p. 1026.*

Figure 32. *(detail) Hopothle Mico, or the Talassee King of the Creeks by John Trumbull, 1790. New York Public Library Digital Collections. The Miriam and Ira D. Wallach Division of Art, Prints and Photographs, Public Domain.*

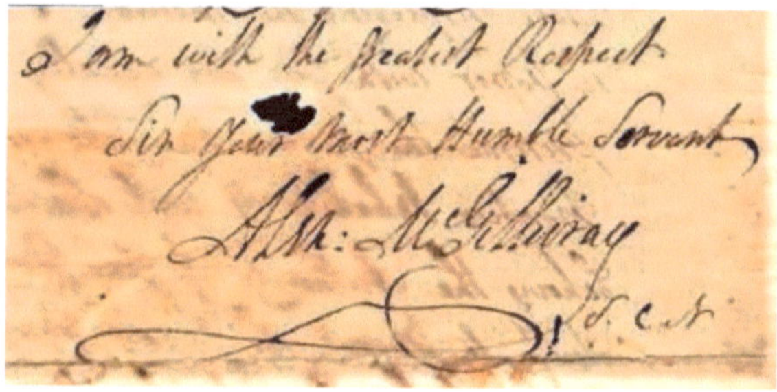
I am with the greatest Respect
Sir Your most Humble Servant
Alex: McGillivray

Figure 33. *Signature of Alexander McGillivray (Creek, Wind Clan) on a personal letter. Source: Papers of the War Department, Creative Commons.*

elaborate turban. When compared to a portrait of William Augustus Bowles (Figure 35), a non-Native American-born defender and self-proclaimed "Director General" of the Creek, here clad in ostrich-feathered turban, buckskins, and cape, they appear to be the same person.

Monticello Awash in Turbaned Guests

Meanwhile, back in Washington, the new President Jefferson was about to have an inundation of turban-headed delegates at his door, both foreign and domestic. While inheriting the tumultuous issues concerning the Creek and Cherokee treaties and delegating the imminent removal of the Southeastern Indians to the Office of Indian Trade (now appropriately within the War Department), another policy issue was coming to a crisis. After the Revolutionary War, the United States lost the protection of the British Navy. "The crisis with Tunis erupted when the USS *Constitution* captured Tunisian vessels attempting to run the American blockade of Tripoli" (Wilson 2003:2). These

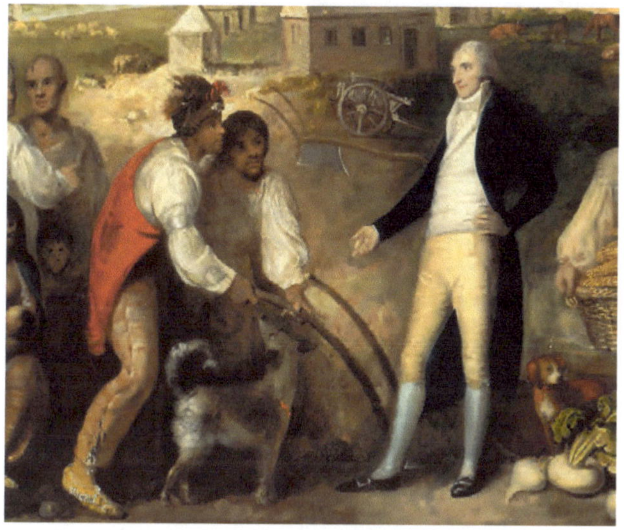

Figure 34. ***(detail) Benjamin Hawkins with the Creek Indians, artist unknown, 1805. Greenville County Museum of Art. Inventories of American Painting and Sculpture, Smithsonian American Art Museum, IAP 48000021, Public Domain.***

Barbary States were provinces of the "turban-wearing" Ottoman (Turkish) Empire along the coast of Africa. Thomas Jefferson sent in his best ships during 1803 to blockade the Barbary ports. The captain and crew of the USS *Philadelphia* were captured and taken as hostages for tribute (Figure 36). The Turks then insisted on sending an envoy to confront the President. Sidi Soliman Mellimelli and his attendants (Figure 37) stayed within the Washington, DC area for six months at federal expense, bringing an unexpected lift to the social season. At the same time, also vying for the president's attention were Cherokee leaders negotiating still another treaty, one they were pressured to sign, the Treaty with the Cherokee of 1806. The gathering of such a variety of exotic turbaned dignitaries drew large crowds of spectators and served to propel the turban as a fashion statement.

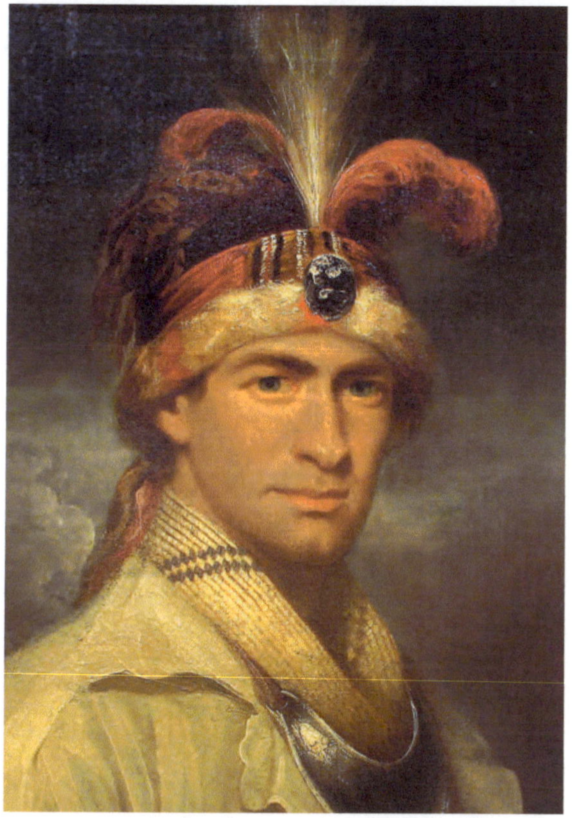

Figure 35. ***(detail) William Augustus Bowles by Thomas Hardy, 1790. State Archives of Florida, Florida Memory Florida Photographic Collection, RC06489.***

James Meigs wrote the following to the editor of the *Washington Intelligencer* that week of November 30, 1805: "Sir, The late arrival of a deputation of Cherokee chiefs [has] from their appearance excited considerable attention." And within the political elite, Dolley Madison (Figure 38), always looking to London and France for the current fashion, thereafter adopted the turban for all her occasions of state. While there, Mellimelli was invited to a dinner on December 9 at Jefferson's Monticello. Also invited was a delegation of Cherokee, Chickasaw, and Osage tribal

Figure 36. *U.S. Commodore William Bainbridge bringing tribute to the Dey of Algiers to avoid capture of U.S. merchant ships, 1800, by Henry Alexander Ogden, Creative Commons. Alamy Stock Photos, used by permission.*

The Creek Confederacy Splits Allegiances

Figure 37. *"Dealings with Mellimelli, Colorful Envoy from Tunis." A nineteenth-century engraving of Barbary State officials in ceremonial garb. Alamy Stock Photos, used by permission.*

leaders who were in Washington to negotiate a treaty. At the table were three cabinet members and Secretary of State James Madison (Sibley 2016:53). During the tension of that elite occasion, both John Jolly (also known as Ah ludi skiaka: Ooluntuskee or Col-lee or Jol-lee) (Figure 39) and his brother Tahlonteeskee signed the 1806 treaty, both being members of the delegation to Washington being coerced into more concessions for roads and settlements on Cherokee lands.

In November of 1811, Tecumseh (Figure 40), of mixed Shawnee and Creek descent and a leader in both the politics and wars erupting in the North, was so moved by the dire issues in the Southeast and the clear, inevitable fate of total land loss within his Creek ancestral territories, that he travelled there to rally them for the return to a single united confederation. He most surely traveled there in his traditional and emblematic turban, for artists who captured his portrait included it in most of their works. The Creeks were headed to war both with the Federal government and among themselves. "This Nativist uprising, which turned into the Creek War of

1813-1814, was, in every sense of the term, a civil war among the Creeks of Alabama" (Wickman 2006:51).

Southeastern leaders as delegates and negotiators representing their people now appeared like the United States statesmen with whom they were dealing. Etomme Tustennuggee (Figure 41) made a pivotal change in his personal policy and signed the 1821 Treaty of Indian Springs where more than four million acres of communally held Creek lands were ceded to Georgia. A counter argument in Washington in late 1825 resulting in

Figure 38. *Portrait of Dolley Madison ca. 1817, by Bass Otis. New York Historical Society, Public Domain.*

Figure 39. *(detail) Col-lee or Jol-lee, a Cherokee Band Chief by George Catlin, 1834. The Smithsonian American Art Museum, Gift of Mrs. Joseph Harrison, Jr., 1985.66.285, Fair Use.*

Figure 40. *Tecumseh , ca. 1812 (Creek/Shawnee). Engraving by Benson J. Lossing (1813–1891), copied from a sketch by Pierre Le Dru, and colored or copied by an anonymous artist. Painting by W.B. Turner. Metropolitan Toronto Library, J. Ross Robertson, T-16600. Thoughtco. com, Public Domain.*

the Treaty of Washington was attended by Yoholo Micco (Figure 42), where he also sat for his portrait. The internal division within Creek ranks is uniquely illustrated in 1827 by Basil Hall who positions the opposing Creek parties, Tastanaki Hopayi, Lower Creek, and Yoholo Micco, Upper Creek, both in formal attire and turbans, in facing chairs being monitored by a gun-toting Georgian squatter awaiting his land takeover opportunity (Figure 43).

There seems to be a striking shift in portraits of Southeastern Indians during the 1800s, as these Indians found themselves in the position of taking long trips to appeal personally to the leadership in Washington, DC. We are able to see the shift from sixteenth and seventeenth century illustrated impressions of Indians as other-worldly children, to Indians as elegant and intelligent citizens of their lands and worthy of being at the American table of nation-to-nation negotiations. Just as their mound-builder ancestors had understood the power of wearing and using exotic imports obtained through long-distance trading networks, so did the new Creek negotiators.

A Separate Seminole Nation Emerges

At this historic crossroads, a separate community of Maskókî (Creek) speakers fled southward along with Black slaves of landholders in South Carolina and Georgia. The Seminole Tribe of Florida today states that

Survivors of that devastating European intrusion amalgamated in the area that is now

18

Figure 41. *(detail) Tustennuggee Emathla (Jim Boy), or Etomme Tustennuggee, by Thomas McKinney and James Hall, ca.1836-1844. Smithsonian American Art Museum, object number 1985.66.1533.19, Fair Use.*

Figure 42. *Yoholo Micco, a Creek Chief, by Charles Bird King. Handcolored lithograph on paper. Smithsonian American Art Museum, 1985.66.153.314, Fair Use.*

Figure 43. *Chiefs of the Creek Nation and a Georgian Squatter. Lithograph by W. H. Lizars (William Home), and Basil Hall. Left, Tastanaki Hopayi (Little Prince), Lower Creek representative. Right, Yoholo Micco, Upper Creek representative. Pl. 28, 4th ed. Forty Etchings from Sketches Made from the Lucida Camera. New York Library Digital Collections, Public Domain.*

known as Florida. Early in the 18th century, the lives and homelands of many more indigenous peoples were similarly disrupted, this time by American colonization efforts. Many were Maskókî speakers, from Indian towns across Georgia and Alabama. Creek, Hitchiti, Apalachee, Mikisúkî, Yamassee, Yuchi, Tequesta, Apalachicola, Choctaw, and Oconee were joined by escaped slaves and others in the pursuit of better lives among the thick virgin forests, wide grass prairies and spring-fed rivers of interior Florida. They shared an instinct for survival and a commonality of

purpose: refusal to be dominated by the white man. The Spaniards called some of these indigenous Florida people cimarrones, or free people, because they would not allow themselves to be dominated by the Europeans. The word was taken into the Maskókî language and, by the mid-1800s, U.S. citizens referred to all Florida people as "Seminoles." (Seminole Tribe of Florida 2018)

The years that followed saw a series of winless wars forced upon the Seminole and a Removal Act led by Andrew Jackson in an effort to relocate all of

the so-called Five Civilized Tribes (Cherokee, Choctaw, Chickasaw, Creek, and Seminole) to today's Oklahoma (Missal and Missal 2004). Ten years later, at Fort Gibson (present-day Muscogee County, Oklahoma), Steeh-tcha-kó-me-co, Great King (called Ben Perryman) (Figure 44) and his brother Hol-te-mal-te-tez-te-neehk-ee (Sam Perryman) (Figure 45), Muscogee Creeks, were portrayed in their traditional turbans by George Catlin. These men were among many "recently removed from Georgia and Alabama to Arkansas, 70 miles west of the Mississippi. Present number 21,000; semi-civilized and agricultural" (Catlin 1848:276).

Figure 44. *(detail) Steeh-tcha-kó-me-co, Great King (called Ben Perryman), a Chief, by George Catlin, 1834. Smithsonian American Art Museum, 1985.66.288_1, Fair Use.*

Figure 45. *Hol-te-mal-te-tez-te-neehk-ee, Sam Perryman, Creek, by George Catlin, 1834. Smithsonian American Art Museum, gift of Mrs. Joseph Harrison, Jr., 1985.66.289, Fair Use.*

Figure 46. *(detail) Os-ce-o-lá, The Black Drink, a Warrior of Great Distinction, by George Catlin, 1838. Smithsonian American Art Museum, gift of Mrs. Joseph Harrison, Jr., 1985.66.301, Fair Use.*

furnished me by Dr. Weedon, the surgeon, who was by him, with the officers of the garrison, at Osceola's request: "about half an hour before he died he seemed to be sensible that he was dying; …he signified by signs that he wished me to send for the chiefs…whom I called in. He made signs…to go and bring his full dress which he wore in time of war…. He then called for his red paint…. His knife he then placed in its sheath under his belt, and he carefully arranged his turban on his head and his three ostrich plumes that he was in the habit of wearing in it. He made a signal for them to lower him down upon his bed…and in a moment smiled away his last breath without a struggle or a groan" (Annual Report of the Board of Regents of the Smithsonian Institution, 1886:219). (Figure 46)

Osceola's Turban Remembered

Artist George Catlin, clearly knowing the risk that Seminole warriors were enduring as captives at Fort Moultrie, stayed alongside their great leader, a very unwell Osceola, as long as he could. The next day, January 30, 1838, Osceola died in a manner which he himself determined. In a note on page 221 of vol. 2, *Catlin's Eight Years*, Catlin gives this account of Osceola's death:

From accounts which left Fort Moultrie a few days after I returned home, it seems that this ill-fated warrior died a prisoner the next morning after I left him, and the following very interesting account of his last moment was

Turbans Still a Tradition at 1840 and Beyond

By 1840, the camera had been developed to a point that it became the most efficient way to record what were thought of as the last days of the American Indian. Fortunately, not all artists were inclined to carry the cumbersome equipment. Heinrich Balduin Möllhausen, topographer and draftsman to Lt. A. W. Whipple's 1853 surveying expedition through southwestern United States along the 35th parallel, was one of these. His sketches of the Choctaw he encountered (Figure 47) show greater detail than any camera at that date could have captured of their continued wearing of traditional turbans into the second half of the nineteenth century, now embellished

Figure 47. *(detail) Choctaw Indians by Heinrich Balduin Möllhausen, engraving. Source: Whipple et al. 1855, p. 24.*

Figure 48. *(detail) Choctaw Indians by Heinrich Balduin Möllhausen, engraving. Source: Whipple et al. 1855, p. 25.*

Acknowledgments. I would like to acknowledge the generosity of Keith and Sara Reeves who made the publishing of this book possible; Dr. William H. Marquardt, whose tireless efforts to ensure that the soundness and clarity of this chapter might endure the test of time; and my son, Garrett Starr Lahan, whose assistance, moral support, and respect for American Indians always encourages me to move forward in efforts to research and write about them.

through imported European updates in cloth material as well as silver or tin headbands (Figure 48). Seminole men in their turbans were also sketched until possibly 1850 and then thereafter photographed throughout the twentieth century and into the twenty-first.

Two Seminole Turbans and the Aura of Museum Objects

The art of American Indians expresses more than just the creativity and purpose of the makers. It also serves to transport us to critical periods in American history when Native artists chose to continue to create beautiful things amid their lives of chaos, displacement, and poverty. Ultimately, each object serves to represent a unique spiritual victory over their oppression, as the interweaving

of foreign, and many times enemy materials into their own traditional art forms creates something new and distinctive in their own art history. In this chapter we have looked beyond the turbans belonging to Doctor Tiger and Jimmie O'Toole Osceola to the place they hold in traditional costume worldwide, as well as their political, social, and economic inferences in eighteenth and nineteenth-century American history. The survival of examples of Seminole/Miccosukee Indian turbans such as the ones we have considered, as well as other objects of regalia and lifeways, become the visual inspiration to contemporary Seminole/Miccosukee artists who work to reflect those ancestral styles, methods, and materials into their own personal expressions, assuring that their voices and traditions will continue to survive.

References

Annual Report
1886 *Annual Report of the Board of Regents of the Smithsonian Institution Showing the Operations, Expenditures, and Condition of the Institution to July 1885.* Part II. U.S. Government Printing Office, Washington, D.C.

Appleton, James L.
2011 Treaty of New York, 1790. *Encyclopedia of Alabama*, Electronic document, http://www.encyclopediaofalabama.org/article/h-1537, accessed March 20, 2018.

Barnett, James F., Jr.
2018 *Natchez Indians. The Mississippi Encyclopedia.* Electronic document, https://mississippiencyclo-pedia.org/entries/natchez-indians/, accessed December 26, 2018.

Baudez, Claude F.
2015 *Maya Sculpture of Copán: The Iconography.* University of Oklahoma Press, Norman.

Bell, Ellen E., Marcello A. Canuto, and Robert J. Sharer
2004 *Understanding Early Classic Copán.* University of Pennsylvania Museum of Archaeology and Anthropology, Philadelphia.

Brown, Virginia Pounds, and Linda McNair Cohen
2016 *Drawing by Stealth: John Trumbull and the Creek Indians.* NewSouth Books, Montgomery, Alabama.

Catlin, George
1848 *Catlin's Notes of Eight Years' Travels and Residence in Europe, with his North American Indian Collection*, Vol.1. Burgess, Stringer, New York.

Chilean Museum of Pre-Columbian Art
2018 *Chile's Indigenous People.* Electronic document, http://www.precolombino.cl/en/culturas-americanas/pueblos-originarios-de-chile/selk%C2%B4nam/, accessed December 25, 2018.

Clark, Niki R., and Amy Oakland Rodman
1994 Ancient Andean Headgear: Medium and Measure of Cultural Identity. In *Contact, Crossover, Continuity: Proceedings of the Fourth Biennial Symposium of the Textile Society of America*, p. 293. Textile Society of America, Inc., Los Angeles.

Clayton, Lawrence, Charles Hudson, John E. Worth, Eugene Lyon, Jeffery P. Brain, and John H. Hann
1995 *The De Soto Chronicles*, Volumes 1 and 2: "The Expedition of Hernando de Soto to North America in 1539-1543." The University of Alabama Press, Tuscaloosa. Electronic document, https://muse.jhu.edu/chapter/308321/pdf (accessed July 5, 2019).

Darnley Fine Art
2022 Electronic document: https://darnleyfineart.com/artwork/portrait-of-a-gentleman-in-levantine-dress/, accessed December 5, 2022.

Englar, Mary
2008 *Dutch Colonies in America.* Compass Point Books, Minneapolis.

Ford, James A.
1969 *Comparison of Formative Cultures in the Americas: Diffusion or the Psychic Unity of Man.* Smithsonian Contributions to Anthropology, Vol. 11. Smithsonian Institution Press, Washington, DC.

Gallardo, Francisco
1993 Wool as a Privileged Substance: Turbans, Power and Symbolism in the Formative Period of Northern Chile. In *Identity and Prestige in the Andes: Caps, Turbans and Diadems.* Museo Chileno de Arte Precolombino, Santiago.

Georgia Historical Quarterly
1920 Oglethorpe's Treaty with the Lower Creek Indians. *Georgia Historical Quarterly* 4(1):3-16, March, 1920. Electronic document, https://www.jstor.org/stable/pdf/40575623.pdf

Krech, Shepard
2009 *Spirits of the Air: Birds & American Indians in the South.* University of Georgia Press, Athens.

Le Page du Pratz, Antoine Simon
1718 *The History of Louisiana or of the Western Parts of Virginia and Carolina.* Electronic document, https://www.gutenberg.org/files/9153/9153-h/9153-h.htm, accessed July 17, 2018.

Leiser, Amy
2005 William Penn and Lenape Chief Tammany. Monroe County Historical Association. Electronic document, http://www.monroehistorical.org/articles_files/110105wmpenn.html, accessed September 12, 2018.

Lewis, Herbert J.
2013 *Clearing the Thickets: A History of Antebellum Alabama.* Quid Pro Books, New Orleans.

Major, Richard H., translator and editor
1847 *Select letters of Christopher Columbus with other Original Documents, Relating to his Four Voyages to the New World.* Bi-Lingual Edition. British Museum. The Hakluyt Society, London.

Martin, Simon, and Nikolai Grube
2000 *Chronicle of the Maya Kings and Queens: Deciphering the Dynasties of the Ancient Maya.* Thames and Hudson, London.

Martin, Jack, and Margaret M. Mauldin
2000 *A Dictionary of Creek/Muskogee: With Notes on the Florida and Oklahoma Seminole Dialects of Creek.* University of Nebraska Press, Lincoln.

Metropolitan Museum of Art
1968 Turquerie. *The Metropolitan Museum of Art Bulletin* 26(5):225-239.

Missall, John, and Mary Lou Missall
2004 *The Seminole Wars: America's Longest Indian Conflict.* University Press of Florida, Gainesville.

Muscogee (Creek) Nation
2018 Electronic document, http://www.mcn-nsn.gov/culturehistory/, accessed December 28, 2018.

Nichols, David Andrew
2016 *Engines of Diplomacy: Indian Trading Factories and the Negotiation of American Empire.* University of North Carolina Press, Chapel Hill.

Norton, Rictor
2002 Cherokee Indians Visit London, 1730. In *Early Eighteenth-Century Newspaper Reports: A Sourcebook.* Electronic document, http://grubstreet.rictornorton.co.uk/indians1.htm, accessed July 28, 2018.

Pennsylvania Gazette
1730 (December 8 issue), Philadelphia. Electronic document, https://www.accessible-archives.com/collections/the-pennsylvania-gazette/, accessed January 15, 2019.

Peters, Ann H.

2004 Nets, Bags and the Transformation of Headdress in the Southern Andes. *In Textile Society of America Symposium Proceedings* 477. Electronic document, http://digitalcommons.unl.edu/tsaconf/477, accessed January 15, 2019.

2014 Dressing the Leader, Dressing the Ancestor: The Longue Durée in the South Central Andes. In *Textile Society of America Symposium Proceedings* 945. Museo Arqueológico San Miguel de Azapa, Arica, Chile.

Rodríguez, José Berenguer

2013 Headwear of the Atacama Desert. In *Chile before Chile* (Catalog). Museo Chileno de Arte Precolombino. QuadGraphics Chile, Santiago de Chile.

Schele, L., and P. Mathews

1998 *The Code of Kings: The Language of Seven Sacred Maya Temples and Tombs.* Scribner, New York.

Schele, Linda, and Elizabeth Newsome

1991 *Taking the Headband at Copán.* Copán Note 96. Copán Acropolis Project and the Instituto Hondureño de Antropología e Historia, Copán, Honduras.

Seminole Tribe of Florida

2018 Electronic document, https://www.semtribe.com/History/IndianRemoval.aspx, accessed January 8, 2018.

Sibley, Katherine A. S.

2016 *A Companion to Ladies.* John Wiley & Sons, Hoboken.

Smithsonian National Museum of the American Indian

2012 *Living Maya Time: Sun, Corn and the Calendar / Bonampak.* Electronic document, https://maya.nmai.si.edu/gallery/bonampak, accessed November 15, 2018.

Sparacio, Matthew J.

2018 *In Time of Iron-Age: The Choctaw Civil War and the Southern Frontier.* Ph.D. dissertation, Department of History, Auburn University, Auburn, Alabama.

Starr, Sandra L.

2012 *Nation to Nation: Treaties between the United States and American Indian Nations.* Exhibition research. Report on file, Smithsonian National Museum of the American Indian, Washington, DC.

Upchurch, John C.

1969 Aspects of the Development and Exploration of the Forbes Purchase. *The Florida Historical Quarterly* 48(2):117-119.

Urban, Patricia A., and Edward M. Schortman

1986 *The Southeast Maya Periphery.* University of Texas Press, Austin.

von Schwerin, Jennifer

2011 The Sacred Mountain in Social Context. In *Symbolism and History in Maya Architecture: Temple 22 at Copán, Honduras. Ancient Mesoamerica* 22:271-300. Cambridge University Press, Cambridge, U.K.

Whipple, L.A., Thomas Ewbanks Esq., and Prof. Wm. W. Turner

1855 *Reports of Explorations and Surveys to Ascertain the Most Practicable and Economical Route for a Railroad from the Mississippi River to the Pacific Ocean, War Department: Route near the 35th Parallel, under the command of Lieut. A. W. Whipple, Topographic Engineers, in 1853 and 1854.* Report on the Indian Tribes, Washington, DC.

Wickman, Patricia R.

2006 *Osceola's Legacy.* University of Alabama Press, Tuscaloosa.

Wilson, Gaye

2003 Dealings with Mellimelli: Colorful Envoy from Tunis. *The Monticello Newsletter* 14(2), Winter 2003. Electronic document, https://monticello-www.s3.amazonaws.com/files/old/inline-pdfs/2003wtunisian_envoy03.pdf, accessed July18, 2018.

Wright, Mark A.

2011 *A Study of Classic Maya Rulership.* Ph.D. dissertation, Department of Anthropology, University of California Riverside, Riverside.

2

A Seminole Indian Warrior's Clothing, 1857

Brent Weisman

In the mid-afternoon of December 3, 1857, two men met on a muddy path in a dense cypress forest in the middle of the Big Cypress Swamp in southern Florida. History knows one of the men. He was Winston John Thomas Stephens, captain of the Florida Mounted Militia, 28 years old, a successful farmer and Florida frontiersman from Welaka, Florida on the east bank of the St. Johns River. The other man, name and age unknown, was a Seminole Indian, probably of or associated with the Billy Bowlegs band. This essay will largely be the story of this man.

History knows enough about Stephens (Blakey et al. 1998; Hodges and Kerber 1978; Patterson 1979)[1] and why, being from Welaka, he found himself far to the south in the Big Cypress

(Covington 1982; Knetsch et al. 2018). History has been less generous to the Seminoles; most of what we know comes through the eyes of others. Names, ages, and determination of sex come from deportation rolls, inventories of loss. Some deemed prominent enough by outsiders left their signatures or marks on treaty papers. A rare few like Billy Bowlegs were photographed, Bowlegs even approaching celebrity status, in the hope of converting him to the white man's ways. The Seminole that is our concern here was none of those; not a celebrity, not a signatory, not a deportee, for he never made it out of Florida alive. He certainly had a name and his death was certainly grieved by his family. But the Seminoles do not speak of the dead, so while their fights with the soldiers have been kept alive in oral traditions,

his name was not, and no soldier or chronicler wrote it down.

On that afternoon of December 3, Captain Stephens and several of his men shot and killed five Seminole Indians on that path through the cypress. These Seminoles were part of a group of warriors who, after ambushing Stephens' scouting party, killing one, were in vigorous pursuit of the retreating Stephens. Stephens, like his adversaries a hunter and woodsman, set a trap of his own. We "concealed ourselves and waited about half hour when we heard them coming," he wrote, "and when they got close we shot two or three down dead and the third one was shot down but he got up to run off and I shot him in the back running from me, and he came very nearly falling on his face but recovered and got into the cypress." Two Seminoles lay dead on the path. Stephens returned to his hiding place, waited about two hours and heard more Seminoles approaching. "When they got around the bodies of the two," recounted Stephens, "we fired and killed three others…making five killed on the spot" (Stephens to Harris, December 4, 1857).

In 1975, two sets of clothing were donated to the Florida State Museum (now the Florida Museum of Natural History—hereafter FLMNH) by Winston B. Stephens, Jr., great grandson of Captain Stephens.[2] One was the Confederate uniform worn by Stephens when he served as lieutenant in the Second Florida Cavalry (often referred to affectionately by the title "colonel" even though he never rose to that rank before the Seminole war). An ardent secessionist and slave-holder, Stephens readily took up arms to protect the sovereignty of his homeland and saw combat at Florida's most significant battle at Olustee on February 20, 1864.

Nine days later in a skirmish at Cedar Creek just west of Jacksonville, Winston John Thomas Stephens was to meet his own fate from the barrel of a gun, felled on horseback by a Union sharp-shooter, dying, speechless, "but with the last look … full of love" by the side of his younger brother Swepston (Blakey et al. 1998:328-29). His uniform survived, and after being curated in the Florida Museum collection in Gainesville, was transferred to the Florida Museum of History in Tallahassee in June 2012.

The other set of clothing was that of a Seminole Indian, for a time after its donation displayed side by side with the Stephens uniform in a glass case in the hallway leading to the Museum's Object Gallery (and where I first remember seeing it in 1982) and now securely conserved in the South Florida Archaeology and Ethnography collections in the Anthropology Division of the Florida Museum of Natural History (Figure 1). Stephens the donor knew that the Seminole clothing dated to his great grandfather's campaign in the Big Cypress but neither the donation paperwork nor the original exhibit label provided specific information about how, where, and when Stephens ended up with it.

Stephens himself apparently never wrote about it; my search of his diaries and letters and those of his wife Octavia in the Stephens-Bryant papers in the Special Collections of the Florida History Library at the University of Florida turned up nothing. Although other possibilities exist,[3] most likely the clothing came from one of the five men killed on that Big Cypress trail on December 3, 1857. Winston B. Stephens, the donor, apparently knew (but did not disclose in writing) that the clothing came from a dead man (Jerald T. Milanich, personal communication 2019) so although never made public, its true origin must have been part of the oral history passed down by Octavia. And it is through this clothing that we must learn who that man was, how he lived, what the world looked like to him, and why he fought to stay in it.

Why Was Winston Stephens in the Big Cypress?

Between 1855 and 1858, combined forces of U.S. army regulars and volunteer regiments of Florida militia were dispatched to the remote swamp forests of southwest Florida to dislodge, capture, and remove those Seminole Indians who had been left alone at the close of the Second Seminole War in 1842, their number deemed too small to impede the march of progress and too difficult to catch to justify the expense.[4] An uncertain peace ensued, with the hope that the Seminoles would confine themselves within a loosely defined reservation and that the push of white settlers south-ward would not encroach upon that territory. When the inevitable frictions occurred (Covington 1993:110-127), alarmist settlers found justification for their removal sentiments and pressed for military action. In the spring of 1855 a series of forts was constructed ringing the nucleus of Seminole settlement in the Okaloacoochee Slough and Big Cypress regions where Billy Bowlegs and Sam Jones were known to live, and probing forays snaked their way in to the heart of Indian Country. On December 20, after finding and vandalizing Billy Bowlegs' camp and discovering another abandoned settlement nearby, Lt. George Hartsuff of the Second U.S. Artillery and his small party of soldiers were ambushed near Bonnett Pond with Hartsuff himself seriously wounded and four of his men killed. The Third Seminole War was on.

In 1856, the army searched for and burned Seminole towns (always abandoned) and destroyed planted fields as they penetrated deeper into the Big Cypress, suffering the occasional ambush (Knetsch et. al 2018:125) but suffering more from the rigors of swamp warfare. What you would call this place depended on who you were. To a soldier it was a wilderness—dark, forbidding, every step mired in mud. Even those soldiers like Winston Stephens, hardened to life on the Florida frontier, didn't know this Florida, a foreign land unto itself. But to a Seminole it was home. Paths connected to trails, trails connected to villages, villages connected to fields and to other villages and to the clearings where the annual Green Corn Dance was held. Dotted along the trails were smaller family camps, nodes in a network of familiarity; not a wilderness, but a landscape made human. To a Seminole this landscape of logic made sense, a coded map of the world. And in a sense too, at a certain level, the army came to understand this and to realize it was their job to break this code, to tear the Seminole world apart into smaller and smaller pieces until it stopped making sense and the Seminoles lost their will to hold on. With every crossing and crisscrossing of the troops through the vastness of the Big Cypress, embedding their footprints even deeper into the mud, with every plume of smoke from a burning village ascending skyward, the Seminole world was piecing smaller and smaller and tearing apart.

Figure 1. *Seminole warrior's clothing taken by Winston Stephens, 1857. Top left: beaded Glengarry-style cap. Center: buckskin shirt, blue faceted glass bead necklace, beaded sash and pouch. Right: beaded garter. Left, top: buckskin pouch. Left center: wooden case and wrapped wooden stick. Left bottom: the two woven palmetto baskets.*

The Big Cypress is a big place. The cypress trees are not big, not the towering giants of the riverine forests, but there are lots of them.[5] The area is about the same as covered by the contiguous metropolitan areas of Baltimore and Washington, DC. Or imagine the streetscape of greater Los Angeles replaced by cypress swamp, wet prairie, pine flatwoods, and tropical hardwood hammock. By 1856 the Seminoles were well established here and had domesticated the land to suit their needs. Hundreds of acres of dry land had been cleared of trees by girdling and burning, this dry land scattered mostly on the hammock islands dotting the prairies or within the deeper strand forests, and then turned into fields of corn, pumpkins, and peas.

Any field with crops growing was burned by the soldiers, all corn cribs and stored produce also burned or scattered on the ground. Surplus rice, most likely harvested in the wild from the wetlands,[6] was also put to the torch or scattered. By May 1857 when Captain Winston Stephens and his company in the Mounted Florida Volunteers was called into service by the War Department and mustered in, significant damage had already been done to the Big Cypress Seminoles. The fear then was that the dispersing bands of Seminoles would thread their way through the eastern reaches of the cypress and filter out into the even more remote Everglades where their capture would require even more time, men, and money.

The men and administrators of state militias, comprised of dubiously trained volunteers enlisted for six months of service, often don't get along well with the officers and men of the regular army.

Chains of command placing the occasionally free-spirited volunteers under the overall authority of West Point-trained army disciplinarians poorly suited both parties. But work together they must, for this war could not proceed without volunteers. Only about 800 soldiers of the regular army were dispatched to Florida; Stephens and his militia company alone put an additional 82 men in the field.[7]

The Events of December 3, 1857

We first see Stephens moving into position on November 17, 1857, at Camp Rogers, within the western margin of the Big Cypress near present-day Deep Lake, on the alert and poised to attack a band of warriors, women, and children, known of but out of sight, somewhere just to the east. Already, even though this was November, tropical illness was crippling the troops; "some of the companies are much weakened by their large numbers of sick," wrote Stephens' commanding officer Col. Samuel W. George Rogers (Rogers to Page, November 17, 1857), struck down by "diarrhea, chill and fever and intermittent fevers." Even so, by November 21 contact had been made, the Seminoles surprised in their secret hiding place, an aged warrior, five women, and 13 children captured, four of them credited to Captain Stephens. A fleeing warrior was shot in the back and killed by the 22-year-old Lt. Richard Stephens, Winston's younger brother; killed also was a twelve-year old boy.

Retaliation struck on November 26 when the Seminoles killed 26 of his horses and four belonging to another company left out to graze in the Devil's Garden area of the northern Big Cypress. Spotting fresh Indian sign leading off into the swamp, Stephens—ordered to take 120 men in pursuit—was delayed by sickness among the troops, and with a reduced force of 87 men finally stepped off on November 30. The next day they passed the trail leading to the village attacked on November 21 and kept going deeper into the swamp. On the evening of December 2, after making camp where they encountered a trail leading toward Fort Shackelford, Stephens sent out scouting parties. One party thought they heard "children playing" and returned with the report that the Seminoles were near.

At first light on December 3, the men moved in that direction. In three to four miles they came upon a small pumpkin patch, then pushing further entered a large town of 50 "neatly built palmetto houses" abandoned, they thought, for three or four days. Nearby were a 10-acre field and a newly cleared field and a crib filled with corn, rice, and peas.[8] By now it was early afternoon and they had yet to spot a Seminole. Again, scouting parties were sent out; this time one returned quickly with the news that eight Seminoles had been seen on the trail ahead. Now the action described earlier unfolded over the next several hours until early evening, resulting in one of Stephens's men killed, the five Seminoles killed, and two more wounded. By December 4, Stephens was back in camp, the warrior's clothing in hand.

Soldiers continued to loop and lace their way through the Big Cypress and the adjacent coastal marshes for the rest of December and into January 1858, ever tightening the knot on the heart of Seminole Country. By January 28 when Stephens mustered out, the pursuit was nearly over. On March 27 Billy Bowlegs came out of the woods. His every camp attacked, his every move done in evasion, his way of life crushed, he had had enough. On May 1 Bowlegs, accompanied by relatives and subchiefs, boarded the U.S. Steamer *Grey Cloud* at Fort Myers (Covington 1993:143; Knetsch et al. 2018:204). It stopped briefly at Egmont Key at the mouth of Tampa Bay, and then steamed off to New Orleans and from there upriver to Indian Territory.

Although estimates vary, probably fewer than 200 Seminoles remained in Florida, some of them in the band of Sam Jones (Abiaka), hidden beyond easy reach in the deepest holds of the Everglades. There the government was content to let them be. Captain Winston Stephens returned to his farm in Welaka, married Octavia Bryant on November 1, 1859, and became a father on October 17, 1860. One year later he enlisted in the St. Johns Rangers, later renamed Company B of the Second Florida Cavalry. Rising in rank again to captain, he was the company commander at the time of his death at Cedar Creek, March 1, 1864. Five days later his son Winston Stephens was born, whose grandson would be the donor Winston B. Stephens.

What the Man Was Wearing

A photograph shows us what Winston Stephens was wearing when he went to war chasing Seminoles (in the Florida Dept. of State, Division of Library and Information Services, "Florida Memory" collection and in Blakey et al. 1998:85). A checkered vest under a long coat, fly-front trousers, Bowie knife slid in behind a broad belt, a revolver holstered on the belt, an Army-issued M1841 rifle, and a powder horn draped over one shoulder—fully weaponed and meant for business but no uniform, essentially dressed the way he would back home in Welaka. The Seminole warrior too dressed in his everyday clothes. Except in a few particulars (a beaded sash for one), his garb little resembled the finery worn by Billy Bowlegs in New Orleans in May 1858 when photographed for *Harper's Weekly* (the newspaper engraving shown in Foreman (1953:380) and numerous other places, including a historical marker in Fort Myers).

On his head, this man was apparently wearing not a silver-banded ostrich-feathered turban but a beaded Glengarry-style cap. Over the shoulder of his worn and stained fringed buckskin shirt was a beaded sash, attached to it at waist level a flapped and beaded pouch or bag. Inside the bag (Seminole clothing had no pockets) were two small woven baskets and a leather wallet-like bag, with one basket and the bag containing personal items carefully wrapped in cloth or deerskin. Also in the pouch were two silver spoons, a pair of silver scissors, and several other small objects and containers. Around his neck was wrapped a single

long strand of blue faceted glass beads and around one (most likely bare) leg an embroidered finger-braided woolen garter. Unlike Bowlegs, no calico shirt, no pants, leggings, shoes, peace medals, or crescent-shaped gorgets. Whatever weapons and ammunition he must have had, most likely a percussion musket and knife, powder horn, possibly even a pistol and bow and arrows, must have been quickly salvaged by fellow warriors or taken as spoils of war by the soldiers and re-used. In his hunting clothes and with a pouch full of personal talismans, he was ready for whatever uncertainties the day would bring.

Individual pieces of nineteenth-century Seminole clothing—beaded sashes and pouches, shirts, embroidered garters—are well known and described (Downs 1995; Goggin 1951; Reeves 2009; Sturtevant 1956a, 1967; Wickman 1991) and are curated in museums in the United States and Europe,[9] but I know of no other intact set of clothing and personal possessions from such a closely dated time and place. We must also acknowledge however that the outfit was collected as a souvenir,[10] a trophy, and was handled many times between 1857 and 1975 and in less than ideal conditions. Winston B. Stephens admitted to taking the clothing to school as a youngster for show-and-tell (Jerald Milanich, personal communication, August 3, 2019) and it was moved with the family from Florida to Massachusetts, spent some time in an attic in Washington, DC, and finally returned to Florida. Even after its donation, parts of the collection were taken to the Smithsonian Institution for identification and were only sent back to the Florida Museum in 2012.[11] Well worn by its original owner and well traveled in its after-life, the clothing nonetheless retains its basic integrity by virtue of its remarkable resilience.

The Hat (E275)

The hat presents both a puzzle and a controversy. A controversy because the beaded floral and bird designs were almost certainly sewn on a woolen Scottish Glengarry-style cap by an Iroquois woman catering to the emerging late 1820s Niagara Falls tourist trade created by the opening of the Erie Canal (Elliott 2003; Harding 1994:36). Does the dating of the style of beadwork and the way the cap was made place it later than 1857? If so, the cap could not have belonged to the warrior and must have been added by a family member later, perhaps after the move to Massachusetts. As we will see, there is no simple answer. It is a puzzle because if the cap was worn by the Seminole and collected by Winston Stephens on December 3, 1857, how did the warrior come to possess it? It is doubly singular; no other such hat is known in collections of nineteenth-century Seminole clothing, no artist or photographer showed any Seminole wearing such a hat, and the Seminoles who have seen the cap do not recognize it as a part of their tradition. And there is no other known and documented cap in museum collections or in online auction inventories exactly like this one.

The hat is a Glengarry-style cap (Figure 2), patterned after the uniform caps worn by Scottish Highland military after 1794, with this particular style achieving dominant popularity after 1841 (Barnes 1972; Suciu 2008). The undecorated caps

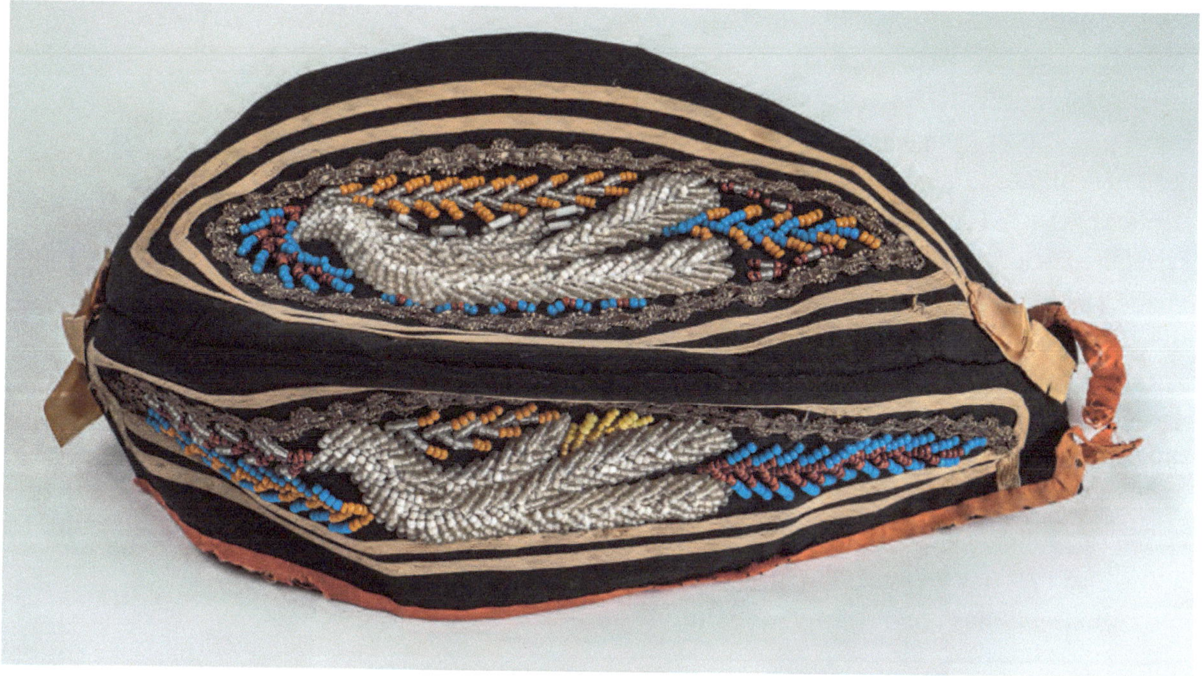

Figure 2. *The Glengarry-style cap.*

were imported for use in the Indian trade. Native beadworkers would then sew beaded designs and other embellishments on to the caps for sale, part of a larger market of "whimsies" crafted for tourists with Victorian tastes. A photograph taken of Iroquois women at Niagara Falls in 1859 shows them sewing elegant beadwork designs on purses, slippers, pincushions, and caps (Elliott 2003:8). This hat features white dove-like bird designs of sewn white and clear beads on a paper backing on sides and top, herringbone or feather-like bead designs in red, blue, orange, and green surrounding the birds, a lace-like beaded trim along the edge of the cap's peak and around the top, and strips of sewn cotton bordering the bead designs and framing the bottom of the hat. Inside the cap is lined with glazed cotton; at its rear cotton strips

dangle toward the wearer's neck in classic Glengarry style. Although beaded bird motifs are rare, they do appear on beaded bags dating to 1855-1875 (Deborah Harding, personal communication 2019). Of the hat styles used for beading, the Glengarry is the earliest, lasting from the 1820s through the 1870s (Elliott 2003:19-20). Cut paper patterns used as templates for beading date to the 1860s, based on a study of beaded bags (Harding 1994:43), but given the limited sample and the lack of specific stylistic study of the caps, the use of paper backing in the 1850s or earlier cannot be ruled out. On the other hand, and not helping the case for legitimate Florida provenance, is Deborah Harding's opinion that the beadwork on the Stephens cap is "classic Iroquois 1870s-1890s."

None of the seven Glengarry-style caps in the Anthropology collections in the National Museum of Natural History, Smithsonian Institution, have bird designs; all are identified by the curators as being Iroquois, in two cases overriding the original donor information. One cap (E395268A-0) was said by the donor family to be of Mexican origin, given to a family member in the Mexican War of 1846-1848. The other (E315439-0), more pertinent to our puzzle, is said by its donor David Bushnell [12] to have been given to General Edmund Gaines by a Creek Indian in Alabama. That is how the accession was recorded in the original handwritten ledger dating to 1920. Subsequent expert opinions (1975, 2007, and 2009, appended to the catalog card) dismissed this attribution and no documentation supporting Bushnell's claim is known. Gaines died in 1849 and most of his interactions with Creek Indians would have occurred when he was commander of Fort Stoddert in Alabama in 1807 and later as appointed commissioner to them just after the War of 1812 (Silver 1949), dates too early for the accepted appearance of the Glengarry cap in North America. Likewise, Gaines served in the Niagara area defending Fort Erie in the War of 1812 (Mahon 1972:277, 279), placing him within Iroquois territory but again too early for a cap. The Bushnell cap, says Deborah Harding, probably dates to the 1850s to 1870s based on the style of beadwork. For now, the mystery of the Bushnell attribution remains unresolved. The single cap with a bird design that I have been able to find was offered in auction by Antique Associates at West Townsend (accessed Dec. 20, 2018) with the following label: "Glengarry cap, Beaded, Native American, Probably Seneca Reservation, Western New York, circa 1880," with no supporting evidence provided.

As improbable as it might seem, if the beaded cap was an original part of the warrior's clothing, how did it get into Florida and into Seminole hands? The dating of the cap, although uncertain, could still place it in the 1840s-1850s range, at least making it possible that it was worn by a Seminole in 1857. We can tell stories about how it got here: one line follows Billy Bowlegs to New York City. In September 1852, Special Indian Agent Luther Blake wined and dined him in Washington, DC and then on to the bright lights of New York, hoping by exposing him to the luxuries of civilized life to soften his resistance to being removed from Florida. Listed among Blake's expenses submitted to Congress are "presents" for Billy Bowlegs and others in the group. [13] A newly minted Iroquois cap might have been one of the presents. After his return to Florida (unsoftened) Bowlegs could have gifted it through family or clan lines to the warrior killed on December 3, 1857. It is also possible that a military man or agent gave the cap to a Seminole sometime in the 1840s-1850s; there was enough interaction between the groups in those years for that gifting to have occurred, perhaps a sign of goodwill. Whatever the case, it is most certain that the cap did not come as a trade item from one of the trading houses operating in south Florida; no other like it is known among the Seminoles and clearly such caps were not part of the regular inventory. Although questions about the cap likely will persist, and its singularity will always raise

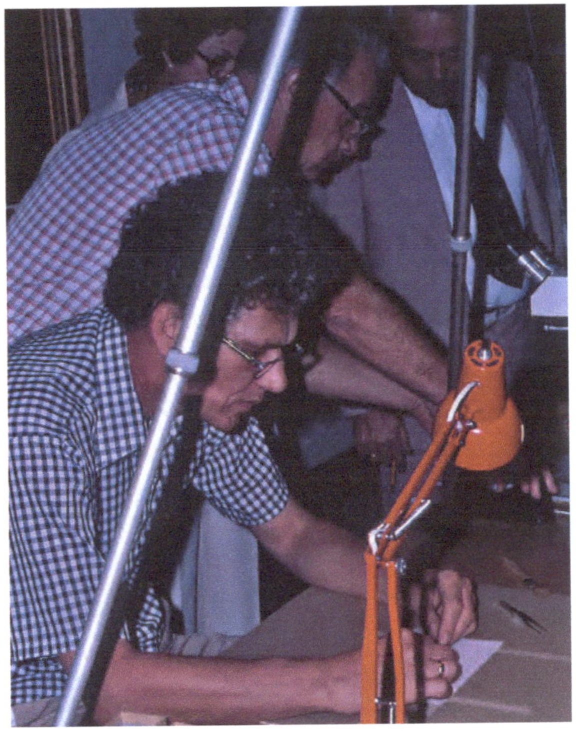

Figure 3. *William Sturtevant at Florida Museum, 1975, examining the collection.*

concern, I treat it here as if it were worn by the Seminole warrior and therefore is a legitimate part of this study, while also admitting that doing so is a stretch of the available evidence.

The descriptions that follow rely heavily on William C. Sturtevant's notecards, written by him in 1975 when he examined the collection at the Florida Museum of Natural History [14] (Figure 3). In most cases, Sturtevant's observations cannot be improved upon; the information I've added largely provides broader context and a comparative perspective. In the heading for each item I also give the FLMNH catalog number. We will look first at the shirt.

Figure 4. *Buckskin shirt.*

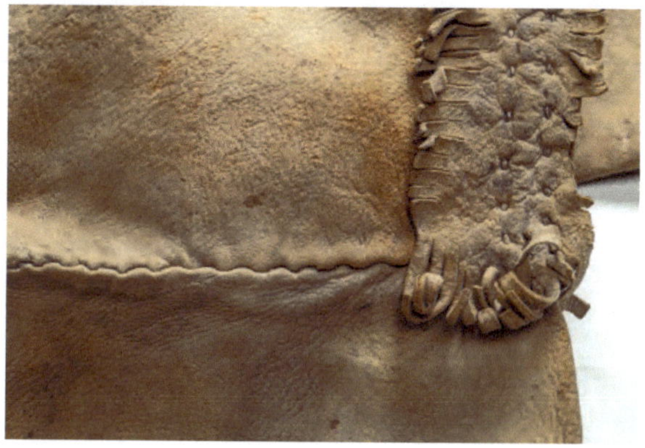

Figure 5. *Stitched body seam of shirt.*

The Shirt (E272)

By the 1830s most Seminole men were wearing long shirts or jackets made of coarse cotton cloth, obtained by trade and cut and sewn in styles that reflected both European and native influences. An 1838 sketch of captured Seminoles near Fort Butler on the St. Johns River shows all but two of the adult men wearing cloth "long shirts" or hunting shirts, with the other two wearing only breechclouts (Sturtevant 1962:75, 78, 79). The photographs of Billy Bowlegs and his retinue in 1852 and 1858 show the men dressed in a variety of shirts, some plain, some calico prints, but none made of leather. They may have had leather

hunting shirts used for everyday life; Osceola seems to have had several, now preserved in museum collections (Wickman 1991:165-169). So it is not entirely unexpected that when our warrior dressed for the day on December 3, 1857 he left home wearing a leather buckskin shirt, made of tanned deerskin (Figure 4). An account from 1881 (MacCauley 1887:518) describes how the Seminoles dressed deer skins using smoke and a paste made from deer brain and shows a simple frame used as a hide stretcher. Both skill and patience were needed to properly prepare a skin, tan the hide, and tailor a garment, a process that took a number of steps, required decisions about what to do, and needed several days.[15] Sturtevant writes that the quality of the tanning is good but

not excellent. The outer surface of the skin was worn toward the body. A light stain left by a purple substance appears on the inside shoulder seams and at the bottom of the shirt, suggesting residue of body paint.

The shirt was made from four pieces of leather: front and back torso-shaped body pieces with a v-shaped slit cut at the neck and two stubs to attach the sleeves, and the two cuffed sleeves, each about 24 inches wide at the shoulder end and tapering about 23 inches to the folded-over cuff. Sleeve and body seams (down the back) were stitched with ⅛-inch-thick deer thong and are tucked under and barely visible (Figure 5). A fringed strip of buckskin stretching across the back of the shoulder holds the front and back pieces together, stitched with a leather thong (Figure 6). Some repair with a newer thong is evident. The shirt is 38⅓ inches long, shorter than the best known Osceola shirt at 43 inches (Downs 1995:30; Wickman 1991:167), probably brushing or just below the man's knees. In design it is simpler than the Osceola shirt and not as well

Figure 6. *Fringed strip of buckskin sewn across shoulder of shirt.*

tailored, hanging more like a parka, in the basic Plain Shirt style influenced by European frontier dress (Sturtevant 1967:167, 171, his Figure 10). The shirt is clean of dirt except at the left cuff and shows sweat stains around the neck and at the shoulder beneath where a sash would have been worn. A scatter of small holes across the surface of the skin, none penetrating, might be from the shots that killed the animal. Damage and sweat stains on the left cuff suggest that the man wore a broad metal bracelet at times, perhaps not on the day of his death. Rusty tack holes punched through the top of the sleeves and at the neckline indicate how the shirt was mounted for display (a technique considered inappropriate and no longer practiced today by museum professionals).

The Sash and Pouch (E-274) (Figure 7)

A beaded shoulder sash with an attached beaded pouch was standard dress for any Seminole man decades before the 1850s. Patterned after the dress worn by eighteenth-century English soldiers, the sash and pouch were widely distributed among the Southeastern Indians and throughout the Eastern Woodlands and are prominently illustrated and prized in museum collections (Downs 1995:43, 60-61, 76, 152-178; Goggin 1951). Worn over one shoulder with the front and back sides joined at the opposite waist by the attached pouch, the sash had decorative and symbolic value and provided a means to secure the pouch. The pouch was meant to carry things, in this case a smaller

Figure 7. *Sash and pouch.*

leather pouch and woven baskets, two silver spoons and a pair of scissors, a wrapped wooden stick, and a small box.

The sash is made of black woolen stroud cloth (Sturtevant calls it dark blue) and is 53 inches long and 3½ inches wide (Figure 8). At 3½ inches from each end the sash is split into two tails. Each tail has an attached woolen tassel. The edges are bound with ¾-inch dark green-brown tape to prevent fraying and the sash is backed by woolen cloth with a blue and white windowpane pattern. A continuous floral pattern sewn with blue, pink, yellow, and green beads showing simple, opposite bay-leaf shaped designs (Downs 1995:174-175) sprouting from a dark green, dark blue, and clear-beaded stem run nearly the length of the sash, ending at a loose diamond pattern of white seed beads at the split ends. A single row of white seed beads is sewn along the edges of the sash all the way around. These beads were strung next to each other on a single piece of cotton thread and tacked down with a stitch between every two or three beads to hold them in place. The diamond beadwork on the two split or forked ends is loose and irregular, suggesting hurried work or perhaps sewn by someone with little experience.

The pouch is square, about 6¼ inches on a side, is made of red cloth, and has a triangular flap (Figure 9). Six strands of four blue-faceted beads hang from the bottom of the pouch, threaded on thick S-twisted cording that extends through the string of beads and is wrapped in tassels of red woolen yarn at the ends (Figure 10). The front of the pouch, except the area covered by the flap,

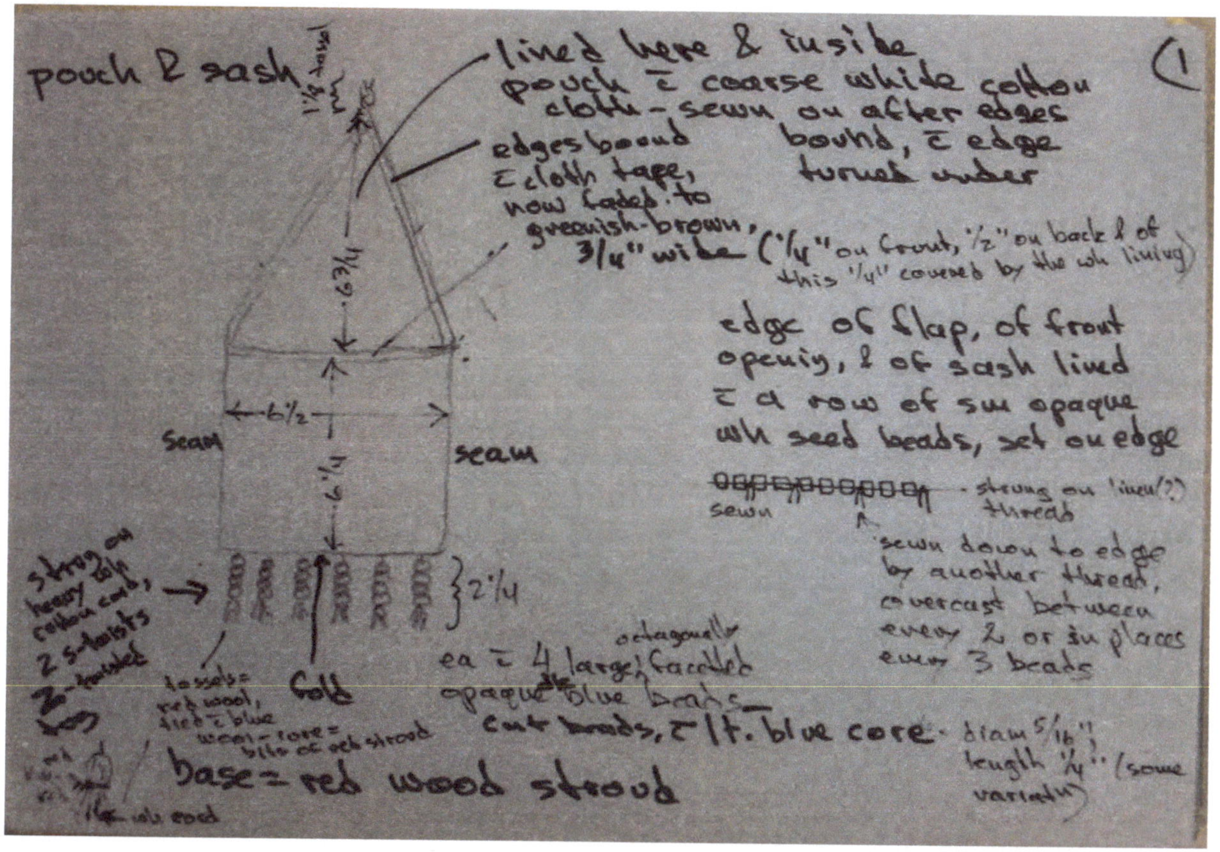

Figure 8. *Sturtevant drawing of sash and pouch.*

Figure 9. *The pouch.*

shows beaded diamond patterns in light blue, dark blue, and white seed beads, tighter in design than the diamonds on the sash but not with the symmetrical precision of earlier known examples (see Downs 1995:Figures 23-27). The flap is edged with the same cloth tape used on the sash and over the tape are sewn two rows of seed beads, white on the edge and a string of blue next to it. A single row of white seed beads lines the underside edge of the flap (Figure 11).

Tied by a knotted 5-inch leather thong to the forked end of the left sash (or to the wearer's right) is a whittled hollow oblong wooden container about

3½ inches long and 0.85 fluid ounces in volume, capped by a tightly fitting wooden lid about ⅜ inch thick (Figure 12). The leather thong from the sash goes through the lid and is knotted on the underside. Fabric fragments from the pouch or sash and residue of charred and uncharred unidentified plant remains are found inside the container, not helping to confirm a use for the object. We can guess but can't be certain that it was a powder measure or powder horn (Pare Bowlegs, personal communication 2019; Pedro Zepeda, personal communication 2019), or

perhaps held the ingredients for a firestarter (Pare Bowlegs, personal communication 2019).

The seamstress, almost certainly a woman, or women, had a variety of materials to work with—textiles of wool and cotton, glass beads, and leather—and the traditional knowledge of what acceptable clothing should look like and what colors to use. What she didn't have was time or safety, due to the constant harassment of soldiers crisscrossing her homeland threatening her daily security, forcing her constantly to look over her

Figure 10. *Beaded tassels at bottom of pouch.*

Figure 11. *Where the pouch and sash are attached.*

Figure 12. *Wooden container attached to the sash.*

shoulder and breaking her concentration on the work at hand.

The Garter (E-276) (Figure 13)

There should have been two garters, one worn around the upper calf of each leg (see, for one example, the famous 1838 Catlin painting of Osceola, reproduced in Downs (1995:Figure 2.6). This one is fingerwoven in tight alternating squares of white seed beads set against each other in a diamond pattern, each set of four diamonds forming a square around a field of blue thread, all set against a background of brown wool (Figure 14). The body of the garter is 10½ inches long and 3½ inches wide. At each end a 10½ to 11-inch length of tassels extends, six on one side, five on the other, with three-strand tightly braided shorter lengths of the brown and blue coming out of the body and flanking the longer, looser tassels. The beaded squares were made by sewing blue thread through a row of four beads, three of these sets to a square, then weaving the blue thread through the weft of brown wool until threading it through the next set of beads. The S-twist weft is characteristic of fingerweaving. Fifteen lines of squares cross the body of the garter from one tasseled end to the other. The edges of the garter appear to be a separate weave (Figure 15). Here we see an 8-strand braid of red wool woven into the outer run of the blue and brown of the body. White beads were threaded in to form triangles with the apex facing the adjacent row of beaded squares.

Fingerweaving is an ancient indigenous weaving technique developed independently worldwide for creating woven textiles and other natural materials without the use of a loom. American Indians perfected this skill long before Europeans came (Dockstader 1978).[16] French colonial women in Canada elaborated on the technique, adding their own embellishments, then supplied their handiwork for the fur trade (Downs 1995:126). In fingerweaving two groups of parallel but separated strands of yarn hang down vertically, suspended from a stick. The right hand gathers strands from the right hand group, turns them horizontally, and laces them through some of the vertical hanging strands that are being held up by the left hand. This is exacting, time-consuming work and there are many ways it can go wrong. It is also more portable than the mechanical warp and weft weaving on a loom, where the vertical warp threads are fixed to a rigid framework and the horizontal weft threads woven through them using a shuttle.

The Seminoles had likely perfected the technique by the 1770s if not long before. William Bartram, writing from that decade, tells us that women, whom he praises as being vigilant, "spin and weave the curious belts and diadems for men, fabricate

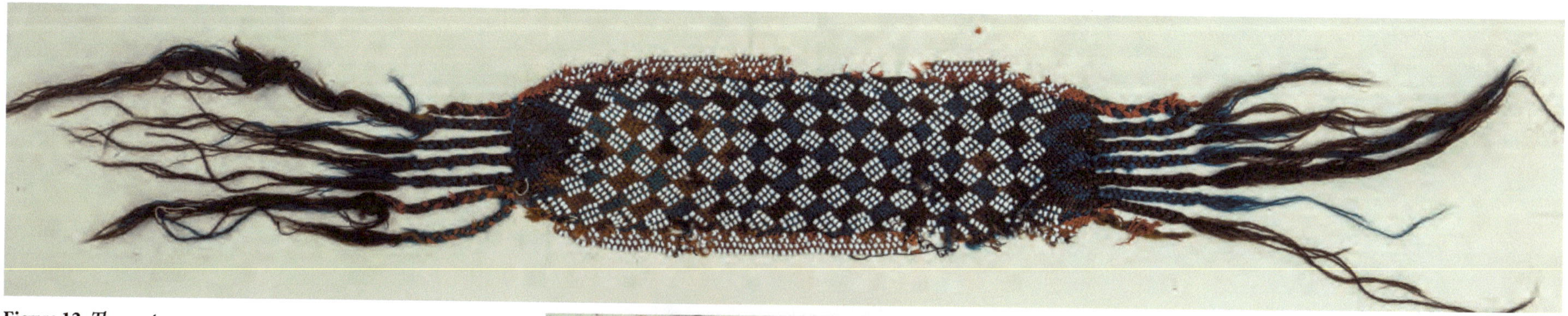

Figure 13. *The garter.*

Figure 14. *Fingerwoven beaded diamond pattern on garter.*

Figure 15. *Garter tassels and red woolen weave on outer edge of garter.*

lace, fringe, embroider, and decorate their apparel" (1996:407). Through careful work, archaeologists uncovered the diamond-patterned seed bead remains of a garter interred with a Seminole in the Fort Brooke cemetery in Tampa, dating most likely from the mid-1830s to early 1840s (Piper and Piper 1982:223). By the mid-1850s, however, fingerweaving was on the decline. Billy Bowlegs was wearing fingerwoven garters in 1852 but Seminole men in photographs from the 1870s onward through the turn of the century lack them (see Sturtevant 1967:Figures 4, 5, 7, 14) with the exception of an heirloom example from 1901 (Downs 1995:177).

The skill shown in weaving the garter presents a different picture than that of the sash. The worn patches and missing beads suggest that it is older and well worn, but the quality of design and overall execution speak of patience and time. Although the decades before 1857 were far from quiet for the Seminoles, the garter may well have been woven during this time.

The Necklace Beads (E-273) (Figure 16)

Around his neck the man wore coils of a 10-foot-long strand of faceted blue glass beads, 420 of them still present, at least five missing. The beads were strung on a brown buckskin thong about 3/32 of an inch wide, knotted in square knots at the ends and in several places throughout the strand. The beads are translucent dark blue on the outside over an opaque light blue core. They are large, about ⅜ inch in diameter and up to ¼ inch or more long, larger but of the same type used in the pouch.

Figure 16. *Blue glass faceted necklace beads.*

Seminole men in the late eighteenth century did not wear necklace beads, to judge from limited archaeological evidence dating to this time (Fitts 2001:150-160; Goggin et al. 1949), but by the early decades of the 1800s this preference changed, as the many portraits of Seminole chiefs clearly indicate. By the 1830s, faceted blue glass beads in particular became popular with the Seminoles. Archaeologists look for them in their excavations to identify Seminole presence from this time period forward (Piper and Piper 1982:210-213; Weisman 1989:70, 76, 92) and with some variation in size and shape they occur at sites in the Big Cypress and Everglades through the end of the nineteenth century.

Specialists classify beads by how they are made. These are tubular drawn beads, meaning they were made by pulling or "drawing" a molten mass of glass into a long tube shape, then chiseling or snapping it into smaller bead-length segments when cool (Karklins 2012:63-65). The facets were cut in by hand or mechanically. There are many sizes and shapes of drawn beads (many of them not faceted) and overall they were the most popular bead in the Indian trade. Often erroneously called "Russian" beads (Ross 1990:36-38), these faceted blue glass beads were made either in Bohemia (now the Czech Republic) or Murano, in Italy, the world center of glassmaking, and were taken worldwide by nineteenth-century colonial powers for gift and trade to native peoples.

Faceted blue glass beads were common and there is nothing unusual about the Seminole warrior's having had them. But they do raise two questions that make us think a little more deeply. First, he was wearing these beads in a necklace, but only these beads. Wearing bead necklaces was then standard dress for a Seminole man; numerous paintings, portraits, and archaeological finds confirm their abundance. The usual necklace, however, was strung with many different types of beads, not just faceted blue. The famous Catlin painting of Osceola shows a variety of bead types in his necklace (Weisman 1989:69-70). Of the more than 9,000 necklace beads found by archaeologists at the Fort Brooke site (Piper and Piper 1982:209), about 90 percent were faceted but other shapes of drawn and another type called wire-wound were also present. Both Seminole men and women wore bead necklaces. A range of necklace bead shapes, sizes, and colors were being traded to Seminoles later in the century based on archaeological collections,[17] so why were only blue faceted beads worn by the Seminole warrior on December 3, 1857?

Now to the second question. Within ten years or so, certainly by the time of Clay MacCauley's visit in 1881, Seminole men stopped wearing necklace beads. Bead necklaces became solely the province of Seminole women, young and old. They aim "to gather about their necks as many strings of beads as can be hung there and as they can carry, "writes MacCauley (1887:487) and are "satisfied with

nothing meaner than a cut glass bead, about a quarter of an inch or more in length, generally of some shade of blue, and costing (so I was told by a trader at Miami) $1.75 a pound" (MacCauley 1887:487-488). Even the aged Chief Tallahassee when photographed in 1901 in all his fingerwork finery (Downs 1995:177) shows no glass bead necklace. A *Harper's Weekly* drawing of No-Kush-Adjo, "brother of old Mrs. Billy Bowlegs," from June 12, 1858 shows strands of beads around his neck (Downs 1995:172). But photographs of Seminole men in 1874 and 1876 show them without (Sturtevant 2000:xvi-xviii). No photograph of a Seminole man from then forward shows them wearing bead necklaces. Why the change? Why did the poundage of beads become a point of pride for female Seminoles and completely abandoned by the men between 1858 and the 1870s? Perhaps the beads are pointing us to a change in Seminole society that our warrior did not live to witness.

What was in the Pouch

Almost everything the man carried was in the beaded pouch sewn to the shoulder sash and worn at his waist. Inside the pouch, carefully wrapped, were a number of items of personal meaning and spiritual significance.[18] He selected these items to give him power over his enemies, to protect him from harm, and to ensure success in the day's journey ahead. No warrior would have set out without them. To respect the wishes of Seminole Tribal reviewers of this essay, these items will not be described further. What we can say here is that these pieces give insight into who

this man was, what meaning he found in the world, what he believed in.

Not everything in the pouch was deemed to be protected information by the Tribal reviewers. Loose in the pouch were two silver spoons (E287, E288). Both spoons fit the time period to have been owned by the Seminole warrior (Figure 17). E288 is six inches long and has three hallmarks, two of them identifiable. One is a lion passant (a walking lion with right front paw raised) and the other probably an eagle with outstretched wings, common trademarks for New York silver made between 1840 and 1865. E287 is stamped with C&S which can refer to several firms operating in New York and Connecticut from about 1836 to 1859 (Robert Alan Green to Jerald T. Milanich, May 20, 1985). Stamped next to the C&S is a sideways fleur-de-lis. This spoon is filigreed shaped and is

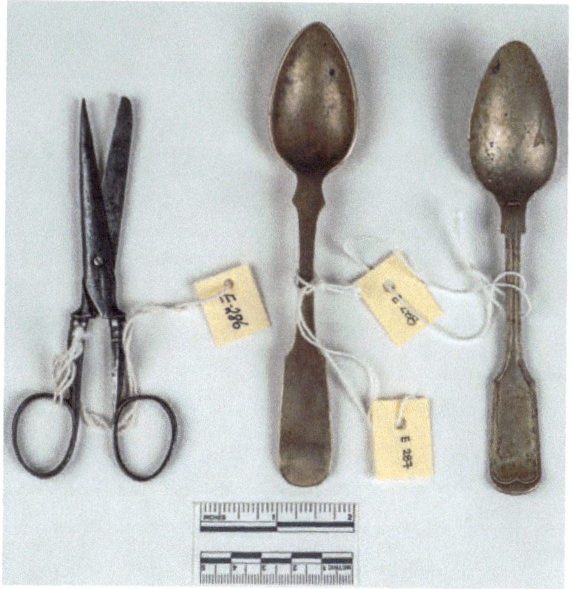

Figure 17. *Silver spoons and scissors.*

5¾ inches long. How the man got the spoons and what purpose or purposes they served are unknown. Two heavily corroded iron spoons were found at Fort Brooke, dating to the mid-1830s (Hardin 1982:274). From the mid to late 1840s Seminole raiding parties attacked encroaching white settlements from the Manatee River area south through the central peninsula (Covington 1993:110-126); the spoons could have been booty.

Increased trading was occurring at newly established forts around the perimeter of Seminole territory around and south of Lake Okeechobee in an attempt to pacify the Indians and bring them out of hiding (Covington 1993:121). New trading posts were opening as far south as Fort Myers, and Indian agents were trading directly with Bowlegs and others (Covington 1993:117, 123), all of which could have been sources of the spoons. Luther Blake's 1854 list of expenditures includes spoons purchased for the Seminoles (see note 13). Although we cannot be sure why the spoons were carried in the pouch, it is possible they were used as measuring aids (Pare Bowlegs, personal communication 2019).

A pair of steel scissors (E286) was also in the pouch (see Figure 17). The scissors are 5 inches long and are stamped with the name Kirschbaum. The blades show use-wear so the scissors were a functioning tool, perhaps for cutting the cloth and buckskin used to wrap the contents of the pouch. Scissors are also included in the Luther Blake list. Scissors were not commercially made in the U.S. until 1877, so it is likely that these scissors were made in Sheffield, England, the center of highest quality scissor manufacturing and export (Beaudry 2006:119, 120).

Conclusion

What do men wear when they go to war? Partly it depends on why they go and what they are fighting for. Neither man who met on that Big Cypress trail in December 1857 wore a uniform. They were not fighting for nation or state. Both, motivated by what they believed their purpose and position in the world to be, were fighting for their homeland. History can judge the rightness of the cause but these men, both of them, with their families, were using their lives to transform the Florida wilderness into the Florida frontier. The captain brought his knife, his powder horn, and his rifle. The Seminole brought the same. Both carried their rightness as a shield. The Seminole warrior did not return home that day in December. The man he encountered, lucky then, had less than seven years to live. And for those Seminoles who survived that day, the time would soon come when their world stopped making sense. Some Seminoles, led by Sam Jones (Abiaka) snaked their way eastward into the fastness of the Everglades and there were left alone, not the perfect solution, thought the authorities, but again, too few to be bothered with, or to be bothers. The others, the followers of Bowlegs, followed him west to Indian Territory, exiled to, yet again, begin as pioneers.

The man who wore these clothes, still and forever nameless, created his image from the skins of tradition and the cloth and glass of the modern world. He set out this day as he had on others, nourished physically and spiritually by the plants, animals, and soil of the world around him. He knew well how to survive in this world; the full corn cribs, the trade beads, and cloth all attest to his powers of adaptation and creation.[19] For him, right then, that morning, life still made sense, this place was where he wanted to be and he would fight to keep his place in it. Unknown, unsung, and forgotten to history if not for his clothes, they remain today to speak of this man, his place, his time.[20]

Acknowledgments. Deborah Harding and Madelyn Shaw gave generous assistance in answering questions about the textiles present in the collection and pointed me to valuable references, as did Stacey Huber. Karen Walker and Donna Ruhl provided access to the collection and shared information about its history. Pare Bowlegs and Pedro Zepeda suggested possible uses for some of the items. Austin Bell responded to questions about his visit to the William Sturtevant collection at the Smithsonian and offered helpful insights. Joe Knetsch and John and Mary Lou Missall provided historical documentation regarding the Winston Stephens campaign in the Big Cypress. Jerald Milanich sent me background information and recollections relating to the original accession. Paul Backhouse opened access to Seminole perspectives on the collection. All photographs of the objects are by Kristen Grace except for Figure 3 made from a slide on file at the Florida Museum, accession 75-81.

Notes

1. The Stephens-Bryant Family Papers include 15 boxes of primary material of letters, diaries, record books, and photographs relating to these families and the history of their lives in rural north Florida, mostly from 1836 through the end of the Civil War. Examined for this study were Boxes 1-2, the Octavia Bryant Stephens Diaries; Box 3, containing the Winston Stephens pocket diary and account books from 1861-1862 and 1862-1864; and boxes 5-7 containing the Stephens Family Correspondence. The bulk of the material was donated by Winston B. Stephens, Jr. to the University of Florida in 1975 and is now curated in the Special and Area Studies Collection, George A. Smathers Libraries.

2. Winston B. Stephens, Jr. donated the Seminole clothing, Stephens' Confederate uniform, and the red silk guidon flag of the St. John's Rangers (Stephens' unit) to the Florida State Museum (now the Florida Museum of Natural History) on October 12, 1975. His correspondence with then assistant curator Jerald T. Milanich covering the appraisal and details of the accession is preserved in folders 2 and 4 of the Winston Stephens Seminole accession in the South Florida Archaeology and Ethnography section, Anthropology Division, FLMNH, Gainesville, along with associated correspondence. The material was accessioned as FLMNH acc. no. 75-81. There are 17 folders in all, containing notes, correspondence, copies of emails, reference materials, photographs and slide sets, and records of visits by outside scholars and Stephens-Bryant descendants.

3. Soldiers often took things from the abandoned Seminole villages they encountered. Andrew Canova, mustered in to Jacob Mickler's company in July, 1857 but with seeming first-hand knowledge of the Winston Stephens December campaign, recounts an earlier episode when he came into an empty village: "Hanging in one of the wigwams," he writes, "were two chiefs' costumes, richly embroidered with beads. Some breast-plates, hammered out of silver dollars, were also found. We made a dash for these, and I was fortunate enough to secure one of these costumes. This consisted of a "waistcoat, a pair of leggings and moccasins, and a sash" (Canova 1906:14). Winston Stephens participated

in the surprise attack led by Captain Cone's regiment on a Seminole village on November 21, 1857 in which an "aged warrior," five women, and 13 children were captured. Winston's younger brother Richard shot and killed one warrior and a 12-year-old boy during this attack. On the morning of December 3 Stephens led his command through an abandoned town noting "fifty neatly built palmetto houses" (Stephens to Harris December 4, 1857). Although it is nearly certain that Stephens obtained the clothing by killing a warrior later that day, other opportunities, however slim, did exist.

4. The Second Seminole War (1835-1842) ended not with a formal treaty but with the U.S. government finally giving up the effort as too costly and without result, pulling out most of the federal troops from Florida by the end of summer, 1842. Despite removing 3,824 Seminoles to Indian Territory and killing untold numbers of others through the nearly seven years of conflict, some 300 evaded the government's grasp (Mahon 1967:318, 321) to survive and rebuild their lives in the Big Cypress and Everglades. Here they were attacked again by army regulars and Florida militia in another attempt at removal in the Third Seminole War, after which fewer than 100 Seminoles remained in Florida. It is clear from the conversations between Billy Bowlegs and Indian agent Luther Blake in the early 1850s that the Seminoles regarded the promise of General Worth to leave them alone at the end of the Second Seminole War as a treaty, therefore the initial incursion of the troops that sparked the third war was essentially a treaty broken.

5. The stunted or dwarf form of pond cypress (*Taxodium ascendens* or *T. distichum var. nutans*) known as hatrack cypress, typical of the Big Cypress savannas, is described and pictured in Ewel (1990:291). Excellent coverage of the ecology of the Big Cypress Swamp is provided by Benjamin McPherson's (1974) chapter in *Environments of South Florida: Present and Past*. Further references are supplied by Linda S. De Mauro's "A Bibliography of the Hydrology of the Everglades and the Big Cypress Swamp, Florida" (1977). Having some grasp of the lay of the land is essential in understanding the military descriptions that came out of the Second and Third Seminole wars and in appreciating how the Seminoles placed themselves

in those environments. Of course, there is no substitute for walking the ground oneself, which is possible on the many trail systems running through the Big Cypress National Preserve. No known archaeological sites correspond to the locations described by Winston Stephens. The village he entered and the scenes of his several skirmishes likely were in the northwestern quadrant of the Preserve, south of I-75 (Alligator Alley) and east of C.R. 839, possibly in the Airplane Prairie or Thompson Pine Island U.S.G.S. topographic quadrangles. The military map produced by Lieut. J. C. Ives dated April 1856, "Map of the Peninsula of Florida South of Tampa Bay," although predating Stephens, shows the area he later traversed including several networks of trails. Specifically, the area south of Billy Bowlegs Old Town and west of the spot labeled Fuse Hadjos is where the action took place.

6. Two and possibly three types of rice were grown or harvested by the Seminoles. Unfortunately, the documents do not distinguish between them and we have no known botanical specimens. William Bartram, reporting to his patron Dr. Fothergill, describes Seminoles living on the east bank of the Suwannee River: "the Whole Town plants in one great field, I suppose containing about 20 Acres, all planted with Corn, Pumkins, Water Mellons, Beans, Pease, Squashes, & some Rice and Potatoes" (Bartram 1996:489). Bernard Romans, writing at about the same time as Bartram, dismissed rice as suitable only for "feeding Negroes, cattle and poultry" but does describe the challenges of cultivation in both wet and dry soils (1999:164-165). Horatio Dexter, visiting Seminole towns in the central peninsula in 1823, notes rice being planted by women, and in a field outside of Opauney's Town near present-day Lakeland, "negro slaves" cultivating rice in such quantity that pack horses carrying the surplus were sent to St. Augustine (Boyd 1958). So here we have the one or possibly two types of rice: the *Oryza sativa*, the domesticated rice introduced by the European colonists, and the second, and more controversial *Oryza glaberrina*, "black rice," also domesticated but coming with the African slaves from West Africa (Carney 2001). Clay MacCauley's report from 1881, more than 100 years after Bartram and from south Florida, states

that "all the rice they need they gather from the swamps" (1887:504), indicating that by this time they were harvesting native wild rice (*Zizania aquatica*).

7. The muster rolls have been transcribed and compiled by Robert Hawk (2019) as Volume 10, *Florida Militia Muster Rolls, Seminole Indian Wars*, Special Archives Publication Number 76, Florida Department of Military Affairs. Now available online, these rolls are very detailed in providing the rank, name, birthplace, height, complexion, color of eyes, color of hair, and occupation for all of the men who enlisted for militia service. The men in Stephens's company are listed on pages 3-8. The majority were farmers. Also listed by the owner's names are the horses killed by the Seminoles on November 27, 1857.

8. The peas were probably the cow pea, *Vigna unguiculata*, or black-eyed pea, very hardy, culinarily versatile, reliably stored when dried, of African origin and introduced into Virginia in the seventeenth century, soon becoming standard Southern fare (Porcher 1863:194). The pumpkins were the legendary Seminole pumpkin, still highly valued by Florida home gardeners. This pumpkin is a form of *Cucurbita moschata*, a winter crookneck squash, and occurs in at least three forms in Florida—the oblong "Hardy" strain, the rounded "Ingram Billie" strain, and a necked variety resembling a crookneck squash (Morton 1975:139). The vining growth crawls over the ground or climbs up and hangs from branches of trees, a condition often remarked upon by travelers to south Florida. Julia Morton (1975) provides an excellent history and botanical appraisal of the Seminole pumpkin (Bartram gets another mention here) and describes its many food uses. Like the cow pea, the hard-shelled Seminole pumpkin stores very well in Florida's heat and humidity and in some form well pre-dates the time of European contact.

9. In addition to the other items in the Florida Ethnographic Collection at the Florida Museum of Natural History, nineteenth-century Seminole Indian clothing can be found in the collections of the Smithsonian Institution's National Museum of the American Indian, the Chicago Museum of Natural History, the British Museum, the Denver Museum of Natural History, and the Seminole Tribe's Ah-Tah-Thi-Ki Museum. Patricia Wickman

provides detailed provenance for the dispersed items associated with Osceola (1991:195-200).

10. Jerald Milanich contacted William Sturtevant of the Smithsonian Institution in 1975, early in the donation process, to help in the appraisal of the Seminole clothing required by the donor Winston B. Stephens, Jr. Sturtevant was the Curator of North American Ethnology at the Smithsonian, had done fieldwork among the Seminoles in the early 1950s leading to his 1955 doctoral dissertation at Yale, and by 1975 was considered the preeminent scholar of Seminole Indian material culture. At Milanich's request, the then chairman of the Florida Museum's Anthropology Department, William Maples, sponsored Sturtevant's visit to the Museum on October 1, 1975 to examine the Stephens donation (Jerald Milanich, personal communication 2019); the appraisal was provided subsequently on October 10. An audio-less videotape of Sturtevant handling the collection is in the Museum files with supporting notes and documentation in Folder 5.

11. Correspondence relating to this transaction and subsequent curatorial efforts are in the Stephens files in the Ethnographic Collection at the Florida Museum of Natural History.

12. David I. Bushnell (1875-1941) was widely active in the early 1900s as a collector, anthropologist, and archaeologist. Not formally trained, he nonetheless was employed by the Harvard Peabody Museum and the Smithsonian Institution's Bureau of American Ethnology and conducted fieldwork in Minnesota and Cahokia Mounds and achieved some credibility as a scholar. He did fieldwork among the Choctaw Indians of Louisiana in 1908-1909 and again in 1917-1918 but it is not clear how or why he would have been in position to have collected the Creek Glengarry cap. The cap was acquired as a loan on September 20, 1920 (cat. no. 315439, acc. acc. no. 65435). Looking at the entries before and after the cap in the original handwritten accession register in the Smithsonian (viewable online), it seems unlikely that a clerical error was made. His papers are housed in the Peabody Museum Archives; perhaps the answer lies there.

13. Luther Blake, formerly the Creek Indian Agent, was hired by Alexander Stuart, Secretary of the Interior, in April 1851 to effect the peaceable removal to

Indian Territory of the remaining Florida Seminoles (Covington 1993:123). He traveled there to hire Seminoles deported during the Second Seminole War to serve as interpreters in his dealings with their Florida brethren, and in September 1852, having enticed Billy Bowlegs to join the delegation, traveled from Florida to Washington, D.C. and then on to New York City in the hope that Billy would be dazzled by and then want to partake in the white man's civilization. Unsuccessful, his services were terminated on May 3, 1853. Fortunately for us, Blake's expenses were aggressively and scrupulously scrutinized and his itemized daily expenditures were listed in congressional documents. Compiled as Senate Executive Document No. 71 (1854), these lists give us a detailed look at the foods, clothing, beverages, and a host of material items purchased for the Seminoles, and therefore also give us a picture of the general kinds of items available for the Indian trade. The level of detail provides some surprises and helps bring people to life in what can otherwise be a dry and impersonal past. On February 17, 1852, for example, a box of raisins was purchased for the Black Seminole interpreter Abraham (p. 47). Mindful that Billy and his retinue were to look presentable when paraded to the urban public, authorities instructed Blake to buy clothes for them. For Abraham (spelled Abram in the documents), a pair of boots and a pair of drawers; for Billy, a pair of pants and calf sewn boots (p. 32). Blake submitted an expense of $40.75 for "presents and making clothes for Billy Bowlegs and others," and a payment of $12.86 to Thomas P. Kennedy for "presents for Bowlegs" (p. 23). Although a hat was purchased on May 20 (p. 47), the documents don't say for whom or from whom and the date does not fit the timeline for the New York trip. Likewise, the cap purchased for Jumper on May 17 (p. 36) well predates the New York trip.

14. As he examined them, William Sturtevant wrote his descriptions of the items on individual notecards. He took these with him back to the Smithsonian in 1975, perhaps hoping to publish on the collection (Jerald Milanich, personal communication 2019). Sturtevant died in 2007. In 2012, Austin Bell, then a student at the University of Florida and working under William Marquardt at the FLMNH, traveled

to the Smithsonian, found and photocopied the cards (now filed in Box 58 of the William C. Sturtevant Papers, NAA.2008-24, National Anthropological Archives). The copies made by Bell are in Folder 15 of the Stephens Seminole Collection (acc. no. 75-81) of the Florida Ethnographic Collection at the Museum (see notes 2 and 10). I matched the photocopies to the items described in my several visits to the collection and used them as a primary source for this essay.

15. Charles Barney Cory, writing in 1896, describes the tanning process of scraping and hand-softening the skins, then rubbing them with animal brains for further softening and curing. Skins to be used for leggings, not brain-tanned, are soaked in a liquid of boiled mangrove bark (1896:14). By 1910, deerskin clothing had all but been given up, with deerskin leggings worn only on ceremonial occasions. The Yale Peabody Museum has a Seminole "beaming tool" (Acc. No. YPM ANT 145559) used for removing hair in tanning a deerskin, made of cypress wood inset with a kitchen knife blade.

16. Fragments of early warp and weft-woven textiles, mostly of simple and diagonal twining dating to the mid-sixth millennium BC, were found in excavations of the famous Windover site in Brevard County, Florida, preserved in the saturated peat soils of the pond (Andrews et al. 2002:133-148, 163). Although we don't know the specific weaving technique or if a supporting rod was used, these pieces, arguably, are examples of fingerweaving. The unique condition of preservation attests to the antiquity of what must have been an everyday technology developed well before simple looms (Miner 1936). As the historic examples prove, elaborate and sophisticated designs can be produced by the skilled artisan and even with the advent of the loom this technique persisted (Dockstader 1978:14, 57-58, Fig. 32).

17. National Park Service archaeologists discovered numerous Seminole camp, garden, and burial sites in surveys of the Big Cypress National Preserve between 1977 and 1983. Particularly relevant for this study is Season 1 (Ehrenhard et. al 1978). Most of the sites date to the time between 1860 and 1940, just after the Third Seminole War and before the modern reservation period (Taylor 1985). Ethnographically this is the period written about

by MacCauley (1887), Cory (1896), Pratt (in 1879, see Sturtevant 1956b), and Skinner (1913). Many of the sites contain faceted blue glass beads (among other types), showing the prevalence and wide time period of this popular bead. Trading houses then operating in the Miami area, especially toward the latter decades of the 1800s and early 1900s (Kersey 1975), supplied these beads in some quantity in what has been described as a "brisk" trade (Carr 1981:181; 1989).

18. Previously published ethnographic references to items similar to those in the Stephens collection can be found in Sturtevant (1955:382, 386, and 394), Sturtevant (1954:37), and Capron (1953:164, 167-168). Downs (1995:167, 168) provides a secondary source. See also Adrosko (1990:71) for other examples. Wissler (1912:246) is a classic source and Zedeño (2008) gives a good contemporary presentation.

19. Cotton and wool were the common materials for clothing in the Indian trade. Tightly woven plain cotton when first introduced to Europe from Calicut, India, became popularly known as calico and in many colored prints of floral and geometric designs came to dominate the clothing of colonial and frontier America (Brackman 1989; Krager 2004; Meller and Elffers 2002). By 1774, English clothing manufacturers figured out how to make quality calico, greatly lessening the demand for cloth from India, and by the early 1800s affordable cotton fabric was being produced in American mills. Chintz, a brightly colored calico, displayed vibrant red floral designs produced by madder, *Rubia tinstorum*, its color fixed (made colorfast) through use of a mordant, a metallic oxide such as alum or iron. The cloth was first painted with the mordant then dipped in a madder bath. Certainly, by the last third of the 1800s calico cloth had become standard dress for the Seminoles. In 1910, Little Billy (Billy Koniphadjo) told Alanson Skinner that leather clothing was "hot too much" and no longer worn daily; he could only remember always wearing calico (Skinner 1913:66). Checked cloth was being produced in New England mills as early as 1810.

Broadcloth or stroud was a wool textile tightly woven on a wide loom. The highest quality broadcloth was made in the west of England where

the mills in Stroud produced a deep scarlet and sturdy cloth. The Yorkshire region of northern England also produced quality cloth. Broadcloth, first developed in England in the late sixteenth century, was widely imported to America which for many years had no domestic wool industry. George Washington ordered a suit made of broadcloth for his inauguration in 1789. Woolen cloth with a striped selvedge was first made in England in the 1820s for the East Indian Company's trade with China.

Osnaburg cloth, listed in the Luther Blake expense report (see note 13), was a coarse fabric first made from linen or hemp originating in Osnaburg, Germany, and used for pants and bags. By the nineteenth century the term was used to refer to coarse cotton fabric with blue and white or brown and white stripes or checks, or sometimes just plain. The source for all of the above is Florence M. Montgomery's *Textiles in America: 1650-1870*, an essential reference for the identification of trade cloth among the American Indians (Montgomery 1984). The textile collection available online from the Winterthur Museum (2019) is also an excellent source for comparison.

As with every aspect of the logistics involved with providing for, removing, relocating, reestablishing, and acculturating the American Indians by the U.S. government's Indian Agent system, greed and corruption infiltrated the supply of cloth and clothing, sometimes in partnership between an Indian Agent and private supplier, and often greatly inflating the cost paid by the government or Indian consumer who would pay for the overpriced cloth from the annual annuity. Concern for the Indian consumer prompted a Commissioner of the Western Superintendency, Henry L. Ellsworth, to investigate trade practices among the agencies under his supervision. His findings of great irregularities and fraud resulted in his compiling of a pattern book consisting of a set of 50 fabric samples with set prices, to be used by the government as a standard reference (Adrosko 1990). The Ellsworth (1834) sample book can be seen online.

20. Editor's note: The collection on which this study is based was donated in 1975 (see Note 2). William Marquardt served as curator in charge of South Florida archaeology and ethnography collections

for 30 years, from 1988 until his retirement in 2018. During that period, steps were taken to curate and protect the collection according to the best museum standards. Concerted efforts – ultimately successful – were made to locate certain items that had been transported to the Smithsonian Institution for study by Dr. William Sturtevant. The complete, reassembled collection was rehoused in new archival materials, kept in a secure location, and never exhibited to the public. The Museum's possession of this collection was not a secret. A color photograph of the entire collection had been published (Milanich 1998:Plate 14); see also discussion by Downs (1995:174-175). Seminole tribal members had viewed the collection upon request. Items in the collection were treated respectfully by Florida Museum personnel, never touched by ungloved human hands. During Marquardt's curatorship, no destructive analyses whatsoever on any items in the collection were allowed. This chapter was completed by Dr. Weisman in 2020 following research done in 2019. The original manuscript included descriptions of certain personal medicines and talismans contained within the pouch of the deceased man's shoulder bag, based largely on Dr. Sturtevant's recorded observations (see Note 14). Dr. Weisman submitted the draft manuscript to the Seminole Tribe of Florida (STOF) in 2020 and was informed that the Tribe approved the chapter as it was. On June 22, 2022, via Paul Backhouse, he received a new request from the STOF to delete descriptions and discussions of certain items contained in the pouch. Dr. Backhouse supplied a strike-through version of the text for Dr. Weisman's consideration. In consultation with the volume editor, the author made 100% of the requested deletions, specifically, 3,861 words (23.9% of the text) and 13 of the 30 images (43.3%). Dr. Backhouse responded, "thank you so much for your understanding of the request to remove the culturally sensitive material we discussed. It is deeply appreciated… thank you for your sensitivity in this matter." Although significant parts of the chapter were removed, the abridged chapter remains a fitting tribute to Seminole resistance during the so-called Third Seminole War. It honors the individual warrior and places him in context with the terrible events caused by the invasion of the Big Cypress Swamp.

References

Adrosko, Rita J.
  1990 A "Little Book of Samples": Evidence of Textiles Traded to the American Indians. *Textile Society of America Symposium Proceedings* 589:65-74.

Andrews, R. L., J. M. Adovasio, B. Humphrey, D. C. Hyland, J. S. Gardner, and D. G. Harding
  2002 Conservation and Analysis of Textile and Related Perishable Artifacts. In *Windover: Multidisciplinary Investigations of an Early Archaic Florida Cemetery*, edited by Glen H. Doran, pp. 121-165. University Press of Florida, Gainesville.

Barnes, R. M.
  1972 *The Uniforms and History of the Scottish Regiments.* Sphere Books, London.

Bartram, William
  1996 *Travels and Other Writings.* The Library of America, New York.

Beaudry, Mary Carolyn
  2006 *Findings: The Material Culture of Needlework and Sewing.* Yale University Press, New Haven.

Blakey, Arch Frederic, Ann S. Lainart, and Winston Bryant Stephens
  1998 *Rose Cottage Chronicles: Civil War Letters of the Bryant-Stephens Families of North Florida.* University Press of Florida, Gainesville.

Boyd, Mark F.
  1958 Horatio S. Dexter and the Events Leading to the Treaty of Moultrie Creek With the Seminoles. *The Florida Anthropologist* 11:65-95.

Brackman, Barbara
  1989 *Clues in the Calico: A Guide to Identifying and Dating Antique Quilts.* EPM Publications, McLean, Virginia.

Canova, Andrew
  1906 *Life and Adventures in South Florida.* Tribune Printing Co., Tampa.

Capron, Louis
  1953 The Medicine Bundles of the Florida Seminoles and the Green Corn Dance. *Bureau of American Ethnology* 151:155-210.

Carney, Judith A.
  2001 *Black Rice: The African Origins of Rice Cultivation in the Americas.* Harvard University Press, Cambridge.

Carr, Robert S.
  1981 The Brickell Store and Seminole Indian Trade. *The Florida Anthropologist* 34(4):180-199.
  1989 Archaeological Excavations at the Stranahan House (8Bd259), Fort Lauderdale, Florida. *The Florida Anthropologist* 42:17-33.

Cory, Charles Barney
  1896 *Hunting and Fishing in Florida, Including a Key to the Water Birds Known to Occur in the State.* Estes and Lauriat, Boston.

Covington, James W.
  1982 *The Billy Bowlegs War.* Mickler, Chuluota, Florida.
  1993 *The Seminoles of Florida.* University Press of Florida, Gainesville.

De Mauro, Linda S.
  1977 *A Bibliography of the Hydrology of the Everglades and the Big Cypress Swamp, Florida.* Report T-501. South Florida Research Center, Everglades National Park, Homestead.

Dockstader, Frederick J.
  1978 *Weaving Arts of the North American Indian.* Thomas Y. Crowell, New York.

Downs, Dorothy
  1995 *Art of the Florida Seminole and Miccosukee Indians.* University of Florida Press, Gainesville.

Ehrenhard, John E., Robert S. Carr, and Robert C. Taylor
  1978 *The Archaeological Survey of Big Cypress National Preserve: Phase 1.* Southeast Archeological Center, National Park Service, Tallahassee, Florida.

Elliott, Dolores N.
  2003 Two Centuries of Iroquois Beadwork. *BEADS: Journal of the Society of Bead Researchers* 15:3-22.

Ellsworth, Henry L.
  1834 The Ellsworth Sample Book. Electronic document, https://americanhistory.si.edu/collections/search/object/nmah_1092188 .

Ewel, Katherine C.
  1990 Swamps. In *Ecosystems of Florida*, edited by Ronald L. Myers and John J. Ewel, pp. 281-323. University Press of Florida, Gainesville.

Fitts, Mary Elizabeth
  2001 Two Eighteenth-Century Seminole Burials From Alachua County, Florida. M.A. thesis, University of South Florida, Tampa.

Foreman, Grant
  1953 *Indian Removal* (new edition). University of Oklahoma Press, Norman.

Goggin, John M.
  1951 Beaded Shoulder Pouches of the Florida Seminole. *The Florida Anthropologist* 4:2-17.

Goggin, John M., Mary E. Godwin, Earl Hester, David Prange, and Robert Spangenberg
  1949 An Historic Indian Burial, Alachua County, Florida. *The Florida Anthropologist* 21:10-25.

Hardin, Kenneth W.
  1982 Utilitarian Grave Goods. In *Archaeological Excavations at the Quad Block Site, 8Hi998*, edited by Harry M. Piper and Jacquelyn G. Piper, pp. 274-296. Piper Archaeological Research, Inc., St. Petersburg, Florida.

Harding, Deborah G.
  1994 Bagging the Tourist Market: A Descriptive and Statistical Study of Nineteenth Century Iroquois Beaded Bags. M.A. thesis, University of Pittsburgh.

Hawk, Robert
  2019 *Florida Militia Muster Rolls, Seminole Indian Wars*, Volume 10. Florida Department of Military Affairs Special Archives Publication Number 76. State Arsenal, St. Francis Barracks, St. Augustine.

Hodges, Ellen E., and Stephen Kerber (editors)
  1978 "Rogues and Black Hearted Scamps": Letters of Winston and Octavia Stephens, 1862-1863. *Florida Historical Quarterly* 57:54-82.

Ives, Lieut. J. C.
  1856 Military Map of the Peninsula of Florida South of Tampa Bay. National Archives Record Group 77, L89-11. Copy available in the P. K. Yonge Library of Florida History, Department of Special Collections, Smathers Libraries, University of Florida, Gainesville.

Karklins, Karlis
  2012 Guide to the Description and Classification of Glass Beads Found in the Americas. *BEADS: Journal of the Society of Bead Researchers* 24:62-90.

Kersey, Harry A.
  1975 *Pelts, Plumes, and Hides*. University Press of Florida, Gainesville.

Knetsch, Joe, John Missall, and Mary Lou Missall
  2018 *History of the Third Seminole War, 1849-1858*. Casemate Publishers, Havertown, Pennsylvania.

Krager, Margo
  2004 Calico Trade Shirts on the Journey of Discovery with Lewis and Clark. *Textile Society of America Symposium Proceedings* 437. https://digitalcommons.unl.edu/tsaconf/437

MacCauley, Clay
  1887 The Seminole Indians of Florida. In *Fifth Annual Report of the Bureau of American Ethnology 1883-84*, pp. 469-531. Government Printing Office, Washington, DC.

Mahon, John K.
  1967 *History of the Second Seminole War*. University Press of Florida, Gainesville.

  1972 *The War of 1812*. University Press of Florida, Gainesville.

McPherson, Benjamin F.
  1974 The Big Cypress Swamp. In *Environments of South Florida: Present and Past*, edited by Patrick J. Gleason, pp. 8-17. Miami Geological Society, Coral Gables.

Meller, Susan, and Joost Elffers
  2002 *Textile Designs: Two Hundred Years of European and American Patterns Organized by Motif, Style, Color, Layout, and Period*. Harry N. Abrams, New York.

Miner, Horace
  1936 The Importance of Textiles in the Archaeology of the Eastern United States. *American Antiquity* 1(3):181-192.

Milanich, Jerald T.
  1998 *Florida's Indians from Ancient Times to the Present*. University Press of Florida, Gainesville.

Montgomery, Florence
  1984 *Textiles in America 1650-1870*. W. W. Norton and Company, New York.

Morton, Julia F.
  1975 The Sturdy Seminole Pumpkin Provides Much Food with Little Effort. *Proceedings of the Florida State Horticultural Society* 88:137-142.

Patterson, Ellen Hodges
  1979 The Stephens Family in East Florida: A Profile of Plantation Life Along the St. Johns River, 1859-1864. M.A. thesis, University of Florida, Gainesville.

Piper, Harry M., and Jacquelyn G. Piper
  1982 *Archaeological Excavations at the Quad Block Site, 8Hi998*. Piper Archaeological Research, St. Petersburg, Florida.

Porcher, Francis P.
  1863 *Resources of the Southern Fields and Forests*. Evans and Cogswell, Charleston, South Carolina.

Reeves, I. S. K., V
  2009 *Art of the Seminole, 1820-1950*. Exhibit catalog, Maitland Art Center, Maitland, Florida.

Rogers, S. St. George
  1857 Letter to Major F. N. Page, December 31, 1857. National Archives and Records Management [NARA], Letters Sent, Registers of Letters Received, and Letters Received by Headquarters, Troops in Florida, and Headquarters, Department of Florida (1850-1858), M1084, Roll 9, Record Group [RG] 393.

Romans, Bernard
  1999 *A Concise Natural History of East and West Florida*, edited by Kathryn E. Holland Braund. University of Alabama Press, Tuscaloosa.

Ross, Lester A.
 1990 Trade Beads From Hudson's Bay Company
   Fort Vancouver (1829-1860), Vancouver,
   Washington. *BEADS: Journal of the Society of
   Bead Researchers* 2:29-67.

Silver, James W.
 1949 *Edmund Pendleton Gaines, Frontier General.*
   Louisiana State University Press, Baton Rouge.

Skinner, Alanson
 1913 Notes on the Florida Seminole. *American
   Anthropologist* 15:63-77.

Stephens, W[inston]
 1857 Letter to Lieut. W.S. Harris, December 4.
   "Letters Received by the Office of the Adjutant
   General (Main Series), 1822-1860, M567, Roll 558,
   1857, Letters Sent, Registers of Letters Received,
   and Letters Received by Headquarters, Troops in
   Florida, and Headquarters, Department of Florida
   (1850-1858, M1084, Roll 9, RG 393).

Sturtevant, William C.
 1954 The Medicine Bundles and Busks of the Florida
   Seminole. *The Florida Anthropologist* 7:31-70.

 1955 The Mikasuki Seminole: Medical Beliefs and
   Practices. Ph.D. dissertation, Department of
   Anthropology, Yale University, New Haven.

 1956a Osceola's Coats? *Florida Historical Quarterly*
   34(4):315-328.

 1956b R. H. Pratt's Report on the Seminole in 1879.
   The Florida Anthropologist 9:1-24.

 1962 A Newly-Discovered 1838 Drawing of a
   Seminole Dance. *The Florida Anthropologist*
   15:73-82.

 1967 Seminole Men's Clothing. *Proceedings* of the
   1966 Annual Spring Meeting of the American
   Ethnological Society, pp. 160-174. University of
   Washington Press, Seattle.

 2000 Introduction. In *The Seminole Indians of Florida*
   by Clay MacCauley. University Press of Florida,
   Gainesville.

Suciu, Peter
 2008 Glengarry: Headgear of the Highlanders.
   Electronic document, https://www.militarytrader.
   com/militaria-collectibles/glengarry-head-
   gear-of-the-highlanders, accessed September 24,
   2019.

Taylor, Robert
 1985 Levels of Significance for the Cultural Sites
   in the Big Cypress National Preserve, Florida. Ms.
   1616, Florida Master Site File, Florida Division
   of Historical Resources, Department of State,
   Tallahassee.

United States Senate
 1854 Senate Executive Document No. 71, 33rd
   Congress, 1st Session.

Weisman, Brent Richards
 1989 *Like Beads on a String: A Culture History of
   the Seminole Indians in North Peninsular Florida.*
   University of Alabama Press, Tuscaloosa.

Wickman, Patricia R.
 1991 *Osceola's Legacy.* University of Alabama Press,
   Tuscaloosa.

Winterthur Museum
 2019 Online collection at museumcollection.
   winterthur.org, accessed September 26, 2019.

Wissler, Clark
 1912 *Ceremonial Bundles of the Blackfoot Indians.*
   Anthropological Papers 7(2), American Museum
   of Natural History, New York.

Zedeño, María Nieves
 2008 Bundled Worlds: The Roles and Interactions
   of Complex Objects from the North American
   Plains. *Journal of Archaeological Method and
   Theory* 15:362-378.

3

Two Seminole Long Coats from the Early Nineteenth Century

Stacey L. Huber

Tucked away in a textile cabinet within the Florida Ethnographic Collection in the Anthropology division, Florida Museum of Natural History are two extraordinary garments that speak of Florida and Seminole history. These are long coats dating to the 1830s-1850s that must have been worn by male members of the Seminole tribe. The museum is fortunate to have two of the earliest surviving long coats. Although both are fragile, they are wonderful examples of these garments and give insight to creative thoughts and expressions of Native Americans during a turbulent time in the history of the Tribe—the Second Seminole War (Mahon 1967). If only these coats could talk, the history they could share! Although that is not possible, we can describe, compare, and contrast these garments to reach a better understanding of how they were made and how they compare with other such garments.

In this chapter, I focus mainly on the two long coats at the Florida Museum and limit my discussion to coats of the nineteenth century. Long coats are sometimes called doctor's coats or councilor's coats, connoting the special status of their wearers. Generally speaking, a long coat is a long-sleeved garment that reaches knee length and has a cape-like collar attached to the neck area. The back of the coat has a slit at the bottom to facilitate ease of movement. Some similarly styled garments are known as "hunting coats," but these are generally made of leather, not cloth.

Acquisition of the Two Long Coats

The first coat, accession number 77-40, catalog number E–595, was obtained by the museum on September 16, 1977. It came from the McMichael Canadian Collection located in Kleinberg, Ontario,

Canada. This coat and other Southeastern objects were exchanged for northwestern Native American objects that the Florida Museum had obtained. A previous descriptive account of the coat was done by Jason Baird Jackson (1991) while a student at the University of Florida. In this chapter, I refer to the coat as the "alligator coat" due to the shape of its cape. Front and back views are shown in Figure 1.

The second coat, catalog number 2019-19-22-1, first came to the museum in July, 2016 on loan for study from then-owner Allison Mantrone-Cardinal, who wanted to learn more about the coat in her possession. The coat originally came her way by her late husband, Don Cardinal (1937-2008), a member of the Sucker Creek Cree First Nation in Alberta. A practicing medicine man, he was conducting a fasting camp in Saugerties, New York in the summer of 2002. A woman with a British accent came to the campsite and gave

Figure 1. *The "Alligator Coat" (catalog number E-595), front and back views. Unless otherwise credited, all photographs in this chapter are by Kristen Grace, Florida Museum of Natural History.*

Mr. Cardinal the coat. Her family was from England and she had inherited the coat but did not know much about it. She wished to give the coat back to a Native American. She left without giving her name and was never heard from again.

During the time the coat was on loan, I was a curatorial assistant in the Anthropology division, working with William Marquardt and Karen Walker. Knowing of my background and training in fabric history, Dr. Marquardt asked me to study the coat and write a report. I did so, and this report was sent to Ms. Mantrone-Cardinal (Huber

2017). In July, 2018 the coat was purchased from Ms. Mantrone-Cardinal by Keith and Sara Reeves of Winter Park, Florida and in December, 2019 the Reeves generously donated the coat to the Florida Museum. I refer to this coat as the "toile coat" throughout this chapter because of the material used to create it. Front and back views of the toile coat are shown in Figure 2.

Both long coats are open down the front and come down to about knee length. The coats have sleeves that come down to the wrists with a cuff. At the back of each coat there is a cape, one with a triangular-shaped cape and the other with both triangular and semicircular-shaped capes. At the bottom of the coats on the back, there is a v-shaped slit. This opening is functional, helping with ease

of movement. Across both coats there are ruffles, trims, and appliqué that style the garment.

Construction of the Garments

Both coats were entirely constructed by hand stitching. Within the two coats various types of stitching can be found. A majority of the stitches are of a type called a **running stitch**, but also used were an **overcast stitch**, a **whip stitch**, and a **back stitch**. (Terms shown in bold are defined in the Glossary at the end of this chapter.)

The **toile** coat is about 47 inches in length and the width (shoulder to shoulder) is about 22 inches. The body of the garment is composed of two

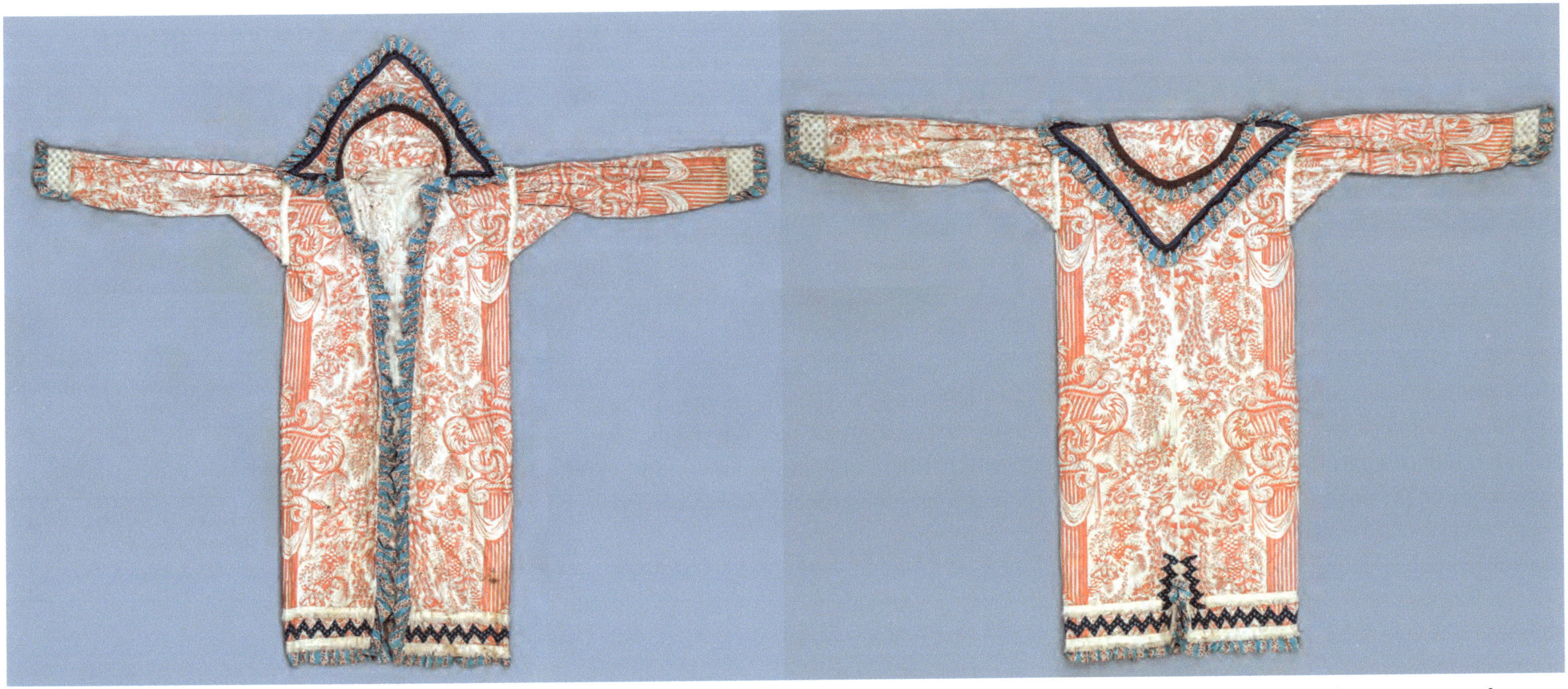

Figure 2. The "Toile Coat" (catalog number 2019-19-22-1), front and back views.

panels of fabric, measuring about 22 inches in width. The panels wrap to the front and are sewn together using a very consistent and tight whip stitch.

The fabric of this garment is a monochromatic pillar print. It is used in both the body of the garment and the sleeves. The print upon this fabric is a highly detailed illustration of architectural columns decorated with swags of fabric and flora (Figure 3). The print is compact, with little white ground showing. The red bleeds to the backside of the cloth. Microscopic examination shows that the fiber is cotton. Printed designs such as this one can be connected to contemporary events. Pillar prints came into fashion between 1800 and 1805. They started as high-quality block prints upon chintzes. These motifs were popular in America because the classical columns represented ideas associated with democratic ideals of the new republic. During the late 1820s, as the United States celebrated the fiftieth anniversary of the American Revolution, the pillar print design was revived. The design faded in popularity with printers in the mid-1830s.

There are similar examples of pillar prints in several textile collections in America. From the detail of the illustration, it cannot be a block print, unlike the alligator coat. This piece was either copper-plate printed or roller printed. In distinguishing between a copper print or roller print, a measurement of the repeat is needed. The repeat measured about 22 inches, which would indicate that this piece of fabric was copper-plate printed. Roller prints are usually 15 to 16 inches. According to Brackman (2009), a finely detailed, monochromatic print on a white ground strongly suggests a pre-1840 origin.

The alligator coat is constructed with solid and printed cotton fabrics of a **plain weave** construction. It is about 45 inches long and 24 inches wide. Like the toile coat, the alligator coat is composed of two panels of fabric to create the body. The main fabric, for both the body of the garment and the sleeves, is tan with a decorative motif print done in red, probably a bright madder dye, a natural dye. Natural dyes tend to fade quickly over time, which is demonstrated with this garment. This decorative motif, a paisley shape, leaf print is extremely faded, making it hard to find. It is most visible at the shoulders.

This print was created by woodblock printing, not with a copper-plate print like the toile coat. The technique of woodblock printing is one of the earliest forms of textile printing, dating as far back as AD 220, but it continued well into the nineteenth century. Eventually by the 1830s, the roller press had completely replaced the woodblock printing technique, a complex and time-consuming process. First the textile designer creates a carved wooden block with the desired design and then applies dye or mordant. A mordant, such as metal oxide, might be required for the color to stick to the raised surface of the block. The block is pressed on to the fabric, applying the colorant, then moving the block to the next desired spot. When examining the alligator coat (Figure 1), there are inconsistencies in spacing of the motif and the motif itself. The inconsistencies, the use of one color on a tan ground, and the simplicity in the design of the motif, give evidence to the print's being of the woodblocking technique.

The sewing construction on these two coats is exquisite and shows that both seamstresses had knowledge of different sewing techniques, those of Europeans.[1] An example of these advanced sewing skills is the technique used to gather the

fabric in a decorative manner. This is especially prevalent on the alligator coat along the cape. The fabric used was a blue calico print with large florals. The printed fabric was then **ruched** in a tight "S" shape all along the edge of the red trim. This piece is closer to the center of the cape. The red trim was **appliquéd** to the main tan fabric, and then the **ruching** was placed along the red trim in a way that hides the seam. It is also apparent that both long coats have ruffles in various size widths along the edges of the garments, such as the opening and all around the bottom. Along the edge of those ruffles, a hem was tightly sewn. Exposed thread measures about one eighth of an inch apart, another characteristic of excellent craftsmanship.

Distinctive Features

The Capes

The toile coat has the decorative element of a double cape (Figure 3). This detail of two capes is astonishing. Usually, there is only one cape, either triangular or round. The question arises, Why did the maker want to draw attention to this area of the garment and why the extra decoration? Both capes are made from monochromatic pillar-print fabric and are edged with the vine floral ruffle print fabric. The triangle-shaped cape lies on top

Figure 3. *Close-up view of the Toile Coat showing detail of the printed design, a monochromatic pillar print.*

of the body of the garment. It measures about 12 inches long, reaching to the middle of one's shoulder blades and extends about 22 inches. The rounded cape is about six inches long and extends to about 13 inches. These capes add extra drama and show evidence that the maker had an eye for style. The use of two capes shows a combination of tribal but also frontiersmen's coats. The rounded cape is similar to the Europeans' coats and the addition of the triangular cape shows tribal influence. The melding of the two creates a statement piece. Although we cannot know the actual intent of this highly unusual feature, it would certainly have drawn attention and stimulated conversation.

The alligator coat is so called because of the cape's shape (Figure 4). The shape is like an alligator head and the majority of the color is tan, the dominant fabric of the coat. As noted by Jackson (1991), the cape dominates the back of the coat. Compared to capes of other long coats, it is long and narrow, measuring 19 inches long. It is decorated with an outer-edge blue patterned ruffle, then a strip of red trim and then another indigo ruching toward the inner part of the cape. The ruching along the inner edge is a different ruching from the outer-edge treatment, looking more like an "S" shape.

Stylistic Trims

An important decorative element of these two coats is located at the bottom. When worn, this portion hangs at the knee of the garment and when walking, a beautiful visual effect occurs with the movement of the decorative element of appliqué. While the two are different in technique, construction, and material, they are similar in overall decorative shapes. When examining the two, the decorative factor is contained in a rectangular box, and within that box, geometric shapes are present, such as triangles, diamonds, and lines. Unlike the print designs on the fabrics used, they are geometric, not organic. Refer to the images of the bottom portions of the toile coat (Figure 5) and the alligator coat (Figure 6).

Figure 4. *Close-up view of the distinctive cape element, which dominates the back of Alligator Coat.*

Figure 5. *Stylistic trim at the bottom of the Toile Coat.*

Figure 6. *Stylistic trim at the bottom of the Alligator Coat.*

is a light blue, mimicking a leaf. The technique of resist printing was used to create this pattern.

Resist printing is the use of a paste to block dye penetration in areas where a pattern is desired. These designs were usually created with a roller printer in which large amounts of fabrics could be printed at a time. This fabric was probably put through another dyebath after the resist was removed to create the light blue design instead of white. The technique was popular from the 1800s to the 1830s before the resist-printing method evolved.

Containing the geometric design appliqué is a border of ecru-colored trims. Along the bottom edge of both sets of trims, the seamstress created a fringe effect. The top portion of the trim is a solid edge where a simple visible running stitch of similarly colored thread is applied to attach the trim to the coat. The width of the trim averages about one inch for both the top and bottom trim. Like the sawtooth appliqué, the two trims encircle the coat with breaks at the front and back. Similar to the sawtooth pattern on the back, the bottom trim follows the edge of the slit in a vertical direction. The top trim, if strung together, would measure in length about 40 inches, while the bottom trim would be about 45 inches in length.

The alligator cape's bottom portion of the design is quite large because the design starts at the color block of red fabric toward the bottom. Like the toile coat, this decorative bottom portion encircles the entire garment from front to back. This bottom portion is almost a precursor to the

As mentioned earlier, the appliqué elements are contained in a rectangular design. The width of the bottom portion for the toile coat's design is about five inches, while the width for the alligator coat bottom portion is about 17 inches. The measurements start from the top of the trim border to the edge of the ruffle for the toile coat, while the alligator measurement is taken from the bottom of the solid red fabric to the edge of the ruffle. While the toile coat's bottom portion of the design and style are not as wide as the alligator's, it is still visually stunning with the beautiful indigo print and appliqué.

The bottom of the toile coat has an eye-catching decorative element, the zigzag (sawtooth) appliqué (Figure 7). This sawtooth design is about two inches high and it wraps around the entirety of the coat with breaks at the back slit opening and the front opening of the coat. There are additional sawtooth appliqués at the back of the garment that run vertically with the slit on both the right and left sides. If the sawtooth pattern ran together, the overall length would be about 40 inches. The appliqué work is of excellent quality. The style of appliqué used is a more common type called overcast or **appliqué stitch**. This stitch holds the two layers of fabric together with tiny visible stitches. Upon close examination, black thread is visible. It is difficult to spot the appliqué stitches against the navy blue calico print fabric. The ground color is a dark navy, while the print design

Figure 7. *View of the back opening of the Toile Coat, showing the zigzag design around both sides of the slit.*

of the ruffle is indigo blue with a large floral print. This print is created by using the **discharge method** of printing. At one time, the leaves in the floral print were green and the floral was pink, but the colors have faded to a yellow and peach. The bottom of the ruffle is not attached to the garment. Instead, it is hemmed along the edge using a tight running stitch. This piece adds dimension and movement toward the bottom of the coat.

Below the indigo ruffle is the decorative element of appliqué (Figure 6), creating a design using two different colored trims, red and brown. The trims are applied onto the main tan ground fabric of the garment using a running stitch with contrasting colored thread. Like the ecru trims of the toile coat, the trims are fringed along one side while the other side is a folded edge where the running stitch is applied. The width of this section is the largest of this bottom decoration, and it is about eight and a half inches in width. This includes the tan area that is covered by the appliquéd ruffle. The design within the tan ground mimics the sawtooth appliqué of the toile coat. When the trims are viewed separately, they create a sawtooth pattern, but together the overlapping trims create a diamond pattern. This band does not fully encircle from front to back because a slit breaks it at the back of the garment.

As noted above, both of these coats have a slit at the back, not for a decorative element but to ease movement of the legs. The slit is created at the center seam on the back of the garment. The toile coat's slit measures about seven inches and the

alligator coat's about eight inches long. The edges of the slit could have been done without the ruffle to keep with a functional design, but the designer/seamstress continued the outer edge ruffle all along the edge. It also shows the concern for an extra design detail, continuing the outer edge of the ruffle up the slit of the garment.

The last band of the alligator coat is the bottom edge ruffle, and the same goes for the toile coat. This decorative element is prevalent in other examples of Seminole long coats. Both sets of ruffles are applied using the same technique, a consistent, tight whip stitch. Figures 8 and 9 show the matching technique. The width of the toile coat's final band is about one and one half inches and the alligator coat's is about three inches. The alligator coat's ruffle is an indigo print fabric. The pattern is of small white florals placed in vertical direction, giving it the illusion of stripes. The toile coat's final band is made up of a floral print design using four different colors: blue, red, yellow, and white. The registration of the print is not precise, for the small prints of blue and yellow do not fit within the intended outline. This mis-registration happened when printers intended to create green, because one way of creating green was to print blue over yellow (Brackman 2009). This dates the fabric to earlier than 1860.

Both coats use trims extensively to accentuate certain areas of the garment. These additions of strips of cloth were not for function but were a detail of style. The toile coat uses the trims to draw attention to the cape, the shoulder, and along the bottom portion of the garment, forming a

modern Seminole garb of the late nineteenth century, with torn fabric bands used to create colorful garments. The rectangular containment of this bottom portion is created by using bands. The first band is the block of solid red fabric, which measures about five inches in width. Below that band is an applied ruffle. This ruffle is about two and one quarter inches wide. Because the ruffle application is on top of the garment, not an edge, the top edge of the ruffle is beautifully gathered together in an "S" formation with no visible thread or raw edges of the fabric. The main fabric color

Figure 8. *Close-up of whip stitch attaching the bottom edge ruffle, Toile Coat.*

Figure 9. *Close-up of whip stitch attaching the bottom edge ruffle, Alligator Coat.*

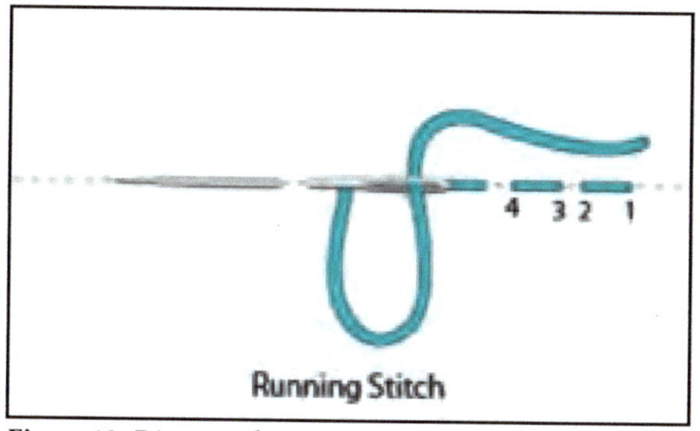

Figure 10. *Diagram showing a running stitch.*

stunning visual detail of appliqué, while the alligator coat uses the trims to outline the cape, draw attention to the shoulders, and serve as a design element for the cuffs of the sleeves and bottom portion of the coat.

The toile coat has three different trims, all of cotton fibers and made with plain weave construction. The maker frayed the sides of the trim and folded them in half before applying them to the coat. At the folded end, the trim is sewn to the garment using a running stitch (Figure 10), the same technique used in the alligator coat to apply the trims. Around the two capes are two different types of trim. The first trim of the toile coat is a navy blue patterned weave trim that is applied to the coat's triangular cape (Figure 11). This navy blue trim outlines the cape, drawing the eye to the edges of the coat. As mentioned before, navy blue is associated with indigo dye and is one of the oldest dyes known. The second trim is a brown fabric that has some shine. Brown was a common color in the nineteenth century because it was an easy color to obtain from vegetable dyes. This trim is located around the round cape.

The last trim is a natural tan color. This trim is placed in several places: around the armhole (Figure 12) and shoulder and at the bottom of the coat (Figure 13). Even though the trim colors blend with the ground color of the main fabric, it draws attention to the shoulder and the appliqué work at the bottom of the coat. In a subtle way the

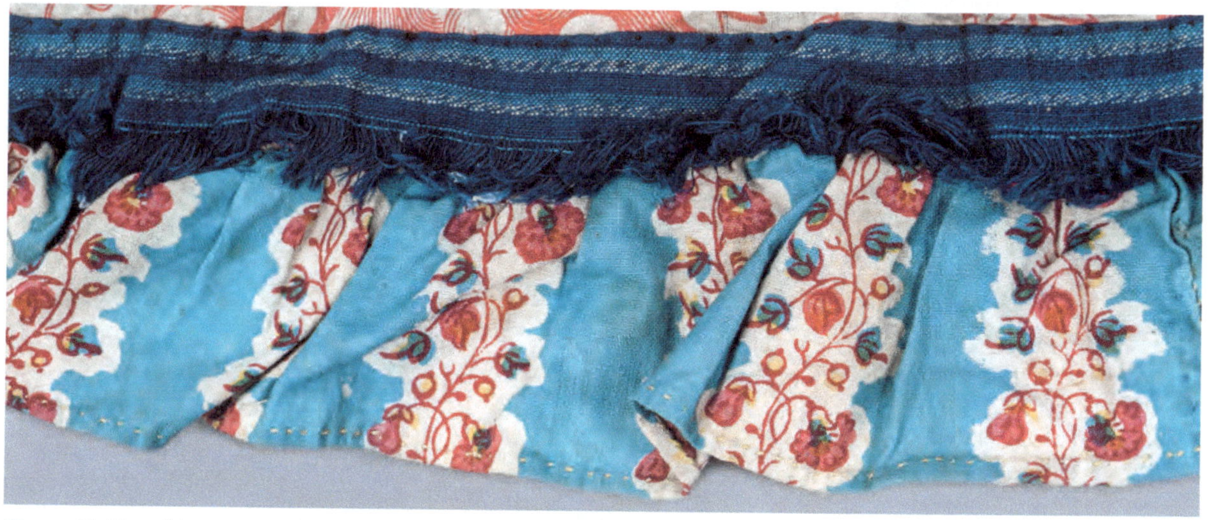

Figure 11. *Navy-blue patterned trim around the Toile Coat's triangular cape.*

Figure 12. *Tan-colored trim at the shoulder of the Toile Coat.*

Figure 13. *Tan-colored trim at the bottom of the Toile Coat.*

One of the trims of the alligator coat creates a diamond pattern, which is placed at the cuff of the sleeve and along the bottom portion of the garment. The red trim is sewn in a zigzag design and then the brown is sewn over the top in a zigzag manner, creating a diamond pattern. See Figure 16, which shows a sleeve cuff with that pattern.

When examining the coats side by side, the trims can be seen to have distinctive purposes. Although trims are decorative elements within the typical style of long coats, the makers used them in subtly different ways. The alligator cape uses its trims to keep the eye moving and is used as a focal point, while the toile coat uses trims to break the busyness of the coat and give dimension, so that the border at the bottom creates a box for the appliqué work.

Dating the Coats

To date the two coats, a comparative method of dating was used. This method is often used to date quilts because most have no provenience history. The comparative method is a compilation of weak or strong clues to build a case for a date. Clues have been presented throughout this chapter, building a strong case that the two coats date from the 1830s to the 1850s. The clues are based on categories such as fabric, techniques, and style.

The first category is fabric, in which the main component fabric pieces for both the alligator and the toile date to the 1830s or earlier. As discussed, the detailed monochromatic print on a white

eye is drawn to aspects of interest: the double cape and appliqué work.

The alligator coat has an interesting use of trim. Unlike other garments seen in collections, it is at the shoulders. The trim at the shoulders creates an illusion of bigger epaulets, making them grander. This illusion is created by using the trims in a diagonal manner, alternating red and brown. This element is not just on the front, but also on the back. Examine Figures 14 and 15 to see the front and back of the shoulder treatment. These trims are applied using a running stitch. The red strip is

sewn with an ecru-colored thread, while the brown trim is sewn with a bluish thread.

A red trim was used to draw attention to the cape on the alligator coat, calling the viewer's attention to the cape's unique shape. The trim is placed in between the edged ruffle and the ruching strip. Like the other trims, it is applied using a running stitch and is flat along the tan part of the cape and around the outer edge. Just like the other trims of this garment and the toile coat, one edge is frayed. Figure 15 shows how the red strip draws viewers into the cape.

Figure 14. *The Alligator Coat, front view of shoulder area.*

Figure 15. *The Alligator Coat, back view of shoulder area.*

Figure 16. *Sleeve cuff with diamond pattern created by overlapping two zig-zag patterns.*

ground suggests a pre-1840 origin. In comparison, the woodblock printing technique of the alligator coat was obsolete by the 1830s. Another part of the fabric category is the thread. Cotton threads were not factory-produced and easily accessible until the 1820s. Both coats used cotton threads, but the construction of the cotton thread gives another clue to the coats being from the 1830s to the 1850s, a three-ply construction. This means that there are three separate yarns spun tightly together to create the thread. When the sewing machine was invented and available, a stronger thread was needed in the second half of the 1840s, and the production of the three-ply thread was halted in favor of a stronger six-ply thread.

The next category examined was technique. The biggest clue is that both garments are entirely hand-stitched. Again, the sewing machine was readily available starting in the 1840s, and we know from journal accounts and artifacts that Seminoles embraced sewing machines. The absence of machine stitches is a clue to a time frame of 1830 to 1850.

Style, the final category of clues, dates this garment to the 1850s or earlier. It is especially important in this category to compare to other long coats. When looking at other pieces from the 1860s to the 1900s, the missing components give clues to the earlier date for the alligator and toile coats. The style is not as evolved and elaborate. An example would be the appliqués becoming more intricate and detailed. During the latter half of the nineteenth century, the artist played with shapes and more than one color/fabric, while the 1830s to 1850s pieces are in the beginning stages of playing with appliqué, creating simple shapes and using one color/fabric.

Compiling these clues with provenience histories points to a strong case that these garments date from the 1830s to the 1850s. To pinpoint an exact date, one would need to have strong clues across the board with better provenience history, but here there is a mix of weak and strong clues leading to a date range. To discover stronger clues, a more invasive and possibly harmful examination would be needed. This is not recommended. No damage should be done to a textile artifact. One way to find stronger clues is to compare these coats to all long coats available for the time interval.

Comparing the Coats to Others

Part of understanding these garments is not only comparing and contrasting with one another, but examining other garments of early Creek or Seminole tribes. Being able to view various pieces in other collections helps create a catalog of specimens and understanding of style trends associated with the community. Searching the online database for "Seminole coat" at the National Museum of the American Indian website resulted in four pieces. The date range of the four pieces is from 1830 to 1930, but here I limit my discussion to the three coats dating to the nineteenth century. The earliest piece, which has been said to be the coat of Seminole war chief Osceola (ca. 1803-1838) is a coat made of deer hide/deer skin. While this garment is not made of cotton, the coat resembles the same tailoring cuts as the toile coat and the alligator coat.

The Osceola Coat

See Figure 17 for front and back images of this coat. Four components match the Florida Museum

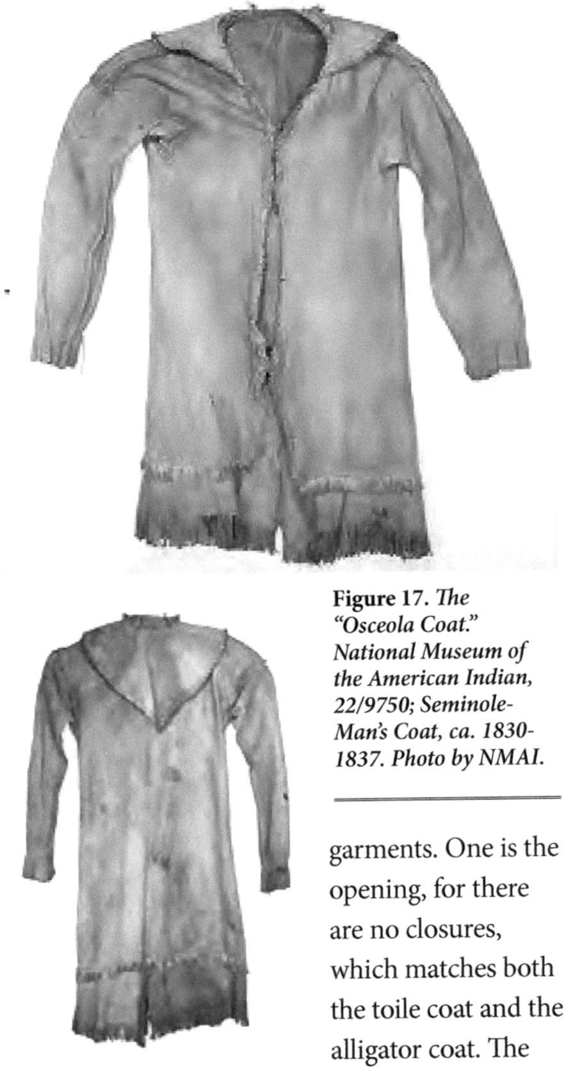

Figure 17. The "Osceola Coat." National Museum of the American Indian, 22/9750; Seminole-Man's Coat, ca. 1830-1837. Photo by NMAI.

garments. One is the opening, for there are no closures, which matches both the toile coat and the alligator coat. The second component is the slit in the back of the garment. A third component that matches the toile and alligator coats is the applied triangular cape piece around the neck. It starts from the front and cuts into a "V" in the back of the garment. This applied cape-like piece matches the applied piece on the toile coat and alligator coat. While the alligator coat cape is a longer and narrower triangle, it is the same basic idea. Finally, there is

the use of fringe. This fringe runs along the edges of the garment around the cape-like piece, the opening, and the bottom edge. The fringe mimics the ruffles used along the edges of the alligator and toile coats. But there is also a decorative element at the bottom portion of the coat, an applied strip of fringe that is not functional but decorative. Having a decorative element at the bottom portion of the coat matches the decorative elements of the alligator coat with the applied trims to create a diamond pattern and the toile coat with the appliquéd sawtooth pattern.

The Second NMAI Coat

The second example found from online collections of the National Museum of the American Indian is similar in tailoring cut to the Florida Museum objects, but also in material (Figure 18). This garment is composed of printed cotton fabrics with the use of plain cotton trims like the toile and alligator coats. The piece has been dated to 1850. There is no collection history because the piece was purchased by NMAI in 1924. Like the deer-hide coat of Osceola, it has an opening without closures, a slit at the back of the garment, and the cape-like piece applied around the neck. One thing that the toile and alligator coats have that is absent in the deer-hide coat and this cotton coat is sleeve cuffs. Both garments are gathered at the cuffs to form a cuff-like appearance. Besides the tailored cuts matching the two Florida Museum coats, material and style are also similar. The main printed cotton fabric is an off-white ground with large floral prints, similar to the toile and alligator coats, which have large prints on a light ground.

Figure 18. *The second NMAI coat. National Museum of the American Indian, 13/5085; Seminole-Man's Coat, ca. 1850. Photo by NMAI.*

On the front, the ruffle lines the bottom half of the opening of the later piece. These ruffles are wider, adding more dramatization. At the bottom of this coat there is a band of appliqué. This appliqué design is of squares within squares, which is a more complicated design than the zigzag (saw tooth) appliqué of the toile coat and the diamond pattern of the alligator coat. This shows the appliqué technique evolving to more complicated designs, from one-fabric pieces to three or four pieces. The trims have a thinner appearance than those of the toile and alligator coats, which shows extra attention to decorative details and the probable use of the sewing machine. There is not just one color of trim, there are two to four strips used to create a decorative trim.

The NMAI coat uses plain strips of cotton cloth to trim and decorate the garment. The trimming is along the applied cape-like piece and along the slit at the bottom of the garment. This trimming resembles the toile coat and some aspects of the alligator coat. One matching feature is the trimming of the slit in the back. The toile coat is trimmed at the slit with the zigzag appliqué. The alligator coat uses trims but doesn't exactly match the location of use. These small similarities in decoration show a trend and style that was forming/formed within the tribe.

The Third NMAI coat

A later example, ca. 1900, shows the continuation of trends and cuts that were established early within the tribe, but it also shows the evolution of the long coat (Figure 19). This garment has the same cuts as the deer hide, the cotton, the toile, and the alligator coats. There is the distinguishable cape-like feature, an opening without closures, and a slit in the back of the garment. There are extra trimmings and decorations. The length of the cape-feature has extended and covers the shoulder blades. Along this piece, there is a ruffle, which is evident on the cotton coat, the toile coat, the alligator coat, and the deer-hide fringe of the Osceola coat. There are other strips of ruffle, but unlike the toile coat's lining of the edges of the coat, ruffles were placed about the center, horizontally and along the opening of the slit. The placement of the horizontal ruffle about the center on the garment is like the alligator coat, which has a horizontal ruffle above the diamond pattern created with trims.

Although comparing and contrasting the two Florida Museum coats to other nineteenth-

Figure 19. *The third NMAI coat. National Museum of the American Indian, 1/8274; Seminole-Man's Coat/Jacket, ca. 1900). Photo by NMAI.*

century examples gives us insight into style and community, it is still just a tiny bit of information. To better understand the community and its story, there needs to be a compiling of all long coats that have survived in order to create a much bigger picture of the community. A database should be created, because databases can not only hold important information, they can also find relationships across data. What is needed is an open, public database with images, measurements, and all pertinent information such as material types, sewing techniques, and provenance where known. Valuable information could be gained, and better communication between collections and researchers would be established thereby.

Long Coats in Cultural Context

Southeastern Native Americans were inspired by the trade shirts acquired from Europeans after contact. They were drawn to the long shirts but importantly also to the hunting coat worn by the southern frontiersmen of colonial and early American times. These coats were loose and knee length and featured a round cape that encircled the shoulders. This characteristic was picked up by members of various southeastern tribes.

As mentioned above, when looking at the two Florida Museum coats, the full view is similar. The shapes, colors, and statements have a similar effect. Both coats show the inspiration of the frock and frontiersmen coats of the Europeans, but the aesthetic of the tribal community is visible not only in the use of multiple colors, patterns, and special cuts, but also in the use of additive pieces.

The details of the coats are similar, and details are what creates styles. For example, consider the fashions of the 1980s street punk movement (Gaget Girl 2014; Pitchfork and Levi 2014). These men and women were inspired by the rebel teens of the 1950s and created the countermovement to the late 1960s time of love and peace with the use of flowing and relaxed wardrobes with the use of leather, tight pants, ripped tees, and anger. However, to gain attention and to create a sense of community, they incorporated additive details in their garments, such as chains, safety pins, and patches. This identified them to one another and showed their community to the world. Similarly, these two Seminole coats, like others in various collections, incorporate additive details such as appliqué designs, trims, and ruffles. All these details conveyed messages about identity and community.

The importance of individuals can be conveyed by their dress. The idea of dressing to impress has been around for centuries and is done by using expensive materials and playing with style. Playing with style is exactly what these two coats do. Both have exquisite capes. This cut style of the capes is rare, not to be seen in other museum collection examples. Imagine walking up behind two renowned Seminole tribal members in the 1830s. How do you know they are great Seminole leaders? It would be their appearance, their dress. Their long coats would draw your attention with the use of colors and patterns but the cape styles of the toile coat and alligator coat would immediately invite special attention. One coat essentially has two capes, a triangular cape that lies on the back with a round cape that lies on top of the triangular cape. The other coat has an alligator-head shape that is extra-long, reaching to the middle of the back. Both coats exhibit "playing with style" while maintaining the fashion of long coats with capes.

Conclusion

One of the biggest takeaways from examining the toile and the alligator coats is the level of craftsmanship demonstrated, not just in technique, but also in design. There have been arguments and suggestions that production of such garments would have required the skills and talents of European settlers, not Seminoles. In fact, these techniques, skills, and eye for design complement the high level of craftsmanship demonstrated in other mediums for the Seminoles. For example, bandolier bags of the same period are exquisite and would have required a high level of craftsmanship. And when looking at present garments of the Miccosukee and Seminole tribes, the attention to high craftsmanship with style and technique is obvious. This focus on craftsmanship has been there from the beginning.

In the end, it is remarkable that two early coats reside in the same textile cabinet, tucked away with their stories. Their hidden narratives are the most frustrating yet magical part of being a material culture researcher. Although the whole history will never be known, continued comparative study can provide insights on the evolution of the unique clothing styles of the Seminole people.

Acknowledgments. I first want to express my most enormous gratitude to the people who made this book happen, Keith and Sara Reeves and Dr. Bill Marquardt. In particular, Keith Reeves's continuous push to preserve and share the history of Seminoles and Miccosukee sponsored this book. Dr. Marquardt's enthusiasm and desire to share the stories of the Seminole and Miccosukee were pivotal in bringing together the scholars of this book. In addition, his continued support and belief in my research kept me going during difficult times. He believed that my research was worth sharing, and I am forever grateful. I am immensely grateful to Allison Mantrone-Cardinal. She saw the importance of this coat and knew that it needed a home—a place where it was kept safe and treated with the respect it deserves, but, most importantly, a place where its story can be told. The Florida Museum is where the toile coat made its home and is where I had the pleasure of working on this project. I am thankful that I had the opportunity to work with such knowledgeable and excellent people at the museum. I had the pleasure of working with and learning from Elise LeCompte, Donna Ruhl, Aaron Ellrich, and Kristen Grace. I also extend my most immense gratitude to former Collection Manager of the Florida Ethnographic Collection, Dr. Karen Walker. She made the collections accessible and helped facilitate my research with her knowledge and support. I also thank Patsy West, Gloria Comstock, and Dr. Christine Meyer for sharing their wisdom and for their attention to detail. Each of you inspires me to be a better researcher and a better contributor to sharing knowledge with all. Finally, I am very honored to be included in this book alongside scholars I look up to and admire in Sandra Starr, Brent Weisman, Patsy West, and Austin Bell. It truly was a beautiful experience, and I am excited that these stories from the collections will be shared.

Notes

1. Dorothy Downs raises the idea that these garments were constructed by runaway slave women who had learned these techniques while living on plantations (Downs 1995:42-45).

Glossary

appliqué – Appliqué is where one material, usually plain, is placed on top of another to create motifs, pattern, or texture. It is layering of fabrics, to "apply" an extra dimension onto the fabric.

appliqué stitch/ overcast stitch – To create an appliqué, a variety of stitches can be used. One is the blind stitch, in which no stitches show, being hidden in the folds of the fabric. The most common stitch is the overcast, or appliqué stitch, that holds the two layers with visible stitches.

back stitch – A back stitch is a basic hand embroidery stitch that creates a line of stitches without a break between them, so it looks like a continuous straight line of thread.

discharge method – a printing technique in which the cloth is completely dyed and then a discharge agent such as bleach is applied by a roller. Where the roller and bleach touch, the figures are produced because the color is destroyed, leaving behind the figures.

overcast stitch – *See* appliqué stitch.

plain weave – the construction technique taking yarns to create fabric. Plain weave is the simplest of weaves to create fabric — interlacing between warp and weft threads, creating a checkerboard. This fabric is balanced and there is no front or back to plain weave fabrics. Because of its smoothness, it is suitable for finishes or for printing.

ruched, ruching – Ruching is gathered overlay of fabric strips that are pleated, fluted, or gathered together to create a ripple-like effect or a ruffle. Often used as trimming.

running stitch – One of the most basic stitches is the running stitch. Done in straight stiches, the needle is inserted into the fabric and taken out in small intervals.

toile – a simply-woven fabric of cotton or flax.

whip stitch – A whip stitch is a simple seaming technique that uses short diagonal stitches to pass over an edge, or in joining, finishing, or gathering fabric.

References

Arnold, Janet
1972 *Patterns of Fashion*. Macmillan, London.

Baumgarten, Linda
1986 *Eighteenth-century Clothing at Williamsburg*. Colonial Williamsburg Foundation.

Blackard, David M.
1990 *Patchwork and Palmettos: Seminole/Miccosukee Folk Art since 1820: An Exhibition Sponsored by the Fort Lauderdale Historical Society, March 1 through September 3, 1990*. Fort Lauderdale Historical Society, Fort Lauderdale, Florida.

Brackman, Barbara
2009 *Clues in the Calico: A Guide to Identifying and Dating Antique Quilts*. C & T Publishing, Concord, California.

Bredif, Josette
1989 *Toiles de Jouy Classic Printed Textiles from France 1760-1843*. Thames and Hudson, London.

Colpitts, George
2014 *North America's Indian Trade in European Commerce and Imagination, 1580-1850*. Brill.

Cooke, Edward S.
1987 *Upholstery in America & Europe: From the Seventeenth Century to World War I*. Norton, New York.

Covington, James W.
1974 Florida Seminoles: 1900-1920. *The Florida Historical Quarterly* 53(2):181-197.

Davis, Hilda J.
1955 The History of Seminole Clothing and Its Multi-Colored Designs. *American Anthropologist* 57(5):974-980.

Downs, Dorothy
1980 British Influences on Creek and Seminole Men's Clothing 1733-1858. *The Florida Anthropologist* 33:46-65.

Downs, Dorothy
1995 *Art of the Florida Seminole and Miccosukee Indians*. University Press of Florida, Gainesville.

Eaton, Linda (author), and Jim Schneck (photographer)
2014 *Printed Textiles: British and American Cottons and Linens 1700-1850*. Monacelli Press, New York.

Emmerson, William C.
1954 *The Seminoles: Dwellers of the Everglades: The Land, History and Culture of the Florida Indians*. Exposition, New York.

Ewers, John C.
1954 *Charles Bird King, Painter of Indian Visitors to the Nation's Capital*. Smithsonian Institution Annual Report for 1953, pp. 463-473. Washington, DC.

Gaget Girl
2014 *Fashion Trends: What Did Punks Wear in the 80s and Punk Fashion Trends Today*. HubPages. Electronic document, https://discover.hubpages.com/style/What-Did-Punks-Wear-in-The-80s, accessed January 18, 2022.

Giambruni, Helen Emery
1966 *The Primary Structures of Fabrics: An Illustrated Classification*. Textile Museum, Washington.

Goggin, John M.
1954 Osceola: Portraits, Features, and Dress. *Florida Historical Quarterly* 33(3):161-192.

1951 Beaded Shoulder Pouches of the Florida Seminole. *The Florida Anthropologist* 4:2-17. Gainesville.

Greene, S. W.
2014 *Wearable Prints, 1760-1860: History, Materials, and Mechanics*. Kent State University Press.

Gordon, Beverly
1986 The Whimsey and its Contexts: A Multi-Cultural Model of Material Culture Study. *The Journal of American Culture* 9(1):61-76.

Harris, Jennifer
1993 *Textiles, 5,000 Years: An International History and Illustrated Survey*. H. N. Abrams, New York.

Huber, Stacey L.
2017 Preliminary Analysis of the Mantrone-Cardinal Toile Long Coat. Report on file, 28 pp. Accession File 2019-22, Anthropology Division, Florida Museum of Natural History, University of Florida, Gainesville.

Jackson, Jason Baird
1991 The Material Anthropology of an Important Seminole Long Shirt. Report on file, 50 pp. Accession File 77-40, Anthropology Division, Florida Museum of Natural History, University of Florida, Gainesville.

Johnston, Lucy, Marion Kite, Helen Persson, Richard Davis, and Leonie Davis
2005 *Nineteenth-century Fashion in Detail*. V & A Publications, London.

Mahon, John K.
1967 *History of the Second Seminole War*. University of Florida Press, Gainesville.

McCall, George A.
1868 *Letters from the Frontier*. Philadelphia.

Montgomery, Florence M.
2007 *Textiles in America: 1650-1870*. Norton, New York.

Pitchfork and Levi
2016 *Rip It to Shreds: A History of Punk and Style*. Electronic document, https://pitchfork.com/features/from-our-partners/9943-rip-it-to-shreds-a-history-of-punk-and-style/, accessed January 18, 2022.

Reath, N. A.
1925 Printed Fabrics. *Bulletin of the Pennsylvania Museum* 20(95):143–153.

Shaw, Robert
2014 *American Quilts: The Democratic Art*. Updated edition. Sterling, New York.

Schoeser, Mary, and Kathleen Dejardin
1991 *French Textiles: From 1760 to the Present*. L. King, London.

Shoemaker, Nancy
1995 *Negotiators of Change: Historical Perspectives on Native American Women*. Routledge, New York.

Sturtevant, William C.
1955 Osceola's Coats? *Florida Historical Quarterly* 34(4):315–328.
1967 Seminole Men's Clothing. *Proceedings of the 1966 Annual Spring Meeting of the American Ethnological Society*. University of Washington Press, Seattle.

Trestain, Eileen Jahnke
1998 *Dating Fabrics: A Color Guide, 1800-1960*. America Quilter's Society.

Weisman, Brent R.
1999 *Unconquered People: Florida's Seminole and Miccosukee Indians*. University Press of Florida, Gainesville.
2007 Nativism, Resistance, and Ethnogenesis of the Florida Seminole Indian Identity. *Historical Archaeology* 41(4):198-212.

Weitenkampf, Frank
1949 How Indians Were Pictured in Earlier Days. *The New York Historical Society Quarterly* 33:213-221. New York.

Wright, J. Leitch
1990 *Creeks & Seminoles: The Destruction and Regeneration of the Muscogulge People*. University of Nebraska Press, Lincoln.

4

Arts from Commercial Craft Programs Represented in the Collections of the Florida Museum of Natural History: Glade Cross Mission and the Seminole Arts and Crafts Guild

Patsy West

The creators of patchwork arts are the *i:laponathli:* (known linguistically as the Elaposhneechaathłi), who speak the language *i:laponki:* (also known as Mikasuki). Persons of Mikasuki-speaking heritage represent about 70 per cent of the combined federally recognized populations across the two Florida tribes. Thus they are the cultural and political majority of the tribal peoples in the State of Florida (Figures 1-3). It was *i:laponathli:* artists who invented and developed the early twentieth-century practice of machine-sewn patchwork. They are responsible for producing the majority of historic Florida native textiles found in museum collections today, including those at the Florida Museum of Natural History.

Since the mid twentieth century, the *i:laponathli:* have lived as federally recognized tribal citizens enrolled in both the Seminole Tribe of Florida and the Miccosukee Tribe of Indians of Florida. The minority population is the post-Seminole War population of Muscogean-speaking Creeks, who, as late as 1938, were placed by the U.S. government within the Mikasuki-speaking Seminole Tribe of Florida. The Creeks reside predominantly on the Brighton Reservation, located on the northwestern shore of Lake Okeechobee. Research presented by this writer in *Florida Historical Quarterly* ties the *i:laponathli:* to a 1540 contact-era town in greater peninsular Florida (West 2016). Indeed, the Mikasuki-speaking peoples' history has only recently begun to be discussed under their own identity as a sovereign native tribal people of Florida in their own right, not as they have often been misidentified, as "Creek" or "Seminole."

Documented as Everglades dwellers a full generation *before* the Second Seminole War in 1835, the *i:laponathli:* were then living in the same well-established settlement pattern on islands in the Everglades inland sea, where they continued to live in post-war days, up to the drainage operations in the eastern Everglades at the turn of the twentieth century. Indeed these indigenous people say that they have been in the Florida peninsula "forever" (West 2016).

Figure 1. *The i:laponki (or i:laposhni: cha thli), the people of Mikasuki-speaking heritage, have been historically documented as residents of Florida Everglades islands since the first purposeful exploration into that area in the early nineteenth century. Photo of Little Billy (Wind clan) with his wife's Panther clan family, ca. 1920. Photo post card, S/MA 701. (Note: S/MA stands for Seminole/Miccosukee Archive; Patsy West, Director).*

Figure 2. *Willie Willie (Bird Clan) poses in a studio photograph in Miami in the earliest image to date that depicts a band of machine-sewn patchwork. It would have been fabricated on a hand-cranked sewing machine by his Bird clan mother or sisters at their island camp north of the future site of the Tamiami Trail, near 40-Mile Bend. Photo post card, John Chamberlain's Studio, Miami, ca. 1904, S/MA 96.1.2.*

The concept of Indian Removal in the Southeast can be seen as America's initial venture towards a national movement of "Manifest Destiny"— the concept of America reaching literally from "sea to shining sea." In Florida, there were more than 6,000 Indian people in residence. It was the Mikasuki speakers who led the fight against America's plan of genocidal removal to Indian Territory beyond the Mississippi River, rather than to relinquish their identity and religion in Florida.

The vast Everglades ecosystem and its interconnecting "water roads," coupled with the bountiful cargoes of ships wrecked from storms on the reefs along Florida's Atlantic seacoast and moved along supply lines, aided in preserving and nourishing the lives and viable culture of the Florida natives during America's three separate Seminole Wars of Removal spanning 1816-1858. The *i:laponathli:* today retrospectively consider that wartime period, accompanied by periods of generational uncertainty and strife between the Americans' three wars, to equate to a 50-year period of war.

The native Mikasuki-speaking majority, under the renowned *i:laponathli:* leader Abiaka (Sam Jones) and his handpicked allies, also provided leadership to the special-interest group of Indians who had fled into Spanish Florida. Most historically prominent was the Creek Osceola, who commanded troops that included Africans who had escaped from the slave states. It was the sovereign Mikasukis' dedicated response — defiant, with force and cunning that thwarted America's plans for their removal, coupled with those natives' knowledge of the Everglades environment, so intimidating to

Figure 3. *Ruby (Mrs. Wilson) Cypress, Panther clan, at her campfire, Big Cypress, 1940s. W. Stanley Hanson Sr. Collection, S/MA 88.5.1433.*

Figure 4. *The* Seminole Queen *tour boat brought tourists from Pier 6 on Biscayne Bay to Musa Isle Seminole Indian Village up the Miami River. Photo post card, March 12, 1942, S/MA 97.3.16.*

outsiders — that resulted in the positive outcome for the Mikasuki-speaking people (West 2016).

In 1858, American troops left Florida to prepare for the future War Between the States. The *i:laponathli:* with their singular, identifying language, emerged from the Seminole Wars as a virtually "intact and unconquered" tribe. Although they had suffered significant losses, they had succeeded in arriving at their ultimate goal: to remain in Florida. Who would think that only 40 years later, in the peace-time of the twentieth century, the still-reticent and government-shunning Mikasuki-speaking people under the U.S. government's generic, imposed name — "the Florida Seminoles" or the "Unconquered Seminoles" — would become as well known to Florida tourists as "Disney World" is today!

In the latter nineteenth century, Southeast Florida was destined to be the state's tourism capital (Figure 4). Standard Oil magnate Henry Flagler constructed his Florida East Coast Railroad down the eastern coast to Miami in 1896, bringing an influx of land speculators and early tourists. Within the next decade, drainage programs in the eastern Everglades initiated environmental destruction of the land (Figure 5). Soon the Mikasuki people saw their established market in furs, alligator and deer hides, and plumes of Everglades birds in jeopardy, while their cypress dugout canoes could no longer easily traverse the eastern Everglades' "water roads" to reach their major riverside trading areas, specifically Miami, due to dikes, ditches, and canals.

Figure 5. *A Mikasuki woman poles her canoe westwards towards the Tamiami Trail Villages, past a sign extolling the selling of drained Everglades land. This was one of the environmental crises that motivated the reticent Mikasuki speakers to engage in the economic boon of Miami tourism early in the twentieth century. Photo by Claude C. Matlack, courtesy HistoryMiami Museum, Matlack Collection, 5-30.*

Figure 6. *Coppinger's Tropical Garden, the earliest "Seminole Indian Village Tourist Attraction," was located on the south fork of the Miami River in a lush hammock of native vegetation with many imported exotic species as well. Botanist and landscape designer Henry Coppinger Sr. imported plants at the same time as his botanist friend, David Fairchild. Photo by Claude C. Matlack, Henry Coppinger, Jr. Collection, S/MA 169.*

Figure 7. *Musa Isle Village on the north fork of the Miami River. View of the village with two cooking chickees, showing the significant popularity of this business with the Mikasuki-speakers, as the attraction could then accommodate families from the two major tribal clans: Panther and Bird. Photo post card, S/MA 95.2.18.*

"Seminole Indian" Commercial Tourist Attraction Villages

Early in the twentieth century, the Mikasuki-speaking people, unconquered in war, strong in tribal sovereignty, and reticent by tribal decree, once more showed themselves most creative in protecting themselves. This time they involved themselves in a unique outreach program for economic survival that allowed them to stand on their own economically and maintain no formal relations with the United States government.

As Miami developed into a tourist destination in the early twentieth century, white pioneer entrepreneurs opened small tourist attractions along the short flow of the Miami River as it exited out of the Everglades. These family businesses, Coppinger's Tropical Gardens and Musa Isle Grove, both on the picturesque river (Figures 6 and 7), soon enabled a novel economic transition for the Everglades-dwelling *i:laponathli:* that was embraced by the women heads of clan camps.

Although retaining the reticence expected of them by their Tribal Council, the Mikasuki speakers were an instant hit in Miami's tourist market. In such facilities, the natives built their traditional palmetto-thatched camps and lived according to their customs for the short (originally only three months) tourist season. Outwardly represented by their outgoing Head Man who spoke a bit of English, the *i:laponathli:* morphed into well-known touristic innovators in the State's early twentieth-century tourist market. They and their

Figure 8. *Charlie Willie (Big Towns clan), Head Man at Musa Isle, early 1920s. Displaced by drainage canals from their long-time home, the women's Bird clan camp on Pine Island in the Everglades west of Fort Lauderdale, the Willies moved to an island north of the future Tamiami Trail near 40-Mile Bend. There Charlie and his son, Willie Willie, operated a successful hide-export business. Claude Matlack, photographer, ca. 1922, S/MA 608.*

culture became enthusiastically branded as "The Florida Seminoles" while producing and evolving their own wearable textile "patchwork arts" and a crafts market, with their wares marketed in the attractions' "trading posts" (Figures 8-13).

Bringing their portable, hand-cranked sewing machines with them, the women fabricated craftwork at the attractions that was of great interest. They sat picturesquely on the chickee platforms (Figure 14), spending hours constructing their clothing in colorful strips which were inserted in skirts, jackets, and the popular Seminole dolls, as eye-catching horizontal bands of patchwork. These natives had, while engaging in their daily lives (Figure 15), begun participating in the lucrative occupation that would bridge the

men's former hunting and trapping economy and engage whole families. It was decades before the term "heritage tourism" would be coined, and long before the Mikasuki-speakers' commercial endeavors of "being on exhibition" were considered a legitimate occupation and not judged to be

Figure 10. *Tourists visit the Bird clan camp of Mona Tiger Billie and her elder sister at Musa Isle in 1925. Photo post card, S/MA 1708.*

Figure 9. *The City of Miami hired the Mikasuki speakers for special events, such as the wedding of Jane Tiger and Jack Motlow in 1932. Here the regular staff (under Head Man Cory Osceola, Big Towns clan) and "extras" brought in for the event, pose at Musa Isle. Photo post card, S/MA 305b.*

Figure 11. *Young women of the Bird clan from "William McKinley Osceola's" camp on the Tamiami Trail pose at Musa Isle (L to R): Mittie Osceola Jim, Annie Doctor Jimmie, Lena Osceola Billie (Big Towns Clan), Annie Billie, Mickey Tiger, Maggie Billie Buster (Bird Clan). Photo by Work Progress Administration photographer Florence I. Randle, ca. 1937. F. I. Randle Collection, S/MA 76.*

Figure 12. *Fifteen children (Bird Clan) pose at Musa Isle Tourist Attraction with the camp's alligator "photo prop" in 1932. They were the first generation of Mikasuki speakers to grow to adulthood in the new tourism economy. Thirty years later, Buffalo Tiger (back row right), facilitated the organization of the federally recognized Miccosukee Tribe of Indians of Florida, and was elected the first, and long-time Tribal Chairman, S/MA 883.*

Figure 13. *At the end of the "Miami Tourist Season" the Mikasuki speakers from the Tamiami Trail Villages were delivered back home by truck. Cory Osceola (Big Towns Clan) and Bert Lasher, foreman of Musa Isle, pose with Mrs. Jimmie Druitt Osceola's Bird clan family, ca. 1930. Mary Osceola Moore Collection, S/MA 00.53.1.*

"demeaning" one by local and governmental critics (West 2008).

It was in the pioneer Miami attractions and other permanent enterprises as far north as Silver Springs near Ocala, Florida (Figure 16) where "Seminole" arts and crafts were enthusiastically proliferated by the Florida natives. Yearly estimates show that more than half of the Mikasuki-speaking population benefited from income related to tourist attractions, including the off-site production of crafts that further supplied the attraction markets (West 2008:29-31). An added bonus of involvement in the Miami attractions was in the form of wages, groceries, rented sewing machines, fabric, and the opportunity for enterprising native men and their male offspring (who were culturally allowed a more

Figure 14. *Jane Tiger Motlow (Otter clan) shows the versatility of the Mikasuki-speaking patchworkers. She sews clothing on a hand-cranked portable Singer sewing machine under a tarpaulin in a temporary camp "somewhere" between the Everglades and Miami, ca. 1927, S/MA 884.*

Figure 15. *Mrs. John Tiger (Bird clan) cuts up a garfish on a palmetto fan in one of the cooking chickees at Musa Isle, ca. 1937, S/MA 243.*

open social latitude), to participate on their own interest and merit in no-hassle, on-the-job training, which resulted in some individuals' early acquisition of the valuable skills of literacy, management, and finance (Figures 17 and 18; West 2008:28-29).

Indian Entrepreneurs

The trans-Everglades highway known as the Tamiami Trail, or U.S. Highway 41, was under construction literally for years across the Mikasuki-speakers' Everglades home (their "Land of Light" *Ka-ha-yut-lee*). The road finally opened to vehicular traffic from Tampa to Miami in 1928. A number of enterprising *i:laponathli*: women, again pursuing their families' economic prospects, approved "moving out to the road" from their tree-island camps to the north and south of the roadway and establishing small tourism-oriented native camps along the Tamiami Trail, complete with a privacy fence and other general features of the city attractions: the native chickee camp, a trading post, sometimes a small zoo, and an alligator wrestling pit (Figures 19 and 20).

Thus from both the city tourist attractions and the Trail village venues, beginning in the 1930s Mikasuki-speakers enjoyed their sovereignty *and* had established an independent source of income

Figure 16. *The popularity of the Miami-based commercial "Seminole Indian Villages" was outstanding. Promoter Ross Allen opened his own Seminole Village at the vintage mid-Florida attraction of Silver Springs near Ocala in the 1930s, hiring Charlie Cypress as Head Man, with wife Lee Cypress and her Otter clan family from Big Cypress. February 12, 1939, Burgert Brother's Studio, Tampa, S/MA 421.*

Figure 17. *Cory R. Osceola (Big Towns), wife Juanita Cypress Osceola (Panther clan), and baby Tahama at Musa Isle. Cory was a literate entrepreneur, Head Man of the village and in charge of the trading post gift shop. He held the premier position for a Florida Native American at that time, ca. 1928, S/MA 1655.*

and a future of economic independence. On the Tamiami Trail there was indeed big business to be had! In the 100 miles across the Everglades from Naples to Miami, the native entrepreneurs commanded all the profits from trans-Everglades sales of crafts, sundries, and village tours. Big Town clan brothers Cory Osceola (wife Juanita, Panther clan, see Figure 17), his brother William McKinley Osceola (wife Sallie, Bird clan) and brother John (wife Ida, Otter clan) were "head men" of tourist villages in Miami while off-season their wives' villages operated on the Trail, continuing to mirror the spirit of these non-reservation Indians who refused to acknowledge, much less receive aid, from the United States government. Indeed, to say "just leave us alone" was the *i:laponathli:*'s only response to governmental overtures. These family businesses, such as that of Ingraham Billie (Panther clan; wife, Effie, Wind clan) represented the earliest economically savvy and successful native entrepreneurs to be found across "Indian America."

The Osceola brothers Cory and William McKinley Osceola further served as craft brokers for the city attractions, making buying trips along the Tamiami Trail and Big Cypress to purchase crafts. They also appear to have made some of the initial efforts to enforce quality control on crafts (West 2008:109-110). Cory Osceola, assuming a wide variety of business dealings, was perhaps the most influential culture broker of his day.

By 1932, John and Nellie Campbell, owners of Musa Isle Seminole Indian Village, took over the concession from the founding manager, Bert Lasher. Nellie assumed Lasher's role as Manager and attempted to instruct and suggest new wares to the *i:laponathli:* women. But, as she noted in a 1981 interview, "[They] did not like anyone to interfere in their affairs: even craft ideas had to be approached very delicately, and not shown, told, or suggested too emphatically. But when one [woman] did something, others eventually, readily followed" (Nellie Campbell, personal communication, 1981).

Glade Cross Mission Arts and Crafts

Episcopalian Deaconess Harriet M. Bedell (Figure 21) came to Miami January 21-26, 1933 on a speaking engagement for the Florida Chain of Missionary Assemblies which highlighted her previous missions among the Cheyenne at Whirlwind Mission in northwestern Oklahoma in 1911 and her sixteen years with Alaskan natives at Steven's Village, 40 miles from the Arctic Circle. She remained in Miami while she waited for the Diocese to appropriate funds for her work in retirement with the "Florida Seminoles." She had received an invitation from the Special Agent for the Seminole Tribe of Florida in Hollywood, Florida, the Reverend James L. Glenn and his wife. According to Bedell's superior, the Bishop Right Reverend John D. Wing, the Glenns were "...exceedingly anxious for you to come down to begin your work among the Indians" (West 2008:99).

Meanwhile, Bedell was taken to a "Seminole Indian Village" in Miami by her local hosts. There, she was appalled when her overtures of "friendship and help" were met with a total rebuff by the tribal peoples, in distinct contrast to the reservation-acculturated peoples she had encountered in Oklahoma. Bedell quickly, but incorrectly, placed the blame for the *i:laponathli:*'s behavior on their "hardened years of life on exhibition!" and she set out to remedy their lot. She did not realize that

Figure 18. *Jack Tigertail (Wind clan). Publicity photo, made into 24-foot billboards to advertise the new town of Hialeah, which was built on drained Everglades land northwest of Miami. R.W. Harrison Studios, 1922, S/MA 166.*

Figure 19. *A sign "Indians Village" advertised an unidentified i:laponathli: camp open for business on the Tamiami Trail, ca. 1940s. The James L. Glenn Collection, History Fort Lauderdale, 5-14,076.*

Figure 20. *Medicine Man Ingraham Billie (Panther clan) with his wife Effie's Wind clan family at their Trail village tourist attraction. Charles G. Washbon Collection, S/MA 64.*

it was she, an overbearing stranger, who had greatly overstepped the tribal natives' bounds of propriety (West 2008:99).

"Exhibit arts and crafts, but not people!" became her mantra, and the good Deaconess worked tirelessly in her career to wean the people away

Figure 21. *Episcopalian Deaconess and nurse Harriet M. Bedell retired from her mission in Alaska to South Florida in 1933 and established headquarters in Everglades City. Her goal was to wean the natives on the Tamiami Trail from their "life on exhibition" at Miami's seasonal Seminole Indian tourist attraction villages, which she thought was harmful. She chose to promote their crafts economy, created additional crafts, established quality control, and established an "all season" economy for their arts and crafts by advertising via the Mission and her supporters' organization's newsletters. Here she points to the "Man on Horseback" design. Unidentified newspaper photograph by McGrath, ca. 1950s, S/MP Newspaper Morgue.*

from the economic need and presumed ill effects of commercial tourism, where, from her perspective, the natives in the Seminole Indian Village attractions of Miami were exhibited "like alligators and monkeys!" (Fort Myers News-Press 1937).

Bedell chose their pre-existing medium of "arts and crafts" to critique into a better saleable product, to stimulate sales by suggesting the making of items "for the home" and promote the product in a "native theme." While she was adamant that the natives would have a more stable income base so that they would not need to rely on the "exhibition" employment that she abhorred, in her 1937 Mission

newsletter she further stated, "An effort is made to develop the native arts and crafts in order to help the Seminole Indians of Florida to be self-supporting *and to make contacts for spiritual work*" (West 1984:61). As can be imagined, it was the economic appeal of arts and crafts that triumphed.

Bedell's "Mission to the Seminole" was granted on a slim appropriation from the Church Service League. Much of her funding and necessities came as gifts from ardent persons who had long supported her work. She was indeed busy, as in addition to her work with the *i:laponathli*: she was also expected to aid coastal Florida fishing families in south-

Figure 22. *Glade Cross Mission, Everglades [City], Florida, 1933, S/MA 88.2.27.*

western Florida, and even inmates in jails. Through the auspices of Barron Collier of the Collier Corporation, Collier County, she was offered a small, rent-free cottage in Everglades City, Florida for the use of her mission work. She named the mission "Glade Cross" (Figure 22).

Bedell fully acknowledged the enormity of her Indian mission: "The field is a large one, extending along the Tamiami Trail 80 miles east to Miami; 72 miles west to Ft. Myers; 40 miles north to Immokalee; villages out in the Everglades, and south on Turner River" (Figures 23 and 24). She was one of the few persons to recognize early on that the "Mikasukis on the Tamiami Trail" were solidifying into an ardently independent group of people.[1]

By 1935 she had leased a former native camp of thatched *chickees* in Immokalee for a mission village and had a large palmetto-thatched assembly hall built for group gatherings such as her Christmas events (Figure 25). In keeping with native tradition, she made sure that each clan family present at functions had its own separate fire for cooking.

Early on, Bedell had stocked the Everglades City mission house with canned goods and when more remote, impoverished natives realized that she wanted to help them, some began to ask for monetary aid, with nothing offered in return. It was then that she implemented her self-help program in earnest, handing out remuneration, foodstuffs, or craft supplies *only* when the recipient brought her a craft item that she could sell in Miami or Fort Myers. She further aided the families by attempting to

Figure 23. *Deaconess Bedell in a canoe poled by Ingraham Billie (Panther clan), a high-ranking practitioner of native medicine and a foremost tribal bundle carrier, 1940s, S/MA 88.2.37.*

Figure 24. *Deaconess Bedell walks to an isolated Everglades camp with two i:laponathli: women, S/MA 88.2.37.*

Figure 25. *Bedell, with the aid of one of her dedicated supporters, distributes gifts to mothers at the Mission's Chickee Village Christmas event in the latter 1930s, S/MA 1581.*

And within Florida, she requested that organizations place her Mission crafts sales lists in their newsletters (Bedell 1935a).

In the initial years of her program, when the quality of crafts was often crude, Bedell was lenient. She noted:

> If this work were commercialized, we would buy only from those doing the best work, but often forlorn Indians come forty or more miles to bring baskets, dolls, etc. too poorly made to offer for sale. They have nothing to eat and must be helped. Each time the work is criticized and suggestions for better work is [sic] made. (Bedell 1935a)

In the same progress Report, included in a survey by the Collier Corporation of "Collier County industries" in 1941, she noted enthusiastically that her program "…has developed beyond our expectations and some wonderful talent is brought out" (Figure 26).

By then, Bedell was in a position to stipulate more emphatically her suggestions for quality control and to introduce new articles, which she did, being remembered as "bossy." She encouraged the Trail craftspeople to "develop an art of their own, not copying that of Western Indians" whose tribal citizens often wintered at the Miami attractions and thereby strongly influenced some of the native Florida craftspeople (Bedell 1937).[3]

Ethel Cutler Freeman from Morristown, New Jersey was an amateur anthropologist who wintered

influence their budgeting for food and fabric. The Collier Corporation again aided her efforts by authorizing an "Indian Account" for Glade Cross Mission at the Collier store, the Manhattan Mercantile Company in Everglades City. She issued her craftspeople checks made out to Manhattan Mercantile, but the account was set up so that they could only purchase coffee, bread, flour, etc. In this manner, Bedell controlled the craftspeoples' earnings, ensuring that they would not procure liquor or sodas (Scott 1937).[2]

For Jimmie O'Toole Osceola (Panther clan), who lived with his family in southwest Florida, Glade Cross Mission became the main source of income. Osceola, who lived in a remote camp near Deep

Lake, recalled that when Bedell's outlet became available, his family actually began their production of crafts for the commercial market for the first time, producing the family's first cash income, and noted, "Then we depend on her for support" (Jimmie O. Osceola, personal communication, 1996).

The Deaconess discussed some facts that were necessary to hold her "self-help" program together: "During the summer when the tourists are gone, there is no market for their goods, so when they come to me for help I buy their things and when my friends buy them from me, their partnership is very real." She would even drive back to her family home in New York to sell crafts there in the summer.

Figure 26. *Woodcarvers display their painted carvings on trays in front of Glade Cross Mission. HistoryMiami Museum, 85-14-12.*

during the 1940s World War II era at the Big Cypress Reservation, Seminole Tribe of Florida. She witnessed the turmoil that mandatory draft registration imposed on these isolated, mostly illiterate, tribal peoples. New to federal reservation life, advantages, and policies since 1937, they had been persuaded by their longtime friend W. Stanley Hanson, who had become Big Cypress Reservation's Civilian Conservation Corps-Indian Division

Program head, to move onto the Reservation (West 1996: 31). The clan mothers refused to let the men register and hid them. Food supplies were then cut off by the Government. Pertinent to this study, Freeman noted that other *i:laponathli:* families went "…either to exhibition camps as a way of getting food or they are enlarging their camps on the Tamiami Trail and bringing their families into them, making a serious business of making souvenirs and nick-nacks which used to be only extra pin money to them, and trying to make a livelihood out of the tourists" (Freeman 1940). During this same period of time, the Government issued the Indians on the Big Cypress Reservation gas ration cards, so that they could drive out and hunt in the Everglades off the Tamiami Trail. But it was Deaconess Bedell who signed their ration cards because the people, by native council mandate since the Seminole Wars, were not "allowed to sign any paper" for fear it would be a treaty. She noted, "I was asked to sign their rationing cards for them and for several days this caused a busy time" (Bedell, Glade Cross Newsletter, undated).

For the Florida Museum of Natural History's Florida Ethnographic Collection, it will be advantageous to be aware of the varied items that were made for the Glade Cross Mission program (see Appendix). There, under the Deaconess' guidance, traditional materials and techniques were redirected into the production of new arts and crafts to be offered in the Mission's inventory. Perhaps this venture was even further stimulated by the natives' consternation over new economic needs during this traumatic period.

Palmetto fiber, from which the bodies of the famous "Seminole dolls" were made, came to be used also in the making of "hotplate mats, whisk broom holders, and "Kodak" book (photo album) covers bound with deerskin" (Bedell 1935a). Cypress wood, used by the men to carve traditional dugout canoes as well as toy dugout canoes was further employed in Bedell's program: "to carve wooden dolls, plaques, Indian busts, 'full sized men and women'; also "bookends, buttons, buckles, napkin rings, salad bowls, forks and spoons, and knitting bag handles" (Bedell 1935a, 1937). The carved dolls and busts are highly sought after by collectors today (Figure 27).

Under Bedell's influence, women began making baskets in "all sizes and shapes, suggested from the native [palmetto-splint] sifting baskets they have long used. This basketry has developed into their making waste, work, market, and picnic baskets," …in which Billie Tommie Jumper and her daughter Ruby Cypress (Bear Clan) excelled (Figure 28; Bedell 1935a).

Bedell, as the catalyst and innovator of crafts, also promoted a more decorative "coiled grass" basket, stitched with colorful embroidery thread, which soon supplanted the sale of traditional palmetto stem baskets in the commercial market (Figures 29 and 30).[4]

Folklorist Robert F. Greenlee observed in 1939 that "Basketmaking for the tourist trade has developed to a surprising extent … under the auspices of [the] Mission" (Greenlee 1952:30; West 1984:63). The round or oval coiled Florida sweetgrass

Figure 27. *Examples of carved and painted figurines made for the Glade Cross Mission program. West Collection, History Miami.*

Figure 29. *Deaconess Bedell watches a craftswoman as she works on a doll-headed lid for a sweetgrass basket. Tamiami Trail, 1930s. Photo by Ethel Cutler Freeman. Special Collections, University of South Florida Library, Tampa. S/ MA 1009.*

Figure 28. *Billie Tommie Jumper, her daughter Ruby Cypress, and children (Bear clan) proudly pose with their new "specialty" baskets. They were made of traditional palmetto splints and in the traditional weaving technique, but were manufactured for non-traditional uses that Bedell ordered, as part of her new marketing strategy. These baskets were sold as "waste," "market," and "work" baskets. S/MA 93.11.8.*

baskets were constructed on a cardboard base covered with palmetto fiber. The coils were then meticulously stitched, one smooth row to the next, with multicolored embroidery thread. This craft style resulted in a more fragile, but a fine decorative product that varied greatly in size, small to large; as baskets with a lid; or even smaller, stuffed for use as a pincushion. They are often topped with a doll-head lid [5] (Figure 31; Doctor 1999:6). Minnie Billie Doctor recalled making and selling just the "doll heads" to basket-makers to attach to

Figure 30. *A demonstrator stitches coils of sweetgrass for a basket at Ruby Clay's demonstration booth at Seminole Fair, Florida Seminole Indian Reservation, Hollywood, Florida, 1990s. Photo by Patsy West.*

their basket lids. For baskets and other Glade Cross Mission crafts, the Manhattan Mercantile Company of the Collier Corporation in isolated Everglades City offered incentive, selling fabric and also small, individual bundles of colorful embroidery thread for making the sweetgrass baskets (Doctor 1999:7).

In 1935, United States Indian Commissioner John Collier had rejected the former administration's notions that Native Americans should be "educated and assimilated into American life" while negating any notion of their encouragement to retain their tribal traditions, language, or rich tribal culture. Instead, Collier wholeheartedly embraced tribal culturalism and immersion, becoming strongly committed to the promotion of *all* aspects of Native Indian life, including arts and crafts (Figure 32). To further this program, he created the Indian Arts and Crafts Board (IACB), whose initial duty was to produce a Survey of Marketing and Production of Indian Arts. The survey was concluded in 1936 (Deloria and Lytle 1984:146; Scott 1936).

Bedell's innovative "List of things made by Seminole Indians" was sent out with the Glade Cross Mission newsletter as early as 1935. Innovative items were "skirts, patchwork samplers, sofa pillow covers and lounge covers, as well as drawstring handbags with sweetgrass basketry bases" (Bedell 1935b). Certainly she was an innovator! The drawstring handbags were still sold as general fashion statements until around the end of the twentieth century.

The Indian Arts And Crafts Board's "Specialist in Arts and Crafts," Alice P. Marriott, was very critical of the introduction of the sweetgrass basketry in

Figure 31. *Linda Beletso, demonstrator, sweetgrass basket-making, "Seminole Family Camp," Florida Folk Arts Festival, Florida Folklife Program, Stephen Foster Memorial, White Springs, Florida, ca. 1990, Photo by Camp Artistic Interpreter, Patsy West.*

Figure 32. *John Collier, Commissioner of Indian Affairs, Washington, DC and creator of the Indian Arts and Crafts Board, visits Carrie Buster's camp at Deep Lake in the Big Cypress in March, 1935. William D. and Edith M. Boehmer Collection, S/MA 91.5.25.*

Bedell's program. She wrote in 1943, "Some attempt had been made by well-meaning white persons to introduce other basket forms to the 'Trail Indians' without great success. The worst of the introduced shapes are globular coiled baskets made of grass and sewn with raffia or colored threads, and the worst of these are those surmounted with the heads of a Seminole doll" (Marriott 1943:47-48, 56).

Without a doubt, the most popular craft in Bedell's program was the female doll, made with colorful traditional cotton capes and skirts with patchwork, which thoroughly covered their stuffed palmetto fiber body. Bedell's mission work with "Seminole" arts and crafts was fully recognized by Collier's Federal Indian Agency. And, although she did not receive government aid for her program, his survey of the "Florida Seminoles" noted that "…Deaconess Harriet M. Bedell, Everglades, Florida has more to do with the actual marketing of dolls than any other one person" (Burton 1937) (Figure 33). In Bedell's program, the larger sized dolls came to be embellished with traditional jewelry. The *i:laponathli:* women's hand-beaten coin silver earrings and bodice jewelry were represented on the dolls by snippets of tin cut from condensed-milk cans, contributed by the women's husbands (Figure 34).

The far more rare "male" dolls required the addition of arms and legs, usually made of rolled and stitched palmetto fiber or of palmetto-covered cypress twigs. Because these dolls required extra time in crafting (from both the men and women), they commanded a higher price and were made by

Figure 33. *Deaconess Bedell poses with a pair of large dolls in front of an unidentified Tamiami Trail Village, ca. 1940. Unattributed photo post card, from Glade Cross Mission, Everglades City, Florida, S/MA 1008.*

Figure 34. *This 16½-inch-tall doll in the Glade Cross Mission style features patchwork bands of "Fire" and "Man on Horseback," also tin-snip earrings. Made by Billie Tommie Jumper (Bear clan), ca. 1940s. Author's personal collection.*

only a few couples (Figure 35). An interesting account was told to me by Cory Osceola's (Big Town clan) eldest son, Pete Osceola, Sr. (Panther clan) in 1981 at "Pete Osceola's Discount Crafts," Tamiami Trail at Miccosukee. It concerned the initial fabrication of a male doll:

A Mikasuki woman was approached by Deaconess Bedell in the early years of the Glade Cross Mission program to fill an order for a male doll. The woman made it, but in the style of the female doll, with no arms and

legs. In exasperation, the Deaconess repeated: "No, No! A MAN!! ARMS! LEGS! …When the woman brought the doll to her, it had palmetto fiber arms and legs, and a penis! (P. Osceola 1981; West 1984:64)

Perhaps the most unusual doll associated with Bedell for her Glade Cross Mission Program was the "Man on Horseback," a clothed male doll riding a realistic-looking horse made of palmetto-fiber with cypress pin legs (Figure 36). In 1951,

Figure 35. *A pair of dolls most probably from the Glade Cross Mission. The woman has tin-snip earrings and cape ornaments, ca. 1940s. Purchased with 76.1.1 "Man on Horse." West Collection, History Miami Museum, 76.2.1a and 76.2.1b.*

Figure 36. *Two Man-on-Horse dolls, ca. 1940. Left: West Collection, History Miami Museum, 76.2.2 (purchased with doll in Figure 35); Right: Fort Lauderdale History Center x538-39 (man) & x538-40 (horse).*

William C. Sturtevant, the future Curator of North American Ethnography, Smithsonian Institution, while working on his dissertation, became familiar with families on the Tamiami Trail. In William McKinley Osceola's, Bird Clan wife Alice's village in 1951, he noted, "Dolls on horseback now on sale

Figure 37. *The Tucker Family brought sweetgrass baskets that they had made to Glade Cross Mission with "horse handles" on the lids! Unattributed Glade Cross Mission photo post card, Everglades City, Florida, S/MA 93.11.9.*

in his store were made by Harley Jumper's mother at Dania [Reservation]" [That was Billie Tommie Jumper (Bear clan) (see also Figure 28)]. (William Sturtevant, personal correspondence, 2000). Figure 37 shows members of the Tucker Family, who made very rare palmetto-fiber "horse handles" for basket lids. This post card image was taken on the site of the Mission.

Indeed, the theme of "Man on Horseback" was significantly important to Bedell. She also "named" an earlier-conceived patchwork design as "Man on Horseback" (Figure 21). Figure 38 shows this design as the centerpiece on a Glade Cross Mission

pillow cover; Figure 39 shows it in the middle row of a Glade Cross Mission jacket in the collection of the Florida Museum of Natural History; and Figure 40 shows it in the middle row of patchwork on a jacket worn in 1942 by the famous singer Bing Crosby. Indeed, Bedell was always eager to stimulate a generic "American Indian" thematic marketing for public consumption in the wares of her craftspeople. She would have been pleased that in 2004, a doll very possibly made in the Glade Cross Mission program *and* wearing a belted shirt with the "Man on Horseback" design was chosen to represent the Florida Seminole and Miccosukee Tribes on a postage stamp (Figure 41).

Figure 38. *A Glade Cross Mission pillow cover. West Collection, History Miami Museum. The pillow cover is believed to have been a gift to Edith Boehmer from Harriet Bedell.*

Figure 39. *Cover Illustration, American Indian Art Magazine, Volume 9, Number 4, Autumn, 1984. Jacket from Glade Cross Mission with an attenuated "Man On Horseback" design, 1950s. Photo by David M. Blackard. Florida Museum of Natural History, Florida Ethnographic Collection, Gainesville, Florida, catalog no. 92784.*

Until about 1960, the craftswomen themselves did not formally give names to designs due to socio-religious teachings. Sometimes however, a design was created on the sewing machine that in hindsight, and over time, resembled, or recalled something. Such a design might then end up in time with a "looks like" name. A good example of a "looks-like" design is "Hog Feces" (Figure 42). It is a relatively popular design, but was obviously not "created" to resemble that substance!

Figure 40. *On November 11, 1942, the popular singer Bing Crosby posed in a three-band patchwork jacket that adheres to the criteria of patchwork produced for Deaconess Harriet M. Bedell's Glade Cross Mission program. The "Man-on-Horseback" patchwork design is the central band. S/MA 96.13.2.*

Figure 41. *U.S. postage stamp featuring a Seminole Doll. The doll, very possibly the product of a Glade Cross Mission craftworker, features the "Man on Horseback" design that Bedell so enjoyed. This doll was selected for a stamp issued August 21, 2004 in a run of 8,700,000, part of a stamp series that highlighted 10 examples of native art from across the United States. West Collection, History Miami Museum 2004.20.1.*

Because "patchwork arts" was where Bedell came to assert her strongest influence, the patchwork for the Glade Cross Mission program has definite, identifiable characteristics at first glance. She allowed *no* rickrack to be used in products for her program, as she considered rickrack to be "tourist, not Indian!" (Charles L. Knight, personal correspondence, September 14, 1983). Her craftsworkers also recalled that the Deaconess' preference of colors for garments did NOT extend to black and white (Johns and Cypress 1996). Most signifi-

Figure 42. *"Looks like" patchwork design: "Hog Feces." Photo by author, S/MA 2022.1.1.*

cantly, she insisted on the retention of the designs that she first encountered in 1935. She encouraged the artists to use what she considered "their best Indian designs." She did not feel that the natural artistic evolution of patchwork arts, which has been identified by David M. Blackard as a definable, *decadal* creative process (Blackard 1990:45-55), was an asset, at least not to her Glade Cross Mission program!

As a result, the same, "Bedell-select" vintage designs continued to be utilized in the wares for Glade Cross Mission long beyond the 1930s when they were in vogue, creating an anomaly within the mainstream development of patchwork arts. This contrasts with contemporary patchwork clothing outside the Mission Program, made and worn by the artists themselves (see Mrs. Poole's skirt in Figure 43), which evolved very innovatively over the decades (West 2008).

Bedell noted in June 20, 1941 in a letter to her Episcopal Bishop, "The designs do not mean anything but are suggestive of running water, a horse's mane, lightning, etc." (West 1984:58-67). The designs that she especially favored were Fire, Lightning, Man-on-Horseback, Waves, Trees, Mountains, and Arrowheads. Because this design anomaly can be readily identified in samplers and clothing produced for the Mission, they might well be historically identified as typical "Glade Cross Mission" designs (Figure 44).

Before leaving the topic of Bedell-influenced designs, more should be said about the "longevity of commercial use" shown to some of those 1930s-era Glade Cross Mission-named designs. As a result of their popularity with the buying public due to their "Indian-name" theme, the capitalization and proliferation of their use assured their continuity. And because a number of the Bedell era-influenced designs remained virtually the same over time, they became ingrained in "cultural branding" and commercialism by select Tamiami Trail area patchworkers and their progeny. Bedell-era designs have been retained by their Glade Cross Mission artists' descendants on the Tamiami Trail, to the present writing.

A very few Trail patchwork artists have specialized, and continue to do so, in the creation of the so-called "named designs" and designs created to be "symbols." This phenomenon has been greatly stimulated over more recent decades through the enthusiasm of a University of Miami scholastic organization, "Iron Arrow." It was begun in 1926 with a "Florida Indian" theme. Hundreds of jackets and coats exist, made for the use of the Iron Arrow membership and initiates, long major clients of a

Figure 43. *John and Camilla Poole Tiger and son. Father and son are wearing typical Glade Cross Mission jackets, older designs, no rickrack. Camilla, however, is wearing a skirt that illustrates up-to-date patchwork styling in design and rickrack. Special Collections, University of South Florida Library, Tampa. Deaconess Harriet Bedell Collection, S/MA 698.*

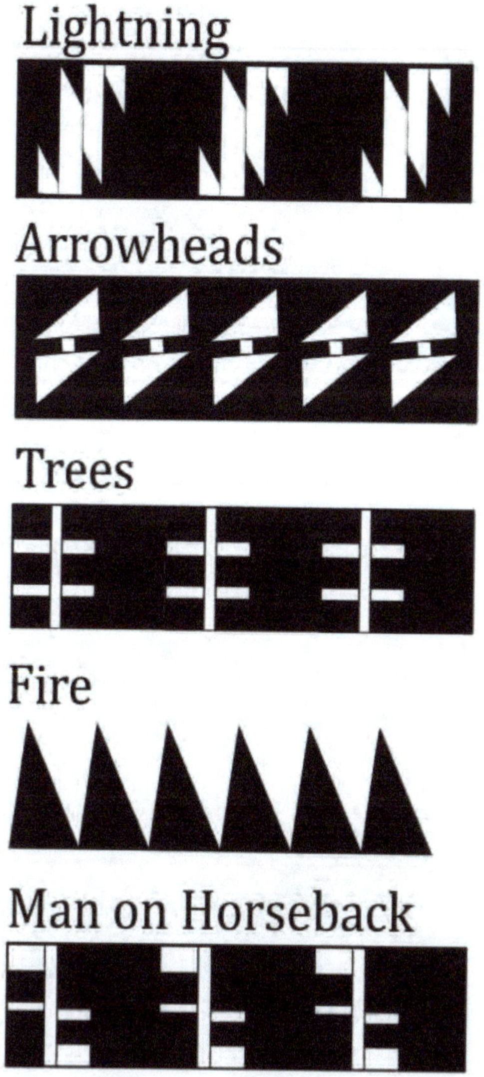

Lightning

Arrowheads

Trees

Fire

Man on Horseback

Figure 44. *Popular designs promoted in the Glade Cross Mission patchwork.*

single village who are citizens of the Miccosukee Tribe of Indians of Florida, for these identifiable patchwork jackets.

Effie Osceola's Bird clan family on the Tamiami Trail has had a strong history of supplying crafts to

Bedell's Glade Cross Mission program, and Osceola's emphasis continued to be strongly focused on "Indian-named patchwork designs." By the 1970s this camp was a commercial anomaly. Dorothy Downs chronicled these designs (1979:32-41, 34-35). Charles L. Knight, a close associate of Bedell's, verified that "Deaconess Bedell would *indeed* name the patterns" (personal correspondence, September 14, 1983). Further research proved that this "naming" phenomenon at the aforementioned Trail camp was not known at all by *i:laponathli:* craftsworkers in other locales (West 1984:58-67).

Under the late Effie Osceola (d. 2020), untold orders have been produced for "Seminole" jackets with specifically created "symbolic, named designs" for Iron Arrow members and initiates who must mandatorily wear their jackets as regalia in Iron Arrow ceremonial campus activities. Often seen in the University's colors of Orange and Green on a White Field, some of the more contemporary jackets are made "coat-length" in order to accommodate more rows of designs (as many as 8 rows), all designs symbolic to University of Miami, "UM," the "Miami Hurricanes," the school's "Hurricane-Bird" mascot, the U.S. maritime "Hurricane Weather Flag," and Iron Arrow, etc. While some vintage and contemporary patchwork jackets worn by members have not been special-ordered with "symbolic" patchwork designs, the Iron Arrow jackets can readily be identified by the identifying "regulation rickrack arrow" on the lapels (Figure 45). The continuous usage has created a further anomaly, a direct commercial carryover of product, linking this Bird clan camp to the commercial production

of vintage, "named" designs, some from the Bedell era (West 1984:58-67).

The Seminole Arts and Crafts Guild, Seminole Tribe of Florida, 1939-1960

The United States government established two reservations for the "Florida Seminoles" in the early twentieth century, but they remained mostly unpopulated into the 1930s. However, the government did not realize that there were two linguistically diverse tribes in Florida, the *i:laponathli:* (the Mikasuki-speakers) living along the Tamiami Trail and in the Big Cypress and frequenting the tourist

Figure 45. *Detail: "Iron Arrow" insignia, on jacket 2015.59.1. Photo by author, West Collection, History Miami Museum, S/MA 2015.59.1c.*

attractions in Miami and Silver Springs, and a minority of Muscogee-speaking Creeks, who lived north of Lake Okeechobee. The two groups seldom cohabited. The Creeks in southern Florida, left largely diminished after the Seminole War period, were not considered a separate people by the government, even though they spoke a completely different language than the 70% majority of the native population in Florida, the *i:laponathli:*. The Creeks had lived "off the grid" around Lake Okeechobee since the end of the Third Seminole War in 1858[6] (Figure 46).

In 1938, a Creek contingent met with government representatives to ask for concessions: a reservation of their own, a school and teacher, and economic opportunities (West 2008:78-79). They represented the first post-war Florida Indians *ever* to negotiate with the United States government. The *i:laponathli:* vehemently opposed the Creeks' overtures and they continued staunchly to follow the dictum of their native tribal council, which remained opposed to interacting at all with the government.

However, the government's representatives were overjoyed at *finally* having a direct and purposeful dialogue with representatives of the elusive "Florida Seminoles" and were eager to grant the Creeks' concessions. One of the Creeks' main requests was for education. William Dyer Boehmer and Edith Meyer Boehmer had joined the Indian Service of the Bureau of Indian Affairs following college, hired as the standard husband-teacher/wife-housekeeper for the United States Department of the Interior. In 1938 they arrived

Figure 46. *Map showing locations of the Seminole and Miccosukee reservations today. Graphic by Roger Mallot, courtesy Florida Museum of Natural History, updated to include Lakeland reservation.*

at the isolated Brighton Reservation in Florida from an eight-year assignment to the Oglala Sioux at Lake Wakpamni, Pine Ridge, South Dakota and became innovative and hard-working champions for the tribal people. The requested school for the Creek-speakers' reservation on the northwestern shore of Lake Okeechobee was quickly built. Under the Boehmers' welcoming tenure, the school at Brighton became a novel attraction to tourists and locals. Even the Audubon Society took the opportunity to bring tours there from Palm Beach.

Edith's introduction into Seminole arts and crafts and the marketing thereof began quite modestly. Tommy Parker, an *i:laponathli:* woman married to a Creek, asked if Bill Boehmer would sell one of her dolls to the tourists who visited the school. That doll sold, then others. Edith received permission from Seminole Superintendent F. J. Scott to formally consign the few handicrafts that were brought to her. Bill Boehmer discussed the state of early crafts:

> Their handiwork down here was used for trading purposes, and there was no set value on how many gallons of gas or bags of groceries the dolls and patchwork could buy. So, as the women brought these things to us, we would get the prices on them and place them on a table in the kitchen…and as the tourists and visitors came, why, they could buy them. We sold them for just the price that the Indians put on them; no mark up. (Love 1967)

The popular crafts market soon outgrew this rudimentary plan. In 1940 John Collier's Indian Arts and Crafts Board sent Specialist Alice Marriott to the Brighton Reservation to help set up the Seminole Arts and Crafts Guild. Edith Boehmer organized the Guild (Figure 47), with the women and men themselves agreeing on "proper markups," while profits were placed in a revolving fund. That money was later paid to the craftworkers, so that they could invest in buying fabric in bulk. Edith recalled, "We taught them to buy supplies in quantity and to watch for sales as well as to insist on good grades of material."

Hollywood Sun Tattler Reporter Rita Love further noted, "Edith's formulas for simplified economics suddenly became big business" (Love 1967).

Interestingly, in her teacher's training classes in college, "Edith had studied sewing and her favorite hobbies were arts and crafts. Little did she dream that some four-score years later, she would be recognized by the United States Department of the Interior for her early talents," Bill Boehmer recalled (Love 1967) (Figure 48).

The objectives of the Indian Arts and Crafts Board and therefore those of the Seminole Guild were "to standardize and improve the quality of Seminole handicrafts; to stimulate interest in Seminole arts and crafts outside local areas and especially outside Florida; to increase the volume of production and sales through the opening of new markets; and to create a revolving fund for the purpose of arts and crafts, especially during the slack season" (United States Department of the Interior, Office of Indian Affairs, Reports and Documents 1943:100). Edith clarified the process: "For instance, if a long tribal skirt sells in the [Brighton school] shop for $20, the woman receives $18 for it and $2 goes into the guild fund" (Sosin 1949).

Because the Creek leaders themselves had asked the government for the reservation and concessions, the Creek-speaking people gradually acquiesced and moved onto the Brighton Reservation, where their life was easier. As a result, they were more malleable and receptive to organized reservation programs and protocol.

Figure 47. *Edith M. Boehmer, René D'Harnoncourt, Director of The Museum of Modern Art in New York City, and Dorothy Osceola pose by the Seminole Crafts Guild sign on the isolated Brighton Seminole Reservation. Photo by William D. Boehmer.*

Figure 48. *Edith Boehmer in the palmetto scrub with craftswomen gathering palmetto husk to make Seminole dolls, the Seminole Craft Guild's first product, early 1939. Photo by William D. Boehmer.*

Edith had little reason to bend to charity when dealing with cases of poor craftsmanship.

When she arrived in 1938, Edith described the quality of Seminole crafts as "not refined." "When they'd run out of one design, they'd just stick a piece of another one in and they did not use the same color thread… as the background" (personal communication, 1982). Bill recalled that Edith "would not accept any shoddy work," gradually bringing the Indian women to realize that if their work "…wasn't the best… If it wasn't good enough, Mrs. Boehmer wouldn't buy it" (W. Boehmer 1971). And, because the artists' peers, the officers of the Craft Guild, backed Edith's efforts, the craftswomen had little choice but to rework any rejected items (Jimmie O. Osceola, personal communication, 1996). It is also significant that the crafts produced for this important tribal program were bolstered by the competent work of the few, long craft-savvy i:laponathli: women who had married Creek men and moved to live with their husbands on the Brighton Reservation. Those few, but important, craftswomen were second, even third or fourth-generation craftswomen who had been raised within the daily craft-producing endeavors of the original South Florida arts and crafts markets at the Miami tourist attractions and Tamiami Trail businesses (Figures 49-51; W. Boehmer 1971; J. Osceola 1996).[7]

As critics of patchwork arts, Boehmer and Bedell shared a strong dislike of rickrack, the colorful manufactured commercial trim. It had been used very sparingly by patchwork artists in the 1930s, probably due to the extra expense, but by the 1940s

Figure 49. *Women participating in the Seminole Arts and Crafts Guild show off their best dolls in 1939 at the Brighton School. Photo by Dwight R. Gardin.*

it was used exclusively by the native patchworking craftswomen for their *own* garments. However, according to Boehmer, "rickrack ruined 'beautiful handiwork' by placing it alongside machine made materials" (Boehmer and Boehmer 1990; W. Boehmer 1971). As for the patchwork designs themselves, Edith Boehmer stated, "I never asked for [particular] designs, I only asked for color… We found that the turquoise jewelry from the

Figure 50. *Annie Tiger (Mrs. Richard Osceola), Panther clan, of the Seminole Arts and Crafts Guild, Brighton Seminole Reservation, poses with her prize-winning doll, ca. 1939. Photo by Dwight R. Gardin, Brighton, Florida. William D. and Edith M. Boehmer Collection, S/MA 91.5.31.*

southwest went with it, so I always suggested that they use some turquoise (E. Boehmer 1982; Boehmer and Boehmer 1990).[8]

Figure 51. *(a) A high-quality standard was set by Edith Boehmer and her craftswomen in the Seminole Arts and Crafts Guild. (b) Detail: The doll has the first hang-tag created for the Guild by Alice Marriott of the Indian Arts and Crafts Board in Washington, DC. It is the popular 1921 image of Jack Tigertail (see Figure 18). Photo by author, William D. and Edith M. Boehmer Collection, S/MA 2022.2.1.*

Edith also had to "…teach the tourists to appreciate quality merchandise," noting that, "Everything that they purchase [from Seminole Arts and Crafts] is authentic and made of lasting material. There are many spurious Indian crafts in the other stores, not only from Japan, but from America as well" (Love 1967).

Indeed, a major goal of Alice Marriott's at the IACB was to protect the distinctiveness and integrity of American Indian craftwork and to promote the success of the Native craft economy. In the 1930s a non-Indian woman had actually attempted to patent the popular Seminole doll! And in March 1937, Deaconess Bedell protested at a meeting of the Florida Seminole Indian Association based in Fort Myers, "…against the sale of imitation Seminole curios, many of which she said were actually manufactured in Japan" (d'Harnoncourt 1938; *Fort Myers News-Press* 1937; Glenn 1932). An IACB investigator sent to Florida from Washington, DC to look into these allegations found that, "All of the four Indian stores in Fort Meyer [sic], Florida have Japanese imitations and real Indian novelties side by side on their shelves" (Burton 1937). In response, the IACB then initiated the trademarking process necessary to protect authentic goods made by Native American tribes, which had been an initial Board mandate in the Act, approved in 1935 (IACB 1943a).

A Tribal-Specific "hang tag" also contributed to the authentication of crafts for an "aware tribal arts-purchasing public." The Seminole Crafts Guild adopted their registered Indian Arts and Crafts Board trademark in 1944. The first trade-

mark was a popular commercial image first created in a Miami photo studio in 1921 of Jack Tigertail (Wind clan), pointing the way to the new subdivision of Hialeah (Figure 51; see Figure 18). Figures 52 and 53 show dolls produced for the Seminole Arts and Crafts program. A later IACB-designed trademark, seen on the Guild's Reservation Billboard (Figure 54), showed the silhouettes of three dolls with their 1940s-style hairboards and patchwork clothing. Some new hang tags also included the name of the maker and documented the provenance and the date that the item was

Figure 52. *An original doll from the Seminole Arts and Crafts Guild, Brighton Reservation. West Collection, History Miami Museum 91.5.211.*

Figure 53. *These paired dolls from the Guild were 18 inches high. William D. and Edith M. Boehmer Collection, Boehmer photographic catalog 536-9-20.*

Figure 54. *The Guild boasted a roadside sign on one of the cross-roads pointing to the isolated, rural setting of the Brighton Reservation and School. The sign shows the new Guild logo of three Seminole dolls developed by the Arts and Crafts Board. Photo by William D. Boehmer, William D. and Edith M. Boehmer Collection, S/MA 91.5.211.*

made. These tags served as proof of authenticity, further separating Seminole arts and crafts from other tourist curios and imports[9] (Figure 55).

It was not until 1939 that Native American crafts were first presented as "art" at the San Francisco World's Fair. On the success of that exhibition, The Museum of Modern Art in New York City (MOMA) in an innovative exhibition curated by the Museum Director and General Manager of the IACB, René d'Harnoncourt, with Frederick H. Douglas, Curator of the Denver Art Museum, mounted a major exhibition of American Indian art. A *New York Times* reviewer stated: "While we all think we are familiar with American Indian art,

Figure 55. *Four examples of various hang tags were developed to identify crafts from the Seminole Craft Guild to serve as price tags, to identify the craftsperson, and—most of all—as "authentication" of a Native-made craft. Photos by author, a: S/MA 91.5.244; b: S/MA 91.5.245; c: S/MA 91.5.246; d: S/MA 91.5.247.*

it has remained for the Museum of Modern Art to bring home to us through its present exhibition the varied richness and startling modernity of the handiwork of these first Americans" (IACB 1943b:135-150, 148-150).

D'Harnoncourt had visited the Boehmer's Guild project in 1941. The "Seminole" items in the MOMA exhibition were a sampler of six patchwork designs, a traditional palmetto splint basket made by Mrs. Billy Osceola (Bert Billie), and a 1940s man's patchwork jacket loaned by Douglas from the Denver Art Museum (IACB 1939-1941).

By 1942, the Indian Service "Housekeeper" Edith Boehmer had added to her job description: "Community Service Employee" (OIA 1942:2). She visited camps in Brighton and Big Cypress, taking boxes of craft supplies, picking up completed crafts, and paying the craftsworkers for sales (Figure 56). Her work was discussed in a *Miami News* article (Sosin 1949) with a photo showing Edith and the Guild's sales-shelf wares of dolls, sweetgrass baskets, a pinafore, and other patchwork items (Figure 57).

While she left patchwork design decisions up to the craftspersons, her own personal mark on the Seminole Craft Guild evolved around the promotion of patchwork clothing as "fashion." Edith wanted to create a greater variety of apparel that incorporated patchwork designs. So, when she realized that the traditional floor-length patchwork skirts were not selling well, she suggested the knee-length skirt (Figure 58). Like Nellie Campbell at Musa Isle, she found it very difficult to commu-

Figure 56. *Edith Boehmer made regular rounds to visit camps on the Brighton Reservation and as far as the Big Cypress Reservation to take supplies of fabrics and settle accounts. Photo by William D. Boehmer. William D. and Edith M. Boehmer Collection, S/MA 91.5.248.*

nicate her wishes, noting, "Of course at the time, the women did not speak English ... and finally to get what I wanted, I had to take a long skirt myself and cut it and have one for a sample" (E. Boehmer 1982; Boehmer and Boehmer 1990).[10] She had no such problem with the only male patchworker of his day, the articulate and affable *i:laponathli:* Jimmie O'Toole Osceola (Panther clan), who was an artistically skilled patchworker (Figure 59). See Figure 60 for an example of his work, and for a close-up view of his "signature" — a tiny "square wedge" of color set within the patchwork design.

Edith was responsible for including a man's sport shirt as a stock item. For this project she engaged

EXAMPLES OF SEMINOLE HANDICRAFT
Mrs. Edith Boehmer Exhibits Some of the Wares

Figure 57. *In October, 1949, reporters visited William and Edith Boehmer at Brighton Reservation on a mission to "survey" all of the three Seminole Reservations. They seemed pleasantly surprised by the Boehmers' strong involvement with education and arts and crafts. Here Edith, holding a pinafore and a doll, stands by the school's modest craft shelf, which gives some idea of the products available. Miami Daily News, article by Milt Sosin, staff writer, photos by Kestly, S/MA 91.5.249.*

Jimmie O'Toole Osceola, whom she lauded as her most talented asset. Jimmie bought a well-designed commercial shirt and took it apart to make the original sample pattern. These sport shirts remained a standard product for decades at Okalee Indian Village's Seminole Arts and Crafts on State Road 7 (U.S. Highway 441) on the Hollywood

Figure 58. *Edith was interested in promoting the Seminole Skirts as "fashion." She had the women make knee length skirts like these, which became popular products of the Guild Program. Two examples are pictured. West Collection, History Miami Museum, a: S/MA 95.1.6a; b: S/MA 95.1.6b.*

Figure 59. *Jimmie O'Toole Osceola was the only male patchworker. Affable and quick to learn, he soon became Edith Boehmer's best and most prolific patchwork artist. Unidentified photographer, William D. and Edith M. Boehmer Collection, S/MA 91.5.250.*

Reservation. This patchwork "IACB Trademarked" shirt (see Figure 61 showing a shirt in its package fold) was still offered in the early 1970s, where it was purchased and worn by many Boy Scouts in the "Order of the Arrow" (J. O. Osceola, personal communication, 1996). It should also be noted that those Boy Scouts of America from Southeast Florida in the organization's National Honor Society, the Order of the Arrow, who were

Figure 60. *A skirt made by Jimmie O. Osceola with detail showing his "signature" on the bottom band, a small square of contrasting color inserted into a patchwork design. Photo by author.*

members of the youth-led O-Shot-Caw Lodge, purchased many individual and at least one bulk order of Seminole jackets for the purpose of visibly singling out their own South Florida dance competition participants at out-of-state conferences. Both the Tamiami Trail Villages and Seminole Arts and Crafts, Hollywood were known suppliers (West, personal knowledge; see also Jon Anderson, jacket donation, Florida Museum of Natural History, Accession number 2010-4). This jacket was part of a bulk order filled by *i:laponathli: craftswomen* in 1963). Edith also engaged a photo

Figure 61. *Edith Boehmer gave Jimmie O. Osceola the project of creating a man's sport shirt as a product of the Arts and Crafts Program, a product that remained popular for decades. Man's patchwork sport shirt in original plastic bag, purchased from Seminole Okalee Indian Village, Hollywood. Photo by author, S/MA 2015.10.3.*

shoot with a fashion model to promote the chic new-length skirts and the world famous "Seminole doll" (Figure 62).

As mentioned, Deaconess Bedell's program had championed "named" designs to bolster sales. Edith Boehmer clarified the fact that the craftsworkers themselves were not the catalyst for such "naming":

> People ask me all the time, just what is the legend of the patchwork on the skirt? I hate to shatter their illusions of Indian lore they

Figure 62. *Fashion shoot for the Seminole Arts and Crafts enterprise. Model unidentified, photographer unidentified, S/MA 91.5.251.*

think is recorded on the material, because there isn't any! The Seminoles like their handiwork to be pretty. They like to experiment and embellish other designs. … Of all the hundreds of skirts they have made, only two have ever been alike – and they were by special order. (Love 1967)

Deaconess Bedell formally retired in 1943 at the age of 68. Glade Cross Mission then was placed under the authority of St. Stephen's Parrish in

Coconut Grove. Bedell functioned essentially as a volunteer parish worker, yet she continued the Glade Cross Mission programs as before, now on a parochial, rather than a diocesan status (Hartley and Hartley 1963:251). Meanwhile, the Annual Florida Seminole Tribal Report in 1954 added to the popular Guild's offerings of apparel "peasant-style blouses, aprons, stoles, swimming trunks [and] pinafores for little girls…" (Seminole Tribe of Florida 1954:14).

Regarding the divisions of expertise within the Guild program between the predominant Creeks on the Brighton Reservation and the *i:laponathli:* in Big Cypress, Jimmie O. Osceola recalled that "Mrs. Boehmer bought dolls from the Creek ladies, but little else, since the Creek women… who were hired to work seasonal jobs picking crops, planting grass, or gathering pine seeds … did not make any [patchwork] clothing" (J. O. Osceola 1996).[11] Indeed, it was the avid crafts-workers on the Big Cypress Reservation, not overly distant from Brighton, who became Edith's major tribal contributors. Because of their decades of experience, they were more adroit workers and were used to handling large orders of crafts for Deaconess Bedell's program. Edith turned to them to bolster the Seminole Tribal IACB program. She distributed clothing orders, as well as bulk materials, when she visited the isolated Big Cypress Reservation to the south. Purchases of beads and cloth in bulk translated into consider-able savings for the women. Sometimes as much as six thousand yards of percale were ordered at one time. The cloth was issued to each crafts-woman on a charge basis. Finished goods were checked in and affixed with the aforementioned label with the name of the maker (E. Boehmer 1958).

In 1953 the Indian Arts and Crafts Board in Washington, DC appointed Edith Boehmer "Instructor, Arts and Crafts." She took over the management of the Guild's business as her full time job. The IACB was responsible for setting standards and encouraging the improvement of craftsmanship. A 1956 Adult Education Series publication, especially targeted to individual tribes, was created for the Seminoles' Guild Program by the Department of the Interior, Bureau of Indian Affairs, entitled "What I Must Know as a Member of My Craft Guild" (BIA 1956). General meetings and an annual meeting in February were arranged for business reports, while Guild trademarking was a commercial advantage to Indian Craft Guild members across Indian America, as well as for the purchasing public at large.

William and Edith Boehmer were extremely proactive concerning the outreach of the Florida Seminole Guild, setting up exhibits around the state at libraries to promote interest in Guild products, and even exhibiting at the 1954 Inter-Tribal Ceremonial in Gallup, New Mexico. While visitors to the school continued to provide revenues, the far greater percentage of the Guild's business was by mail order, as the Washington office of the IACB aided the Guild greatly by forwarding inquiries from prospective buyers, often museum gift shops as far away as Paris.

Edith believed first and foremost in the potential benefits for Seminole women and their families from an arts and crafts economy. She noted in 1957 that the production of crafts "is a form of home industry and means a great deal in their economic life. If this program is not encouraged, it might die, and will mean that the Indians will be the losers by at least ten thousand [dollars] a year" (E. Boehmer 1957). Like Bedell, Boehmer showed a great deal of interest in how the monies earned by the Indian women might be put to what she perceived as "appropriate and ameliorative use," especially in the latter 1950s when, during the federal recognition movement, progressive reservation dwellers and politicians were install-ing non-Indian housing and establishing new reservation communities. "It is through this increased income," she observed, "that the Indian women are buying improvements for their homes. They do not show interest in learning about home improvements until they can get some of the things to better their living conditions. [They] have to pay for the things that they want. It is up to the woman to provide the other necessities she wants." Because the Guild issued checks rather than script to their craftspeople, there were no external controls exerted over the craftsperson's purchases (J. O. Osceola 1996).

In 1957 the new federally recognized Seminole Tribe of Florida was created. The Tribe's business interest, The Seminole Tribe of Florida, Inc., bought out the craftworkers' former Guild in 1960 for $25,000 (W. Boehmer 1971:15). In 1961 the Tribe's new business, "Seminole Arts and

Crafts," installed its merchandise in the federal government-built, modern A-frame facility designed by Fort Lauderdale architect William G. Crawford on the Florida Seminole Reservation in Hollywood, Florida facing State Road 7, U.S. 441 (Figure 63). *Miami Herald* Fashion Editor Beverly Wilson noted in an article on Seminole arts that year that, "Nearly 75 percent of the total yearly output from the three [Seminole] reservations is shipped for sale out of the state." Thus a major goal of the IACB's business projection for the Seminoles' Guild had been met (Wilson 1961).

In 1960, Glade Cross Mission and its programming were totally destroyed by Hurricane Donna. The elderly Deaconess entered the Episcopal Retirement Home in Davenport, Florida, where she died in January, 1969.

In 1961, there was a special exhibition of clothing and demonstrations of Seminole patchwork held at the exclusive Jordan Marsh Department Store in Miami that evoked Edith Boehmer's expertise. The *Miami Herald's* Fashion Editor declared: "Meet [the] Real Pioneers of Florida Fashion," while noting as a fashion statement (and a nod to Edith!) that the clothing had been "adapted for street wear or patio entertaining from traditional Seminole garb" (Figure 64; Wilson 1961).

However, on the downside for a perfectionist like Edith, she had by then witnessed the liquidation of the Seminole Craft Guild by the newly reorganized, self-governed, and federally recognized Seminole Tribe of Florida (Figure 65). When the business division of the Tribe bought out the Guild and

formed "Seminole Arts and Crafts," the new tribe sought to structure and manage its own affairs. The change of command and the loss of the communal responsibility of the "Craft Guild" lessened the strict quality control due to the leniency of Seminole Tribal managers (E. Boehmer 1957).

Meanwhile, Edith Boehmer was busy promoting the use of satin for the famous "top of the line" Seminole jackets. Rita Love (1967) noted that in the Seminole Craft Guild Program, "satin instead of percale is used for the vivid and handsome Indian coats." A jacket attributed to Mary Osceola,

an excellent Creek craftswoman, was worn by Joe Dan [Jaudon] Osceola, her nephew, who was elected President of the Seminole Tribe of Florida in 1967 (Figure 66). According to Jimmie O. Osceola, Mary was "known on the Hollywood Reservation for her 'Baby' designs" (J. O. Osceola 1996). While on that same subject, Edith Boehmer noted that of all the Mikasuki-speaking crafts-women, those "in Big Cypress made the designs smaller [than those in other areas]" (E. Boehmer 1990). Figure 67 shows a fine example of what I term a "postage stamp jacket," with the postage stamp to illustrate the small width of the patch-

Figure 63. *Seminole Okalee Village's Seminole Arts and Crafts showcase, U.S. highway 441, Hollywood, Florida was the new outlet for Seminole Arts and Crafts from the early 1960s. The U.S. Government built Okalee Village as a tourist attraction when the Seminole Tribe of Florida became a federally recognized tribe in 1957. Painting by Oklahoma Seminole Fred Beaver. The architect for the modern A-frame was William G. Crawford, Sr. Photo by J. F. Capicotto, S/MA 2012.13.16.*

Figure 64. *Agnes Johns (Bird clan) poses in a designer layout of ten Seminole Arts and Crafts skirts, ca. 1955. William D. and Edith M. Boehmer Collection, S/MA 443-7.*

Figure 65. *Bill and Edith Boehmer examine a large sweetgrass basket in the "Seminole Okalee Indian Village" gift shop, Hollywood, Florida. Photographer unidentified, S/MA 91.5.252.*

work band (detail). The patchwork on these jackets is so small and narrow that I suggest it was probably conceived and utilized for dolls long before it was utilized in fine-quality jackets.

At her retirement in March 1967, Edith Boehmer received an award from Secretary of the Interior Stewart Udall for "meritorious service." Frederick J. Dockstader, Chairman of the Board of the Indian Arts and Crafts Commission, and René d'Harnoncourt, Director of the Metropolitan Museum of Modern Art in New York City sent her wishes on

her retirement. Udall stated, "She has contributed greatly to the development of Seminole crafts, into one of the most expressive and vividly colorful tribal art forms in America today" (Love 1967).

Edith's last major contribution before her death in 1990 was as a virtual participant in the first comprehensive Symposium on Seminole and Miccosukee Arts, March 31, 1990. Sponsored by the Seminole/Miccosukee Photographic Archive, which I had begun and directed since 1972, the Symposium was held at the Fort Lauderdale

Museum of Art, in conjunction with the exhibition "Patchwork and Palmettos: Seminole-Miccosukee Folk Arts since 1820," conceived and curated by David M. Blackard at the Fort Lauderdale Historical Society, March 1-September 3, 1990 (Blackard 1990).

In effect, Bedell's initial instruction and demand for quality goods and work ethics greatly benefited the Seminole Arts and Crafts Guild's program with the Department of the Interior's Indian Arts and Crafts Board, assuring continued sponsorship, and bolstering the long-term economy of both the *i:laponathli:* and Creek tribal citizens in the federally recognized Seminole Tribe of Florida. Meanwhile, Edith Boehmer's IACB-backed Seminole Arts and Crafts Guild program would in time come to exemplify all of the Indian Arts and Crafts Board's criteria. This was a win-win for both of these selflessly dedicated, activist women, Deaconess Harriet M. Bedell and Edith M. Boehmer (Figure 68).

Acknowledgments. In pursuit of data included herein, I engaged in active discussion with the following persons who were still or who had been, highly involved in *i:laposhni cha thli:* arts projects: William D. and Edith M. Boehmer, Minnie Burt, David M. Blackard, Carol Cypress, Billy L. Cypress, Executive Director, Ah-Tah-Thi-Ki Museum, Seminole Tribe of Florida; William and Ellen Hartley, Mary Frances Johns, Charles L. Knight, Jimmie O. Osceola, Pete Osceola, Sr., and William C. Sturtevant, Curator of North American Ethnography, Smithsonian Institution.

President, Seminole Tribe of Florida, Inc.
The youngest American Indian to be elected as his tribe's leader.

Figure 66. *Joe Dan [Jaudon] Osceola (Panther clan) poses wearing a satin Seminole jacket, probably made by his Aunt Mary Tiger, when he was elected President of the Seminole Tribe of Florida Board in 1967. Joe Dan was the youngest American Indian in the country to hold such a major tribal position. Photo post card, S/MA 2012.13.17.*

Figure 67. *A "Postage Stamp Jacket," maker unknown, ca. 1960s. Four bands of "postage-stamp" size patchwork were used in this satin jacket. This outstanding work is a fine example of a product produced by the Tamiami Trail-Big Cypress craftsworkers, who had made crafts and clothing for both Glade Cross Mission and the Seminole Arts and Crafts enterprises. Such jackets were satin lined and zippered. Detail (at right) shows a postage stamp resting on a patchwork band to indicate narrow width and precision work. Maker unknown. West Collection, History Miami Museum, S/MA 81.1.1a and 81.1.1b.*

Figure 68. *Edith Meyer Boehmer with Deaconess Harriet M. Bedell, Glade Cross Mission, Everglades City, Florida, late 1950s. Photograph by William D. Boehmer. These two dedicated women aided in the formulation of Florida native arts and crafts as an industry, producing self-sufficiency and world-wide acclaim.*

Appendix

Criteria of the Two Major Commercial Tribal-wide Craft Programs Operating in the Twentieth Century: Glade Cross Mission and the Seminole Arts and Crafts Guild

An aid to the interpretation of the arts and crafts of the i:laponathli: (Mikasuki-speaking) artists within the Florida Ethnographic Collection, Florida Museum of Natural History, Gainesville, Florida

ABSENCE OF RICKRACK

- The initial indicator for patchwork arts produced in both the Glade Cross Mission and the Seminole Crafts Guild/Indian Arts and Crafts Board-trademarked programs is the absence of rickrack. Instead, a thin appliquéd trim of contrasting color was utilized above and below the bands of patchwork.
- The thread color should match the top-stitched trim.
- Only solid-colored fabrics were used for the garments and crafts.

PATCHWORK

Both Glades Cross Mission and Seminole Craft Guild/Indian Arts and Crafts Board:

- Only vintage standardized designs were used and generally the bands were the same width.

Glade Cross Mission:

- Only older, simple (considered "standard") designs were permitted, many with names suggested by Deaconess Bedell, such as Man on Horseback, Fire, Trees, Arrowheads, Waves, Lightning, Mountains. Bedell's original naming for designs saw a rebirth in sales for a Bird Clan camp (historically that of William McKinley's wife) on the Tamiami Trail in the 1970s.

Seminole Arts and Crafts Guild/Indian Arts and Crafts Board:

- The color "turquoise" often appears in the patchwork designs.
- Skirts often featured a black background.
- Intricate, small designs and additional styling were common.
- Early use of satin fabric in jackets.

Notes

1. Due to the Wheeler-Howard Bill in the early 1950s which would abolish certain native tribes, these people would form the Miccosukee Tribe of Indians of Florida in 1962, agreeing to govern themselves as a federally recognized tribe.

2. Annie M. Tiger recalled that embroidery thread (for sweetgrass baskets) and fabric were bought at the Manhattan Mercantile Co. in Everglades City. Ah-Tah-Thi-Ki Museum Oral History Project, Seminole Tribe of Florida, Doll Exhibit, May 13, 1999. Interviewee: Annie M. Tiger (Panther Clan); Carol Cypress, Interviewer, translator, and transcriber. Language: I:laponki:, p. 7. Seminole/Miccosukee Archive, Gainesville, Florida.

3. Buffalo Tiger (Bird clan) grew from childhood at the Musa Isle attraction with a career of painting hide drums, small and large, with Southwestern Indian "symbols," learned from a wintering Southwestern tribal citizen. Tiger grew up to lead the Trail Miccosukees in their tribal formation and was elected the first Miccosukee Tribal Chairman in 1962, a position he retained for many years.

4. The Mikasuki coiled grass baskets are of the type long made by the Gullah-Geechee of African origins who live in coastal South Carolina. It is entirely possible that Bedell visited that area in her annual trips back to her home in New York or acquired a sample basket elsewhere. Either way, she would have seen the value of this craft, so well suited to Everglades sweetgrass manufacture and would have realized how this highly decorative basketry would give the i:laponathli: women a new economic design outlet. The i:laponathli: coiled baskets have not been recorded in collections *prior* to Bedell's program.

5. The women generally complain that this grass is coarser than it looks and abrades their fingers. Minnie Billie Doctor said in an interview with Carol Cypress that, "It hurt my hand so much …" (Doctor 1999:6).

6. Statistically, in the rather uncommon circumstance of a Mikasuki-speaking woman marrying a Creek man, she would move to the Creek Reservation at Brighton. Economically this was more feasible, because the Creek men, who had asked the U.S. government for economic concessions in 1938, then had a strong, active economic base.

7. It should be noted that a Mikasuki-speaking woman did not bring a Creek-speaking husband to live with her people in southern Florida.

8. Edith sold turquoise jewelry on consignment from a southwestern dealer to accessorize the Guild's clothing.

9. Edward Malin, "Trademarks" United States Department of the Interior, Indian Arts and Crafts Board, "Smoke Signals" 43/1965, 3-18, 17; "Seminole Craft Center" USDI, IACB, "Smoke Signals" 47-48/Spring 1966, 21-23, 22; Data from the collections of the Seminole/Miccosukee Archive, Hang tags: 91.5 and 96:4 1-2. The earliest photographs of crafts from the William D. and Edith M. Boehmer Photographic Collection (early 1940s) show the first official hang tag in use. In 2019, the Ah-Tah-Thi-Ki Museum, Seminole Tribe of Florida, adopted a version of this tag attached to Arts and Crafts Guild items in their historic collection for new craft items sold in the Museum's Gift Shop. Ah-Tah-Thi-Ki's hangtag also includes the name of the craftsperson, which the staff sees as an important asset to their purchasing clientele (personal communication, February 5, 2019).

10. These short skirts are featured in the Craft Guild Guide (p. 15), 1956, Seminole/Miccosukee Archive 91.5.269.

11. William Sturtevant (1967:160-173) credits the Mikasuki-speaking Seminoles, the i:laponathli:, with the invention of machine-sewn patchwork. In the early 1950s Jimmie O. Osceola noted that only the Mikasuki-speaking women who had married Creek men were making patchwork at Brighton. See also E. Boehmer (1958).

References

Bedell, Harriet M.
1935a Glade Cross Mission Report. Included in a letter to Commissioner of Indian Affairs John Collier. File 6975, Seminole-150, U.S. Department of the Interior, Office of Indian Affairs, Washington, DC.

1935b List of Things Made by Seminole Indians. Glade Cross Mission, Everglades, Florida, 2 pp.

1937 Price List. Glade Cross Mission Report.

1941 Glade Cross Mission Report. William and Ellen Hartley Collection. The Charlton W. Tebeau Library of Florida History, History Miami Museum.

1953 Glade Cross Mission Report, Christmas, 1953.

BIA (Bureau of Indian Affairs)
1956 What I Must Know as a Member of My Craft Guild. Adult Education Series publication created for the Seminole Guild Program. Department of the Interior, Bureau of Indian Affairs, 27 pp. On file, Seminole/Miccosukee Archive 91.5.269.

Blackard, David M.
1990 *Patchwork & Palmettos: Seminole-Miccosukee Folk Art since 1820*. Exhibition Catalog. Fort Lauderdale Historical Society, Fort Lauderdale.

Boehmer, Edith M.
1957 To Anna Mae Sikes, State Home Demonstration Agent, Florida State University, May 14, 1957:1-2, 1. National Archives – SE, RG 435 – IACB, Box 1 [unmarked folder].

1958 Report of Work - 1958. National Archives – SE RG 435 – IACB, Box 1.

1982 Interview by the author. Seminole/Miccosukee Archive, Gainesville, Florida.

1990 Taped interview, Mount Dora, Florida (March 12, 1990) for her participation in the "Patchwork and Palmettos" symposium, Fort Lauderdale, Florida, September 8, 1990. Sponsored by the Seminole/Miccosukee Photographic Archive.

Boehmer, William D.
1971 Interview by John K. Mahon, February 23, 1971:1-49. 1. Indian Oral History Project, Doris Duke Foundation, University of Florida, Gainesville.

Boehmer, William D., and Edith M. Boehmer
1990 Video interview by the author, Mount Dora, Florida, March 12, 1990.

Burton, Lucius W., Jr.
1937 A Preliminary Report on the Seminole Indians. National Archives, RG 435, Records Relating to Technical Assistance, 1932-1934, Box 1, Misc. Reports (ca. 1937):1-2:2.

Craft Guild Guide, 1956. Seminole/Miccosukee Archive, Gainesville, Florida.

Deloria, Jr., Vine, and Clifford M. Lytle
1984 *The Nations Within: The Past and Future of American Indian Sovereignty*. Pantheon Books, New York.

d'Harnoncourt, René
1938 Gen. Mgr. IACB, to Hon. Conway P. Coe, Commissioner of Patents, Dept. of Commerce, April 9, 1938. National Archives, RG 435, Records of the IACB, Records Relating to Technical Assistance, 1932-48, Box 2, Misrepresentation Violations of Sec. 6, PL 74-355 1936-1943.

Doctor, Minnie Billie
1999 Ah-Tah-Thi-Ki Museum, Oral History Project, Seminole Tribe of Florida, "Doll Exhibit" [not mounted]. Interview with Minnie Billie Doctor, May 14, 1999. Okalee Museum, Hollywood. Interviewer: Carol Cypress. Seminole/Miccosukee Archive, Gainesville, Florida.

Downs, Dorothy
1979 Patchwork Clothing of the Florida Indians. *American Indian Art Magazine* 4 (Summer 1979), pp. 32-41.

1995 *Art of the Florida Seminole and Miccosukee Indians*. University Press of Florida, Gainesville.

Freeman, Ethel Cutler
1940 Ethel Cutler Freeman Papers, Series 5, Box 43, National Anthropological Archives, Smithsonian Institution.

Fort Myers News-Press
1937 Seminole Souvenir Industry Menaced by Jap Imitations, Deaconess Bedell Declares; Indians Developing Real Art, Association Told; Tribesmen Exhibited in Miami Like Alligators and Monkeys. *Fort Myers News-Press* (March 5, 1937). News clipping in the collection of the Seminole/Miccosukee Archive, Gainesville, Florida.

Glenn, John L.
1932 Seminole Commissioner, Florida, to Commissioner of Indian Affairs John Collier, November 19, 1932. National Archives, RG 435 Records of the IACN, Misc. Files, 1930-1935, Box 4, Seminole.

Greenlee, Robert F.
1952 Aspects of Social Organization and Material Culture of the Seminole of Big Cypress Swamp. *The Florida Anthropologist* 5(3-4):25-31.

Hartley, William, and Ellen Hartley
1963 *A Woman Set Apart: The Remarkable Life of Harriet Bedell*. Dodd Meade, New York.

IACB (Indian Arts and Crafts Board)
1939-1941 National Archives, RG 435, Records of the IACB, Records Relating to Exhibits and Exhibitions, 1939-1941, Box No. 24 (Old Box 32); Box 28 (Old Box 36), captioned: MOMA.

1943a Public – No. 355 – 74th Congress [S2203] An Act to promote the development of Indian arts and crafts and to create a board to assist therein, and for other purposes, pp. 89-91. Approved August 27, 1935. U.S. Department of the Interior, IACB, "Reports and Documents," Section VI, 33-35, December 1, 1943.

1943b U.S. Department of the Interior, Reports and Documents, X – Educational Activities of the IACB, 1943.

Johns, Lena Cypress, and Betty Cypress
1996 Interview with the author, April 2, 1996, Brighton, Florida. Mary Frances Johns, Interpreter. Seminole Oral History Project in conjunction with Ah-Tah-Thi-Ki Museum, Seminole Tribe of Florida, Hollywood.

Love, Rita
 1967 Teacher Turned Tribal Crafts into Big Business. *Sun Tattler* (July 7, 1967). Hollywood, Florida. Clipping in the William D. and Edith M. Boehmer Collection, Seminole/Miccosukee Archive, Gainesville, Florida.

Marriott, Alice R.
 1943 Arts and Crafts of the Florida Seminole. Reports and Documents concerning the Indian Arts and Crafts Board 7 (December 1):47-58. Department of the Interior, Washington, DC.

OIA (Office of Indian Affairs)
 1942 United States Department of the Interior, Annual Report, 1942.

 1943 United States Department of the Interior, Annual Report; Reports and Documents, 1943.

Osceola, Jimmie O'Toole
 1996 Interview with the author. Seminole/Miccosukee Archive, Gainesville, Florida.

Osceola, Sr., Pete
 1981 Interview with the author, at Pete Osceola's Discount Crafts, Tamiami Trail, 1981. Seminole/Miccosukee Archive, Gainesville, Florida.

Scott, Ed
 1937 Manager, Deep Lake Company, to Deaconess Harriet M. Bedell, December 20, 1937. William and Ellen Hartley Collection, The Charlton W. Tebeau Library of Florida History, History Miami Museum.

Scott, F. J.
 1936 Superintendent, Seminole Agency, Dania, Florida to Louis C. West, General Manager IACB, Oct. 6, 1936. National Archives R 435 – Records of IACB. Records Relating to Technical Assistance, 1932-1948, Box No. 2 ["Nationwide Survey for Potential Directory of Currently Produced Indian Goods"].

Seminole Tribe of Florida
 1954 Annual Report, 1954. Hollywood, Florida.

Sosin, Milt
 1949 Vocational Guidance Is Need of Seminoles at Brighton. *Miami Daily News* (October 4, 1949). Clipping in the William D. and Edith M. Boehmer Collection, 91.5, Seminole/Miccosukee Archive, Gainesville, Florida.

Sturtevant, William
 1967 Seminole Men's Clothing. Reprinted from *Essays on the Verbal and Visual Arts: Proceedings of the 1966 Annual Spring Meeting of the American Ethnological Society*, pp. 160-174. University of Washington Press, Seattle.

West, Patsy
 1984 Glade Cross Mission: An Influence on Florida Seminole Arts and Crafts. *American Indian Art Magazine* 9(4):58-67. Scottsdale, Arizona.

 1996 I.LAPONKI.: The Florida Seminoles in the 1930s. *Native Peoples* 9(3):26-32.

 2008 *The Enduring Seminoles: From Alligator Wrestling to Casino Gaming*. Revised and expanded edition. University Press of Florida, Gainesville.

 2016 Abiaka, or Sam Jones, in Context: The Mikasuki Ethnogenesis through the Third Seminole War. *The Florida Historical Quarterly* 94(3):366-410.

Wilson, Beverly
 1961 Meet Real Pioneers of Florida Fashion. *Miami Herald* (April 18, 1961). Clipping in the William D. and Edith M. Boehmer Collection, 91.5, Seminole/Miccosukee Archive, Gainesville, Florida.

5

Pairing Faces with Names: A History and Typology of Seminole Dolls

Austin J. Bell

Introduction

In many respects Seminole dolls seem to embody certain cultural characteristics of the people who create them. The dolls are at once traditional and contemporary, both rooted in a rural landscape and outfitted with cosmopolitan panache. They are symbols of cultural identity and tribal autonomy (Archer 2005), conceived as a commodity in response to decades of oppression and poverty, their artistic integrity still intact more than a century later. They are a medium through which traditional art forms and lifeways are sustained while communicating important cultural values to broader audiences (Figures 1 and 2).

Yet a single doll does not represent any specific person, for it is taboo for Seminoles to recreate anyone in literal form (Downs 1995:211). Nor does a doll, at least on an individual basis, repre-sent much more to its maker than a means to an end. As Seminole artist Pedro Zepeda explains, "Seminole items are made to look beautiful and appealing to the eye. When you look at the Seminole item, there's not a whole lot of meaning to it, other than to look pretty" (Tobias 2009). Or, as Seminole dollmaker Mary Billie puts it, "the reason she does it is it's the only income she gets"

(Billie 1980a:4). The dolls have neither ceremonial nor spiritual roles in Seminole culture, say as *katsina* dolls do among the Hopi of the American Southwest (McQuiston and McQuiston 1995:49-61). And yet, Seminole dolls of all ages, sizes, and types are highly prized collectibles and have been so practically since their inception (Figure 3).

Figure 1. *Three Type 1 dolls. Photo by Eric Zamora. Collections of the Anthropology Division of the Florida Museum of Natural History, FLMNH cat. nos. 88-6-4, 88-6-6, 2006-19-1.*

Figure 2. *An unidentified Seminole woman making dolls with a Singer sewing machine (1954). Courtesy of the State Archives of Florida.*

Figure 3. *An unidentified Seminole woman selling dolls and sweetgrass basketry at the 1983 Florida Folk Festival. Photo by Larry Coltharp (May 1983). Courtesy of the State Archives of Florida.*

Historically, Seminole dolls have been lumped into larger discussions about Seminole arts and crafts but seldom given singular attention or study. This may be due in part to their lack of ceremonial importance or perceived "deeper meaning," or perhaps even a disrespect for doll artistry due to their commercialized existence, which often emphasizes salability over artistic perfection. The most in-depth examinations of Seminole dolls are either complementary chapters in larger volumes (Blackard 1990a:56-57; Downs 1995:211-219; Roberts 2001:148-160), relatively obscure (Archer 2005; Johnson 2008), or presented as public-facing interpretation (FLMNH 2021a). Apart from Johnson's thorough but loosely structured classifications (2008), previous sources describe various types of Seminole dolls only in limited detail and generalities. None attempts a standardized lexicon or typology.

In this chapter, I attempt to establish a typology and lexicon by which to describe and classify the likely thousands of dolls that exist in museums and private collections. In doing so, I focus solely on the types known with certainty to be the handiwork of Seminole or Miccosukee artisans. Anglicized Seminole dolls of unknown provenance, such as plastic dolls, Cabbage Patch dolls, Precious Moments dolls, Troll dolls, Skookum dolls, papier-mâché dolls, commercial rag dolls, and the like are therefore not included unless explicitly documented as Seminole or Miccosukee (Blackard 1990a:57; Sieg 2018:112-116). The same applies to limbed "all palmetto" dolls, some of which are "folk art dolls made by non-Native Americans for the tourist trade" (Johnson 2008:20-21, 74). Also excluded are incomplete dolls or accessories, such as Seminole doll "kits," unfinished examples of dolls in the process of fabrication, as well as at least two examples of unworn doll outfits.

The term Seminole is broadly applied to all dolls in this study, including those that might be considered Miccosukee, because any such distinction was seldom documented by early collectors, especially prior to federal recognition of the Miccosukee Tribe of Indians of Florida in 1962 (Miccosukee Tribe 2021). However, it is important to note a linguistic distinction between and within the two tribes. The *i:laponathli:* – or *Mikasuki*-speaking Seminoles – make up a two-thirds majority of both tribes. The *ci:saponathli:* – or Muscogee-speaking Creeks – comprise the remaining third and live primarily at the Brighton Reservation north of Lake Okeechobee (Sturtevant 1971:111-117; West 1998:1-3) with some noted exceptions (see West, this volume). The *i:laponathli:* are primarily responsible for the emergence of the Seminole tourism economy in the early 1900s, but the *ci:saponathli:* did make forays into the market, as evidenced in dolls collected at Brighton. Some distinct cultural or regional preferences may be apparent in these dolls, as hinted at by anthropologists in museum records.

Historical Overview

Despite their seemingly straightforward roles as cultural commodities, Seminole dolls were not always made to be bought and sold. The first Seminole dolls were children's playthings, observed by Clay MacCauley in early 1881. "The Seminole has a doll, i.e., a bundle of rags, a stick with a bit of cloth wrapped about it, or something that serves just as well as this. The children build little houses for their dolls and name them 'camps'" (MacCauley 1887:506). These dolls were intentionally ambiguous and simple in form, perhaps in part due to Seminole taboos (Downs 1995:215), but perhaps also due to a lack of resources, the absence of an established doll tradition, and the simple fact that they were made for children to handle and play with (Figure 4). These dolls, classified here and elsewhere as "rag dolls," still exist in museum collections (Downs 1995:213, Figure 9.1).

By the early 1900s, Seminole dolls were still toys for children, but had taken a more well-defined form. Carved cylindrically by men from a single piece of soft wood, usually cypress, they typically had round heads, which were sometimes adorned with carved or drawn-in facial features (Roberts 2001:148). If clothes were not painted on by men, the dolls were outfitted by women in the conventional clothing of the time: capes and skirts for

Figure 4. *A young Seminole girl holding a rag doll. Courtesy of the Ah-Tah-Thi-Ki Museum, ATTK2001.32.1.*

female dolls and "big shirts" for males, often with strips of calico fabric included (Downs 1995:211-212; West 1998:51). These early wooden dolls were generally made prior to 1920 but initiated a trend in which Seminole dolls would often don the popular styles of their time.

By 1918, ever-increasing numbers of Florida tourists began to take an interest in the dolls as souvenirs. Northerners had been pouring into the southern portion of the peninsula, soaking up its sunshine and subtropical climate. Seminoles, having lived in relative poverty and isolation for most of the decades following the Seminole Wars and facing a loss of hunting ground and natural resources due to the draining of the Everglades, recognized an opportunity to capitalize on an otherwise unwelcome encroachment (West 1998:4-9). "Indian villages" began popping up around more populated areas in South Florida, such as Miami and Fort Lauderdale. The villages were white-run tourist attractions at which the Seminoles effectively granted access to themselves to generate income, much of which came through the sale sof arts and crafts (West 1998:50-57). The dolls were a small but integral part of that larger effort, "authentic" in that they were made by Seminole artisans, but not actually a traditional art form.

The first village to sell dolls was Coppinger's Tropical Gardens in Miami, where women began producing the first palmetto dolls (Roberts 2001:149), again changing the medium. Rosalee "Rosie" Tiger Huff made the first palmetto doll as a child's toy, having previously made rag dolls (Billie and Jumper 1982). Ada Tiger, her cousin, along with

Annie Tommie, saw the doll and thought it had potential as a tourist item. So, Tommie replicated the doll while Tiger created a skirt for it. They placed it in a "little store," where a tourist bought it (Billie and Jumper 1982). Thus, Tiger, Huff, and Tommie became the pioneers of palmetto doll-making (Jumper 1988:1 [Downs 1995:215; West 1998:52]), their early dolls reportedly 20 centimeters in height and costing $0.50 apiece. By 1922, the palmetto dolls were being sold in gift shops at Coppinger's, Musa Isle, and other locations (Downs 1995:215; see Figure 5, this chapter).

Palmetto was likely chosen as a medium for several reasons, including that it was already an important locally available plant (MacCauley 1887:517; Oehlbeck 1997:51-58), less labor-intensive than woodcarving, and possessing a coloration more closely resembling that of a Seminole person's skin than white cypress wood (Downs 1995:215). Palmetto fiber is collected from the trunk of a wild saw palmetto (*Serenoa repens*), the search for which is typically an all-day affair (Billie 1980b:4-8; Cypress 1999:11-12). The already arduous task has become increasingly difficult in recent years due to a proliferation of private landowners (Cypress 1999:12) and the customary practice of burning the palmetto plant prior to collecting fiber, which now requires permitting to prevent wildfires (Billie 1980b:6; Cypress 1999:14); see Figures 6 and 7.

Once collected, it is dried and cut into strips that can be rolled into balls (for heads) and cylinders (for torsos) using the fiber's natural curl (Downs 1995:216; Roberts 2001:149). The body is stuffed

Figure 5. *Rosa Johns (left), Cecil Jones (center) and Mary Parker (right) at the Toby Johns camp on the Brighton Reservation. Rosa Johns is making palmetto dolls. Photo by William D. Boehmer (1939). Courtesy of the Ah-Tah-Thi-Ki Museum, ATTK2009.34.1.*

Figure 7. *Mary B. Billie harvesting palmetto fiber for dollmaking. Photo by Doris Dyen (July 15, 1980). Courtesy of the State Archives of Florida.*

Figure 6. *Claudia C. John and her mother, Mary B. Billie, search for a wild palmetto to harvest. Photo by Doris Dyen (July 15, 1980). Courtesy of the State Archives of Florida.*

with either palmetto fiber or cotton and a circular cardboard base seals off the bottom end of the cylinder (Billie 1980b:13-14); see Figures 8 and 9. Palmetto fiber was a more common stuffing in the early days, but the use of cotton as a stuffing – sometimes from old, discarded mattresses (Cypress 1999:4) – increased after World War II. The spherical head is made separately and attached to the body before its facial features are sewn on (Billie 1980b:12-14; Downs 1995:216; Libhart 1989:40).

Once the palmetto doll's "naked" body is formed, it is outfitted in Seminole regalia. Clothing is made separately, sometimes by different women (Billie

1980b:19-20), usually with a sewing machine. A female doll is dressed skirt first, followed by a cape, hair, and accessories (Billie 1980b:20). Large orders are often done assembly-line style, making them a communal effort (Cypress 1999:10) and an important part of Seminole life. Cotton fabric is the typical cloth material, which, prior to 1920, was arranged in alternating colorful bands and appliqué work (Blackard 1990a:42). Calico and gingham fabrics were also commonly incorporated into garments until they became difficult to obtain during World War I (Zerkel 2014:58-59). However, the Seminoles are best known for their colorful patchwork, first introduced around 1920, which comes in a variety of patterns and forms (Blackard 1990a:45-55, 1990b:77-82; Downs

Figure 8. *Mary B. Billie making dolls at the Big Cypress Reservation. Photo by Doris Dyen (July 15, 1980). Courtesy of the State Archives of Florida.*

Figure 9. *Seminole dolls at various stages of completion. Photo by Doris Dyen (July 15, 1980). Courtesy of the State Archives of Florida.*

Figure 10. *Deaconess Harriet Bedell with Seminole dolls at the Glade Cross Mission in Everglades City. Photo by Don Marks (March 1960). Courtesy of the State Archives of Florida.*

1995:83-119). Many Seminole dolls feature at least one row of patchwork (45.1% of the 683 dolls in this study). Four-to-six-inch dolls do not usually have a row of patchwork, but dolls eight inches or taller do (Billie 1980b:20). Notably, the *ci:saponathli:* did not begin making patchwork until the 1930s (Blackard 1990a:46).

Seminole patchwork designs are an oft-cited means to dating Seminole dolls (Blackard 1990a:56; Roberts 2001:150). The patterns sometimes correspond with different eras in Seminole craft making, particularly those that occurred under the direction of Deaconess Harriet Bedell at the Glade Cross Mission (1933-1960) and William and Edith Boehmer's Seminole Arts and Crafts Guild (1939-1960); see West, this volume. It was

under these programs, particularly Bedell's mission, that patchwork designs were standardized for commercial purposes (Figure 10). Bedell was strict in her quality control, accepting only the dolls she deemed of a certain quality and "traditional" style (Lenz 1986:82; Downs 1995:215). The patterns became more uniform under her direction, but still evolved over the decades, becoming increasingly complex and more colorfully diverse (Figure 11). Despite Bedell's insistence that the Seminoles adhere to her models, artistic preference led to experimentation and variations. Some patterns were simply easier than others to make, meaning they could be produced more quickly, especially helpful when dealing with large orders (Cypress 1999:10).

Figure 11. *Annie Tiger Bowers shows Lawanna Osceola Niles how to sew a doll at the Brighton Reservation (1958). Courtesy of the State Archives of Florida.*

Figure 12. *Mary Motlow holding a Seminole doll. Photo by William D. Boehmer (ca. 1960). Courtesy of the Ah-Tah-Thi-Ki Museum, ATTK2009.34.1381.*

Hairstyles and personal accouterments are also telling indicators of when a doll was made, as they too were incorporated into the dolls depending on what was in style (Blackard 1990a:56). For example, rolled hair on female dolls is generally indicative of an early 1930s date, while a pronounced crescent-shaped hairboard is more typical of the 1940s (Roberts 2001:149); see Figure 12. By the late 1960s, dolls began to have pigtails and ponytails, much like their Seminole makers (Roberts 2001:149). Of course, the final appearance of each doll is up to its artist and some more recent dolls are done in "traditional" styles, so patchwork and accessories are not always a reliable means of dating them.

Doll Artists

Each doll in this study was presumably made by one or more Seminole or Miccosukee artists. Traditionally, palmetto dolls are made by women, although men are sometimes involved in collecting the plant fiber directly from a wild palmetto (Downs 1995:216; Cypress 1999:12). Wooden dolls are more typically carved by men, but their clothes, if made from cloth, are usually sewn by women. Painted features on dolls are typically done by men. Not every palmetto doll is made entirely by the same woman. In fact, a woman – or whole family unit together – may collect the fiber and sell it to someone else who makes the

body, which may then be outfitted by an entirely different person (Cypress 1999:12). The Seminoles are proud to have had assembly-style operations from which the highest yield of dolls could be produced (Tara Backhouse, personal communication, 2020). In these instances, it would be unlikely to track the doll makers because there can be several per doll. However, some dolls are made entirely by the same person, from fiber collection to final decoration. Beginning in the 1940s, some dolls were affixed with tags that named the individual artist responsible for the work. However, many thousands of dolls were made before that innovation, and most dolls still do not list a maker.

Unfortunately, this makes a doll with a known maker among the rarest of all Seminole dolls; only 97 (14.2%) of the 683 in this study have a known maker (Appendix A). That figure is likely skewed higher than the overall figure for all Seminole dolls in existence, because many of the dolls in this study were collected by anthropologists who obtained artist information in the field. Still, doll tags, museum records, and oral histories have left some of the names of artisans responsible for doll work, including Elaine Aguilar (Downs 1995:209-210), Annie C. Billie, Bird Billie (Cypress 1999:5-6), Lena Billie, Lucy J. Billie, Mary B. Billie (Dyen 1980), Mary R. Billie, Robert Billie (Cypress 1999:9), Ruby Jumper Billie, Lizzie Buck, Barbara Clay, Agnes Billie Cypress, Carol Cypress, Ida Cypress, Mary B. Cypress, Minnie Doctor (Figure 13), Donna Frank (Downs 1995:204-209), Lena Osceola Frank, Connie Frank Gowan, Bobby Henry,

Alice Huff, Rosalie Tiger Huff, Mrs. Istimathli Ingraham (possible duplicate), Elsie Roberts Jimmie, Claudia C. John (Dyen 1980), Lucy Johns, Rosa Johns, Sally Johns, Shula Jones, Loretta Micco, Mina Osceola Micco, Yolanda Ortero, Alice Osceola, Effie Osceola, Mrs.

Figure 13. *Minnie Doctor and an unidentified child with dolls at the Okalee Indian Village on the Dania Reservation. Photo by Charles Lee Baron (September 1961). Courtesy of the State Archives of Florida.*

George Osceola (possible duplicate), Henry Osceola, Ida Osceola, Mrs. John Osceola (possible duplicate), Mabel Osceola, Maggie Osceola, Mary Osceola, Mary Jane (Cypress) Storm, Ada Tiger, Annie Cypress Tiger, Doctor Tiger, Mary Tiger, Mrs. Tommie Tiger (possible duplicate), Annie Tommie, and Dorothy Tucker.

Some artists had unique styles or innovations in their work, such as Annie Tiger Jim, who is known for her "snowflake" patchwork design (Downs 1995:117), or Paul Billie, who introduced step patterning in his sweetgrass basketry (Livingston 2014). This posits the tantalizing idea of retroactively attributing artist identities to certain works based on physical characteristics – information valuable not only for posterity and to tribal descendants, but also to the artists themselves, perhaps opening the possibility of retrospective exhibitions of their work. Yet, as Carol Cypress points out, while possible in some instances, particularly with tribal elders, that sort of task is exceedingly difficult even for someone who has been around dollmaking their entire life (Cypress 1999:8). However, by establishing this typology, I hope that perhaps certain rare combinations of traits may tease out some new possible artist attributions.

Methodology

Seminole dolls are held in museum collections across the United States. They are highly collectible, and have been basically since their invention, having been accessioned into museum collections as early as 1910. To build an appropriately compre-

hensive tiered lexicon by which to classify and date specific dolls, I elected to study a large sample of dolls across multiple institutions (Appendix B). In total, I examined 683 dolls at five institutions, including the Florida Museum of Natural History (275), the Ah-Tah-Thi-Ki Museum (260), the National Museum of the American Indian (92), the National Museum of Natural History (35), and the American Museum of Natural History (21). These institutions were selected not only for the diversity and scope of their collections, but also for their lengthy collecting histories, general notoriety, and affiliated collectors (some of them prominent anthropologists more inclined to collect important provenance, such as "artist" or "maker," along with objects).

Those collections from American Museum of Natural History (AMNH), the National Museum of Natural History (NMNH), and the National Museum of the American Indian (NMAI) were studied virtually through images in online collection databases, thereby introducing a greater possibility of error in type attributions. For example, the presence of limbs (arms under capes) on wooden female dolls could not always be ascertained with certainty from pictures alone. The collection at the Ah-Tah-Thi-Ki Museum (ATTK) was studied virtually and in person in October 2021. The collection at the Florida Museum of Natural History (FLMNH) was studied in person in November 2021.

Table 1. Lexicon for the Establishment of a Seminole Doll Typology.

Gender	Body Material	Body Type	Style
Female	Cloth	Cylindrical	All Palmetto
Male	Palmetto	Head Only	Basket
	Wood	Horseback	Big Shirt
		Limbed	Lapel Pin
			Necklace
			Pin Cushion
			Rag
			Rancher
			Traditional
			Other

I established a lexicon (Table 1) based on easily observable physical characteristics in these dolls, beginning with the most obvious dichotomy: **gender**. Most, if not all, dolls are easily identifiable as either male or female due to their manner of dress (typically cape and skirt for females, shirt and/or pants for men), body type (typically cylindrical for female, limbed for male), and various gender-specific accessories (e.g., earrings, necklaces and hairboards for women, turbans and neckerchiefs for men). While this model excludes nonbinary genders, I have not known or observed an intentionally non-binary portrayal of a Seminole doll to date. One male doll wearing a big shirt at the FLMNH (2018-15-3) has arms but a (typically-female) cylindrical base, presenting the only possible representation of a non-binary gender. It may also simply represent a unique form or style or the resourceful adaptation of a previously made female body into a male one. According to Johnson (2008:57), "some early [1918-1933] male dolls were made with the cylindrical body." Non-binary could easily be added as a third gender category in the future if necessary. The term "Two-Spirit" would be an appropriate term for such dolls (Blais-Billie 2021:7-8). Female dolls are far more common than male dolls, comprising 81.6% of the 683 dolls in this study.

The second tier further separates dolls by primary **body material**, as both genders of dolls have been portrayed in all three mediums; palmetto, wood, and cloth, with palmetto being the most common (89.8% of the 683 dolls in this study).

The third tier, **body type,** refers generally to the doll as if it were "naked," absent any clothing and accessories. *Cylindrical* is the term generally applied to most palmetto and wood dolls, predominantly female and limbless, with a tubular torso that often has a wider base than top, making it slightly conical. *Limbed* refers to those dolls, male and female, with distinct arms and/or legs, regardless of torso shape. Because Seminole women typically kept their hands and feet hidden, limbs were generally not included on female dolls (Barbour 1944:53-54), but there are exceptions. *Horseback* refers to those rare dolls (usually male) attached to and seated on top of a horse. *Head only* refers to torso-less doll heads, usually pieces of larger composite crafts such as lapel pins, pin cushions, baskets, and other objects.

The fourth and final tier, **style,** is less demarcated than the preceding three by necessity. *Traditional* refers to the most classic Seminole doll outfit: the cape and skirt, outfitted exclusively on female dolls. The *big shirt* and *rancher* styles apply only to male dolls, usually either one or the other depending on the doll's outfit. *Ranchers* typically wear pants, while those in *big shirts* do not. *Rag* refers to both early featureless rag dolls and later commercial rag dolls. The latter has been excluded from this study, but I noted seven (five female, two male) across three museums (ATTK, FLMNH, NMAI), each made of cloth and limbed. *All palmetto* refers to those dolls wearing clothing made entirely from palmetto fiber. *Lapel pins*, *pin cushions*, *baskets*, *necklaces,* and *other* are composite objects, usually featuring *head only* dolls, that function primarily as something other than a doll. In these instances, the doll is more of an accessory than the primary object. Any of these four tiers may be expanded in the future to include new genders, body materials, body types, or styles.

Results

Out of this four-tiered hierarchy and the 240 unique doll possibilities it presents, I was able to identify 24 different types of dolls across five museum collections. This list is not meant to be exhaustive and is open to additions from other collections. Should other new classifications be found or invented in the future, such as new body types or styles, I hope that they might easily be amended to the lexicon presented here. For instance, during the course of writing this chapter, I observed two additional types outside the scope of this study and thus preemptively included them as Types 25 and 26.

Date ranges are approximated based on museum catalog records and my own observations and are not necessarily fixed. Many of the dolls in this study have known creation dates thanks to the anthropologists who collected them in the field, which aided in establishing a range for certain characteristics. While no single characteristic provides a perfect method for dating dolls, a combination of clues can establish a narrower timeframe for those dolls lacking provenance. These include cloth types (especially patchwork patterns), facial features, hairstyles, accessories, and rickrack. All of these characteristics were noted on each individual doll in order to establish a general date range for each whenever possible.

The 26 types I have determined thus far are outlined here, in order from most to least prevalent (Appendix C).

1. **Female: Palmetto: Conical: Traditional**
   a. No. of examples: 397
   b. Height range: 6.4 – 149.9 cm
   c. Median height: 22.0 cm
   d. Date range: 1920 – Present
   e. Known artists: (26) Lena Billie, Lucy J. Billie, Mary R. Billie, Lizzie Buck, Ida Cypress, Mary B. Cypress, Minnie Doctor, Lena Osceola Frank, Connie Frank Gowan, Alice Huff, Mrs. Istimathli Ingraham, Elsie Roberts Jimmie, Sally Johns, Shula Jones, Loretta Micco, Mina Osceola Micco, Ida Osceola, Mrs. John Osceola (possible duplicate), Maggie Osceola, Mary Osceola, Annie Cypress Tiger, Mary Tiger, [unknown] Tiger (possible duplicate), Dorothy Tucker, Ethel [unknown]
   f. Discussion: The traditionally dressed limbless female palmetto doll is far and away the most common type (Johnson 2008:16). It comprises 58.1% of all the dolls in this study. There is extraordinary variation among dolls of this type, particularly in clothing and accessories (Figures 14-18).
   i. Seventy-six (19.1%) dolls have some sort of nose, 47 (11.8%) have black thread eyebrows, and 27 (6.8%) have "teeth" (white thread in between red thread "lips"). Detailed facial features can sometimes be an indicator of age (Johnson 2008:36).
   ii. Two hundred sixty-one (65.7%) dolls have hairboards, 258 (98.9%) of which are wrapped in cloth and three (1.1%) of which are wrapped in real hair. Thirteen hairboards are embel-

Figure 15. *A Type 1 doll with real hair and three rows of patchwork (ca. 1950-1960). Photo by Aditi Jayarajan. Graphic by the author. Collections of the Anthropology Division of the Florida Museum of Natural History, FLMNH cat. no. 2012-50-25.*

Figure 14. *Three Type 1 dolls. The doll on the left was made by Connie Frank Gowan and Minnie Doctor. Photo by Eric Zamora. Collections of the Anthropology Division of the Florida Museum of Natural History, FLMNH cat. nos. 2006-20-19, E663, E806.*

lished with bangles and/or beadwork. Ninety-seven (24.4%) dolls have rolled hairstyles, 88 of which are cloth (one velvet) and nine of which are yarn. Three of the rolled hairstyles are embellished with beaded hairnets. Thirty-five (8.8%) dolls have "other" hairstyles, which include braided, bun, pigtails, and ponytail. Four of these "other" styles also wear beaded headbands and one wears a feather in its hair. Twenty-three of these dolls have yarn hair, 12 have nylon hair (one has both yarn and nylon hair), and one has a cloth ponytail. Five dolls' hairstyles were either damaged or otherwise indiscernible.

iii. One hundred forty-six dolls have rickrack (36.8%) and 199 (50.1%) feature at least one row of patchwork. Patchwork appears on dolls in the 1920s and escalates in the 1930s after the arrival of Deaconess Bedell at the Glade Cross Mission in 1933 (Roberts 2001:150). Narrow rickrack generally appears with greater frequency after 1950 (Johnson 2008:28; Roberts 2001:150).

iv. Two hundred forty-one (60.7%) wear monochromatic beaded necklaces, 145 (36.5%) wear multicolored beaded necklaces (one wears both monochromatic and multicolored necklaces), and 13 (3.3%) have no necklace. Multicolored beaded necklaces are typically indicative of a post-1950 date (Johnson 2008:33; Roberts 2001:150-151). There is evidence that some of the 13 dolls

Figure 16. *A Type 1 doll with a cloth hairboard, silver bangles, and two rows of patchwork (ca. 1940-1950). Photo by Aditi Jayarajan. Graphic by the author. Collections of the Anthropology Division of the Florida Museum of Natural History, FLMNH cat. no. 2017-41-1.*

Figure 17. *A Type 1 doll with beaded pendant earrings (ca. 2000-2007). Photo and graphic by the author with permission of the Ah-Tah-Thi-Ki Museum, ATTK2007.9.28.*

Figure 18. *A Type 1 doll with an embellished hairboard and a "baby" doll brooch (ca. 2000-2007). Photo and graphic by the author with permission of the Ah-Tah-Thi-Ki Museum, ATTK2007.9.29.*

missing a necklace may once have worn one.

v. One hundred twelve (28.2%) wear traditional drop-style bead earrings, which first appear after 1930 (Roberts 2001:151), and 67 (16.9%) wear hoop-style bead earrings, which are more common after 1950 (Johnson 2008:33; Roberts 2001:151). An additional three (0.8%) wear more specialized earrings, including beaded pendants, silver pendants, and pin-style earrings. The remaining 216 (54.4%) dolls have no earrings.

vi. Twenty-five (6.3%) dolls have relatively uncommon accessories, including silver bangles (14) and/or small lapel pin dolls (presumably representative of babies) or brooches (13).

vii. Forty-two (10.6%) of the dolls have an attributed artist as part of their provenance.

2. Male: Palmetto: Limbed: Big Shirt

a. No. of examples: 96

b. Height range: 8 – 81 cm

c. Median height: 29.1 cm

d. Date range: 1930 – Present

e. Known artists: (5) Annie C. Billie, Lucy J. Billie, Ida Cypress, Effie Osceola, Maggie Osceola

f. Discussion: The second most common doll type, the limbed male palmetto doll, wears a traditional "big shirt" as opposed to the more contemporary jacket and pants (Johnson 2008:63); see Figures 19-21. Some, apparently, also wear undershorts (Downs 1995:217), although none was observed in this study.

Figure 19. *A Type 2 doll with a circular coiled sweetgrass base (ca. 2000-2007) possibly made by Maggie Osceola. Photo and graphic by the author with permission of the Ah-Tah-Thi-Ki Museum, ATTK2007.9.30.*

Figure 20. *A Type 2 doll with a rectangular palmetto base. Photo by Aditi Jayarajan. Graphic by the author. Collections of the Anthropology Division of the Florida Museum of Natural History, FLMNH cat. no. 2012-46-6.*

According to Johnson, "not many male dolls" were made prior to Bedell's intervention (Johnson 2008:58). These dolls are sometimes created with a female counterpart and sold as a pair, a practice that began in the 1940s (Johnson 2008:70). Due to a cultural taboo, only women past menopause are supposed to make male dolls (Downs 1995:217).

i. Twenty-two (22.9%) of the dolls stand upon a handcrafted base or platform, usually attached to the lower limbs and designed to make each doll stand upright on its own. Eleven of these bases are circular wood pieces, six are square or rectangular palmetto pieces, three are circular coiled sweetgrass pieces, and two are circular palmetto pieces. Dolls with bases or "platforms" were likely created post-1950 (Johnson 2008:63).

ii. Sixty-two (64.6%) of the dolls have simple "bowl" haircuts (56 cloth, 3 yarn, 3 real hair), while 33 (34.4%)

Figure 21. *A female (Type 1) and male (Type 2) doll pair (ca. 1930-1940). Photo and graphic by the author with permission of the Ah-Tah-Thi-Ki Museum, ATTK2005.76.1 and ATTK2005.76.2.*

wear cloth turbans. Eleven of the turbans feature silver bands and seven feature a row of patchwork. One doll (FLMNH 2012-50-28) wears a cap rather than a bowl cut or turban.

iii. In terms of facial features, most of the dolls (60.4%) have sewn-on noses, 30 (31.3%) have eyebrows, and three (3.1%) have teeth.

iv. All of but three (96.9%) of the dolls wear a neckerchief tied around the neck. Of those 93 neckerchiefs, 41 (44.1%) have a beadwork woggle fastened around the knot.

v. Seventy (72.9%) dolls have at least one row of patchwork sewn into their

big shirts, a significantly higher percentage than seen in the more common Type 1 doll (49.8%).

vi. Twenty-two (22.9%) of the dolls wear rickrack.

3. **Female: Palmetto: Head Only: Lapel Pin**

a. No. of examples: 52

b. Height range: 4.5 – 11 cm

c. Median height: 7 cm

d. Date range: 1940 – Present

e. Known artists: (1) Connie Frank Gowan

f. Discussion: These small bodiless dolls are generally designed as brooches for personal adornment, but sometimes also appear on larger dolls. They are typically fastened with safety pins. They have the same appearance as a traditional cylindrical female palmetto doll but usually have no body underneath the skirt. Exceptions have been reported (Johnson 2008:17) but none were found during this study (Figures 22-23).

i. Five dolls (9.6%) are outfitted in a felt papoose or cradle instead of a skirt and/or cape. These papoose pin dolls were introduced in the 1970s (FLMNH 2021c; Johnson 2008:17) but Seminoles historically did not use papooses (Johnson 2008:66).

ii. Twenty-six (50.0%) dolls have rolled cloth hairstyles, 25 (48.1%) have hairboards (two of which are embellished with beads), and one (1.9%) has nylon pigtails (with a beaded headband).

iii. Twenty-five dolls (48.1%) wear traditional beaded necklaces, 22 (42.3%) wear multicolored beaded necklaces, and five (9.6%) wear no necklace.

iv. Eleven (21.2%) wear drop-style bead earrings, five (9.6%) wear hoop-style bead earrings, and 36 (69.2%) have no earrings.

Figure 22. *Five Type 3 dolls. Photo by Eric Zamora. Collections of the Anthropology Division of the Florida Museum of Natural History, FLMNH cat. nos. 2007-7-4 through 2007-7-8.*

Figure 23. *Four Type 3 "papoose" dolls made by Connie Frank Gowan. Photo by Eric Zamora. Collections of the Anthropology Division of the Florida Museum of Natural History, FLMNH cat. nos. 2006-20-9 through 2006-20-12.*

v. Twenty-four (46.2%) of the dolls have rickrack.

4. **Female: Wood: Limbed: Traditional**

   a. No. of examples: 25

   b. Height range: 22.9 – 50.8 cm

   c. Median height: 28.6 cm

   d. Date range: 1900 – 1950

   e. Known artists: (1) Bobby Henry

   f. Discussion: This is primarily an older (pre-1930) type. Some of the first dolls of this type were created in the early 1900s for the Convention of Doll Land in New York City (Downs 1995:212; Johnson 2008:18). It is essentially the same as the

Figure 24. *A Type 4 doll (ca. 1940-1950). Photo by Aditi Jayarajan. Graphic by the author. Collections of the Anthropology Division of the Florida Museum of Natural History, FLMNH cat. no. 2012-50-35.*

Type 8 doll, save for two small wooden arms attached to the torso (typically by nails) underneath the cape of each doll (Figure 24). It is possible that some of the dolls identified (remotely) as having "limbs" in this category in fact only have cloth sleeve limbs (with no wood underneath). However, the artist's intent to depict limbs remains the same. Johnson (2008:18-19) distinguishes between later (1920s to 1940s) "primitive" and "detailed" female wooden commercially produced

dolls, noting that "carved arms might be absent" on the more "primitive" dolls.

   i. Facial features are generally painted on and 24 (96.0%) of the dolls have painted hair (one 1910 doll from AMNH has no hair).

   ii. Nineteen dolls (76.0%) wear some sort of beaded necklace.

   iii. Three of the dolls (12.0%) wear other accessories, including a beaded pendant, silver bangles, and turtle shell bangles.

   iv. At least 10 of the dolls (40.0%) wear calico cloth, which is generally consistent with a pre-1920 date (Downs 1995:88).

   v. The only known artist of this type is a male, which is generally in keeping with Seminole woodworking traditions. Four of the dolls (16.0%), however, wear cloth patchwork clothing, which was likely produced for dolls by women sometime after 1930 (FLMNH 2021d).

5. **Female: Palmetto: Head Only: Basket**

   a. No. of examples: 20

   b. Date range: 1930 – Present

   c. Known artists: (7) Elaine Aguilar (Downs 1995:209-210); Agnes Billie Cypress; Donna Frank (Downs 1995:204-209); Lucy Johns; Alice Osceola; Yolanda Ortero; Mary Jane Storm

   d. Discussion: This doll type includes female palmetto doll heads adorning the tops of lidded pine needle or (more typically) sweetgrass baskets, usually acting as decorative "handles" (Downs 1995:204). Deaconess Bedell first

Figure 25. *A Type 5 doll. Photo by Aditi Jayarajan. Graphic by the author. Collections of the Anthropology Division of the Florida Museum of Natural History, FLMNH cat. no. 2017-9-14.*

Figure 26. *A Type 5 doll with a sweetgrass cape and skirt. Photo and graphic by the author with permission of the Ah-Tah-Thi-Ki Museum, ATTK2002.166.61.*

introduced the concept to make baskets more "decorative and appealing" (Downs 1995:208-209). The dolls also represent the women of the Seminole Tribe because basketry is mostly women's work (Figure 25).

i.   All examples in this study wear some variety of beaded necklace and most (70.0%) wear earrings.

ii. Thirteen (65.0%) have hairboards, six (30.0%) have rolled hairstyles, and one (5.0%) has yarn pigtails. Two of the hairboards are embellished with beadwork. Two also wear sweetgrass hats on their heads, an apparent artistic innovation of Alice Osceola.

iii. It is possible that some of the dolls were made by artists other than the basket makers (Downs 1995:209). One basket (FLMNH 97-8-1), for example, has two different known artists.

iv. One unusual doll (ATTK 2002.166.61) is less a functional basket and more a cylindrical doll with a connected sweetgrass cape and skirt (but no underlying torso); see Figure 26. It might also be classified as Female: Palmetto: Head Only: Other.

6. **Male: Wood: Limbed: Big Shirt**

   a. No. of examples: 13

   b. Height range: 13 – 50.8 cm

   c. Median height: 27.9 cm

   d. Date range: 1900 – 1960

   e. Known artists: (3) Bobby Henry, Henry Osceola, Doctor Tiger

   f. Discussion: These generally early male dolls are carved primarily from a single piece of wood (aside from the arms, which are sometimes attached separately) with facial features carved and painted on (Johnson 2008:56-57). The hair or turban is also typically carved and painted on, but some wear cloth turbans (Johnson 2008:57); see Figure 27.

      i.   Eleven (84.6%) of the dolls wear turbans while two (15.4%) have painted bowl cuts (no turban). Nine of the turbans are painted and two are cloth.

      ii. Ten (76.9%) of the dolls wear necker-chiefs, two with beaded woggles around the knots.

      iii. Six (46.2%) of the dolls have circular wooden platforms or bases.

      iv. Six (46.2%) of the dolls wear cloth big shirts with patchwork while one (7.7%) wears a painted big shirt with patchwork.

      v.   One of the dolls (ATTK 2002.166.74) is holding a sofkee spoon.

      vi. All of the known artists are male.

7. **Male: Palmetto: Limbed: Rancher**

   a. No. of examples: 11

   b. Height range: 15.1 – 55.6 cm

Figure 27. *A Type 6 doll. Photo by Aditi Jayarajan. Graphic by the author. Collections of the Anthropology Division of the Florida Museum of Natural History, FLMNH cat. no. 88-6-9.*

c. Median height: 29.5 cm

d. Date range: 1937 – Present

e. Known artists: (1) Mabel Osceola

f. Discussion: These dolls are similar to Type 2 dolls, the primary difference being the style of outfit worn. Instead of a long one-piece big shirt, this doll wears a more contemporary jacket with pants (Figure 28). Previously thought to be a post-1950 innovation (Johnson 2008:63),

at least three examples in this study are likely pre-1950.

i. All but one of the dolls wear the classic bowl haircut, but a higher percentage of these (60.0%) have yarn hair rather than cloth hair (40.0%). One of the dolls (Figure 28) wears yarn pigtails (and a top hat), which is highly unusual for male dolls.

ii. Eight (72.7%) of the dolls have noses, seven (63.6%) have eyebrows, and six (54.5%) have teeth, all of which are

Figure 28. *A Type 7 doll made by Mabel Osceola. Photo by Aditi Jayarajan. Graphic by the author. Collections of the Anthropology Division of the Florida Museum of Natural History, FLMNH cat. no. 2000-8-1.*

higher percentages than observed in the big shirt dolls.

iii. Three of the dolls hold or wear uncommon accessories, including a lasso, a wooden pole or stick, and a silver woggle. Only one doll has a platform or base.

iv. Most of the dolls wear neckerchiefs (90.9%) and at least one row of patchwork (72.7%). Only one of these dolls wears rickrack.

8. **Female: Wood: Cylindrical: Traditional**

a. No. of examples: 10

b. Height range: 13 – 34.3 cm

c. Median height: 25.4 cm

d. Date range: 1900 – 1950

e. Known artists: none

f. Discussion: The female wooden doll was originally created as a toy for Seminole children in the early 1900s (Downs 1995:212). Some dolls of this type were also created for the Convention of Doll Land in New York City (Downs 1995:212; Johnson 2008:18). It consists primarily of a single cylindrical piece of wood with a round head. Most notably, this type lacks limbs of any kind, distinguishing it from the very similar (and more common) Type 4 doll (Figure 29).

i. Four of the dolls (40.0%) have a documented provenance prior to 1941.

ii. Nine dolls (90.0%) were likely carved by men and later outfitted by women in keeping with Seminole social norms. Four of the dolls (40.0%) wear patchwork, likely created for dolls by women sometime after 1930

(FLMNH 2021d). One doll at the FLMNH (92885), however, has painted-on patchwork clothing, which may have also been done by a male artist.

iii. Seven of the dolls (70.0%) have painted hair, two have no hair, and one has cloth hair.

iv. Seven (70.0%) wear a beaded necklace.

Figure 29. *A Type 8 doll. Photo by Aditi Jayarajan. Graphic by the author. Collections of the Anthropology Division of the Florida Museum of Natural History, FLMNH cat. no. 88-6-8.*

9. **Female: Cloth: Head Only: Rag**

a. No. of examples: 9

b. Height range: 7 – 47 cm

c. Median height: 32 cm

d. Date range: 1900 – 1930

e. Known artists: (1) "Four-year-old girl"

f. Discussion: These faceless, limbless dolls (Figure 30) are early examples of children's playthings (Johnson 2008:22). In two cases, the dolls seem to have also

Figure 30. *A Type 9 doll. Photo by Aditi Jayarajan. Graphic by the author. Collections of the Anthropology Division of the Florida Museum of Natural History, FLMNH cat. no. 2012-50-6.*

been made *by* children. The body type is classified as *head only* due to the lack of a defined cylindrical "body" (or stuffing of any kind) underneath the skirt, but there is sometimes a relatively small stuffed torso beginning just below the head and terminating just above the waist. Thus, this type might alternatively be classified as Female: Cloth: Cylindrical: Rag. The featureless heads are made from cloth, sometimes patterned but usually (66.7%) black. Johnson (2008:22) describes them as cape-less with long skirts, which is generally true, but one example (NMAI 227722.000) does wear a cape.

i. Five of the dolls (55.6%) exhibit empty arm sleeves. All the dolls are described as female, but it is conceivable that some of the one-piece outfits with arm sleeves are misinterpreted big shirts, which would make the dolls male.

ii. Eight of the nine dolls are from the NMAI's collection. The other doll, at the FLMNH, wears a multicolored beaded necklace that was apparently added later. Multicolored beaded necklaces are more typically seen on dolls after 1950 (FLMNH 2021e; Roberts 2001:150-51).

iii. Not included in this study is one well-known 44.1-cm doll at HistoryMiami (formerly the Historical Museum of Southern Florida).

iv. Two of the dolls at NMAI had no measurement data available.

10. Female: Cloth: Head Only: Lapel Pin

a. No. of examples: 9

b. Height range: 5 – 7.8 cm

c. Median height: 7.5 cm

d. Date range: 1950 – Present

d. Known artists: (2) Barbara Clay, Connie Frank Gowan

f. Discussion: This type is generally the same size as its female palmetto lapel pin counterpart (Type 3) but the cloth head is probably a more recent innovation (Figure 31). The earliest known (with certainty) of this type was created in 1970 by Barbara Clay, but it is possible that some are older. This type may be what Johnson (2008:51) terms "bee dolls."

   i. All of the dolls except for Clay's (88.9%) exhibit rickrack, and all but

two (77.8%) wear multicolored beaded necklaces, indicative of a post-1950 date.

   ii. Eight (88.9%) have rolled cloth hairstyles, the other wears a hairboard.

   iii. Six (66.7%) wear drop-style earrings.

   iv. The doll at NMAI had no measurement data available.

11. Female: Palmetto: Limbed: Traditional

a. No. of examples: 9

b. Height range: 21.5 – 77 cm

c. Median height: 33.0 cm

d. Date range: 1930 – Present

e. Known artists: (3) Ruby Jumper Billie, Alice Osceola, Mabel Osceola

f. Discussion: This doll is essentially the same as the Type 1 doll but with limbs. The limbs (arms) are generally made from palmetto and attached to the torso underneath the cape. Dolls of this type are frequently more complex, more decorated, or more outfitted with accessories than other types (Figures 32 and 33).

Figure 31. *A Type 10 doll made by Connie Frank Gowan. Photo by Aditi Jayarajan. Graphic by the author. Collections of the Anthropology Division of the Florida Museum of Natural History, FLMNH cat. no. 2006-20-15.*

Figure 32. *A Type 11 doll made by Ruby Jumper Billie. Photo and graphic by the author with permission of the Ah-Tah-Thi-Ki Museum, ATTK1997.36.2.*

Figure 33. *A Type 11 doll made by Mabel Osceola. Photo and graphic by the author with permission of the Ah-Tah-Thi-Ki Museum, ATTK1999.53.2.*

i. Seven of the dolls have eyebrows (77.8%) and six (66.7%) have noses.

ii. Two (22.2%) have embellished hairboards.

iii. A majority of the dolls (66.7%) are holding or associated with uncommon accessories such as babies, a basket, a mortar and pestle kit, a lone pestle, and a sofkee spoon, which offer possible motivations for creating limbs.

iv. Five of the dolls (55.6%) wear patchwork clothing.

v. One of the dolls (FLMNH 2013-31-1) is notable in that it is a so-called "square-headed doll." It is very similar in appearance to those reported by Johnson (2008:66-67, 72-73), which resemble commercially made cloth rag dolls but instead are made entirely of palmetto. The nose is black thread sewn in an inverted V-shape. Johnson (2008:73) argues that despite their resemblance to anglicized dolls, some of the known square-headed dolls were certainly made by Seminole artisans, or possibly even by the same one. Although not included in this study, the Logan Museum of Anthropology has two of these dolls (08802; 31211) in its collections (Beloit College Digital Collections 2022). These dolls generally wear larger beads and may have been made between 1925 and 1945 (Johnson 2008:73). An alternative classification for this doll type might be Female: Palmetto: Limbed: Rag.

12. Female: Palmetto: Head Only: Other

a. No. of examples: 7

b. Date range: 1940 – Present

c. Known artists: (4) Minnie Doctor, Maggie Osceola, Mrs. George Osceola (possible duplicate), Mrs. Tommie Tiger

d. This type is a varied assortment of "head only" dolls that are composite pieces of unique objects and are not known to have been duplicated (Figure 34). The seven examples in this study are part of two hair ties, two silver bells, a patchwork hat, a sash, and a display mannequin.

i. The hair ties were both made in 1965 by Minnie Doctor. They feature two 6-cm dolls each on either end of a long piece of cloth that could be

Figure 34. *A Type 12 hair tie made by Minnie Doctor. National Museum of the American Indian, Smithsonian Institution (255345.000). Photo by NMAI Photo Services.*

tied in a knot and used as a hair accessory. The hair tie connects to the tops of the dolls' heads.

ii. The two bell dolls range in height from 12.7 to 16.5 cm. One wears a row of zigzag patchwork dating it to between 1940 and 1960. In her notes about an unrelated object at the AMNH (50.2/6413), anthropologist (and donor) Ethel Cutler Freeman remarks, "I have a picture of Mrs. George Osceola in the deep cypress dressing a bell as a doll and showing me how it rang." It is possible that the dolls in this study were also made by Osceola, but that is uncertain. The dolls look like typical cylindrical palmetto dolls when standing upright but have bells for bodies under their skirts.

iii. The hat (24 cm in height) was made by Mrs. Tommie Tiger sometime between 1959 and 1968. The doll's head adorns the top of the hat, which is otherwise decorated like an oversized skirt (with rickrack and patchwork) and designed to be pulled down over the wearer's head.

iv. The sash was created in 1965 by Maggie Osceola and features one row of patchwork along the length of the sash. It is very similar in form to the hair ties created by Minnie Doctor, with 5-cm dolls connected by the head on both ends of the sash.

v. The display mannequin head is large (67.3 cm) and was created specifically as an ATTK museum exhibit piece.

13. Female: Palmetto: Head Only: Pincushion

a. No. of examples: 5

b. Height range: 7 – 17.8 cm

c. Date range: 1940 – Present

d. Known artists: none

e. Discussion: This type is generally similar in form to the coiled pine needle and sweetgrass baskets that have female dolls and doll heads as "handles" (Type 5). However, in this case, the hollowed interior of the basket is filled with palmetto stuffing and capped with a smooth palmetto fiber surface in which to stick pins (Figure 35). The circular (often semi-spherical) surface piece is sometimes outlined by a string of beads. In one case (FLMNH E994), the surface piece is velvet cloth instead of palmetto. The doll's head typically projects from the center of this circle.

Figure 35. *A Type 13 doll. Photo by Aditi Jayarajan. Graphic by the author. Collections of the Anthropology Division of the Florida Museum of Natural History, FLMNH cat. no. 2012-50-1.*

i. These five examples all wear beaded necklaces and don 1940s-style hairboards.

ii. Four (80.0%) wear some style of earring, indicating a post-1930 date (Johnson 2008:33).

14. Female: Cloth: Cylindrical: Traditional

a. No. of examples: 4

b. Height range: 15.1 – 52.7 cm

c. Date range: 2010 – Present

d. Known artists: (2) Minnie Doctor, Shula Jones

e. Discussion: These dolls resemble the classic and prevalent female palmetto doll (Type 1) in both aesthetic and form. However, in a modern twist, the doll's head and body are created from a palmetto-colored felt cloth rather than actual palmetto (Figures 36 and 37). This innovation is likely due to increasing difficulty of obtaining palmetto (Bidney 2013; FLMNH 2021c; Tara Backhouse, personal communication, 2020).

15. Female: Palmetto: Cylindrical: All Palmetto

a. No. of examples: 3

B. Height range: 15.2 – 21 cm

c. Date range: 1960 – 1970

d. Known artists: none

e. Discussion: There are three examples of this doll type, one at the ATTK (2007.28.7), one at the NMNH (E409750-0), and one at the FLMNH (2018-10-1). The ATTK and NMNH dolls feature rickrack and multicolored beaded necklaces along with hair materials (yarn and nylon) and styles (ponytail and wild) that indicate a likely origin date in the 1960s. The NMNH

Figure 36. *A Type 14 doll made by Shula Jones. Photo by Aditi Jayarajan. Graphic by the author. Collections of the Anthropology Division of the Florida Museum of Natural History, FLMNH cat. no. 2013-11-6.*

Figure 37. *A pair of Type 14 dolls made by Minnie Doctor. Photo and graphic by the author with permission of the Ah-Tah-Thi-Ki Museum, ATTK2012.9.2 and ATTK2012.9.3.*

doll was acquired at the Brighton reservation sometime after 1959 and prior to March 22, 1968. The NMNH and ATTK dolls may have the same maker. The highly unusual FLMNH doll features eyebrows and wears beaded hoop earrings and a *palmetto* cape and skirt decorated with beads. It also wears an embellished hairboard (Figure 38).

i. Note: These dolls are decidedly Miccosukee/Seminole in appearance compared to two other similar doll types (Female: Palmetto: Limbed: All Palmetto and Male: Palmetto: Limbed: All Palmetto) that were not included in this study due to lack of provenance. The two excluded doll types are more likely folk art created by non-Native individuals (Johnson 2008:74). However, should definitively Miccosukee/Seminole-made examples of these types be determined in the future, they should be added to this typology.

16. Female: Palmetto: Cylindrical: Basket

a. No. of examples: 3

b. Date range: 1940 – Present

c. Known artists: (2) Alice Osceola; Mary Jane Storm

d. Discussion: Identical in function to "head only" basket dolls (Type 5), these dolls come complete with a full cylindrical body attached to the top of a sweetgrass basket (Figure 39). All three examples in this study wear rickrack and some variety of beaded necklace. Two wear rows of patchwork. One, by an unknown artist, is accompanied by two "child" dolls and has yarn pigtails. A doll and basket by Mary Jane Storm appear to be the very same pictured in *Second Jumper: Searching for his Bloodline* (Second-Jumper 2011:192), circa 2005.

17. Male: Palmetto: Horseback: Big Shirt

a. No. of examples: 3

b. Height range: 26.7 – 36.0 cm

c. Date range: 1940 – 1960

d. Known artists: (2) Ida Cypress; Maggie Osceola

e. Discussion: The male on horseback doll is one of the rarest and most complex

Figure 38. *A Type 15 doll. Photo by Aditi Jayarajan. Graphic by the author. Collections of the Anthropology Division of the Florida Museum of Natural History, FLMNH cat. no. 2018-10-1.*

Figure 39. *A Type 16 doll made by Alice Osceola. Photo and graphic by the author with permission of the Ah-Tah-Thi-Ki Museum, ATTK2007.9.128.*

Figure 40. *A Type 17 doll made by Ida Cypress. American Museum of Natural History/Division of Anthropology (50.2/6409).*

dolls in existence (Figure 40). Both the rider and the genderless horse's bodies are made from palmetto, usually with thread or cloth "reins" extending from the horse's muzzle to the rider's hands. The horse's legs are made from wood and covered in palmetto (Johnson 2008:69). Deaconess Bedell oversaw the creation of this type (Lenz 1986:82). According to Reeves and Reeves (2009:92; 2018:43), between five and "twelve or so" examples are known to exist, all made by the same artist. However, this study identifies at least two different artists and five different horse-back dolls (of three types, including one *female* on horseback). Anecdotally, I have observed at least six additional dolls in private collections, so without question there are no fewer than 10 male on horse-back dolls in existence. According to Ethel Cutler Freeman, "cattle from the west were introduced on the reservations in 1940 and horses for the cowboys. Junior Cypress

[Ida Cypress's husband] was a cowboy." The cattle-raising industry took off at the Brighton Reservation and probably was the doll's geographical source of inspiration (Downs 1995:218-219).

   i.   Of these three dolls, two are wearing neckerchiefs atop their big shirts.

   ii. Two have cloth "bowl cut" hair, while the other, created by Maggie Osceola, wears a cloth turban.

18. Female: Cloth: Head Only: Other

  a. No. of examples: 1

  b. Height: 6 cm

  c. Date: 2006

  d. Known artists: (1) Connie Frank Gowan

  e. Discussion: This doll is essentially the same type as the female cloth lapel pin (Type 10) but is part of a larger composite object, in this case a beaded necklace (Figure 41). The multicolored necklace emanates from the top of the doll's head.

19. Female: Palmetto: Cylindrical: Pincushion

  a. No. of examples: 1

  b. Date: 1949

  c. Known artists: none

  d. Discussion: This unique type is similar in function to the "head only" pincushion, but the lower body of the doll itself serves at the pincushion. Instead of the typical coiled pine needle or sweetgrass "basket" structure, the cylindrical palmetto "torso" of the doll is simply exaggerated in size to fill the traditional patchwork skirt's interior completely (Figure 42). This particular doll was collected from the Big

Figure 41. *A Type 18 doll made by Connie Frank Gowan. Photo by Eric Zamora. Collections of the Anthropology Division of the Florida Museum of Natural History, FLMNH cat. no. 2006-20-8.*

Figure 42. *A Type 19 doll. American Museum of Natural History/Division of Anthropology (50.2/6413).*

Cypress reservation in 1949, where Ethel Cutler Freeman noted "more innovation in their handicraft."

20. Female: Palmetto: Horseback: Traditional

a. No. of examples: 1

b. Height: 30.5 cm

c. Date: 1950 – 1960

d. Known artists: (1) Maggie Osceola

e. Discussion: This doll is nearly identical to the male on horseback dolls but with a traditional female palmetto doll seated on the horse. The rickrack, multicolored necklace, and patchwork design indicate an origin date in the 1950s or later (Figure 43).

21. Female: Palmetto: Limbed: Other

a. No. of examples: 1

Figure 43. *A Type 20 doll made by Maggie Osceola. Photo and graphic by the author with permission of the Ah-Tah-Thi-Ki Museum, ATTK1999.54.2.*

b. Height: 69 cm

c. Date: 1999

d. Known artists: (1) Carol Cypress

e. Discussion: This highly unusual form (ATTK 2014.7.2) is referred to at the ATTK Museum as a "palmetto frond root doll." It is an abstract representation of a human figure, completely featureless and clothing-less (Figure 44). It is created entirely from the leaves of a saw palmetto frond rather than the more typical palmetto husk. It may represent a revival of an extremely early doll-making practice. It has two "limbs" and is part of a female/male pair (see Type 22).

22. Male: Palmetto: Limbed: Other

a. No. of examples: 1

b. Height: 73 cm

c. Date: 1999

d. Known artists: (1) Carol Cypress

e. Discussion: Nearly identical to the Type 21 doll and part of a pair, this doll (ATTK 2014.7.1) is identified as male because it has four "limbs" (two arms and two legs) instead of the two (arms only) apparent on the female doll (Figure 45). This pattern is in keeping with most other limbed dolls.

23. Male: Palmetto: Horseback: Rancher

a. No. of examples: 1

b. Height: 45.7 cm

c. Date range: 1950 – 1960

d. Known artists: (1) Maggie Osceola

e. Discussion: Nearly identical to the male on horseback wearing a big shirt (Type 16), this lone example instead wears a rancher style shirt with blue pants, leather shoes, and a patchwork turban (Figure

Figure 44. *A Type 21 doll made by Carol Cypress. Courtesy of the Ah-Tah-Thi-Ki Museum, ATTK2014.7.2.*

Figure 45. *A Type 22 doll made by Carol Cypress. Courtesy of the Ah-Tah-Thi-Ki Museum, ATTK2014.7.1.*

46). The large facial features, rickrack, and patchwork design indicate an origin date in the 1950s or later. The turban may have been an artistic preference of Maggie Osceola, as it seen on all five of the male dolls in this study that she is credited with creating. This doll originated from the Hollywood reservation.

Figure 46. *A Type 23 doll made by Maggie Osceola. Photo and graphic by the author with permission of the Ah-Tah-Thi-Ki Museum, ATTK1996.46.1.*

24. Male: Wood: Limbed: Rancher

a. No. of examples: 1

b. Height: 16.5 cm

c. Date range: 1930 – 1950

d. Known artists: none

e. Discussion: This unique and relatively small doll (FLMNH 2012-50-39) is carved entirely from one piece of wood (Figure 47). It has no cloth elements and wears a painted patchwork jacket, neckerchief,

Figure 47. *A Type 24 doll. Photo by Aditi Jayarajan. Graphic by the author. Collections of the Anthropology Division of the Florida Museum of Natural History, FLMNH cat. no. 2012-50-39.*

pants, and shoes. It has an unusual posture, hands on its hips, with its feet standing on a rectangular wooden base. The hair, which has a part carved into it, is painted. Like the more common wooden limbed big shirt dolls, its facial features are also carved and painted. According to Johnson (2008:61), not all of these "hard to find" dolls were necessarily carved by Seminole or Miccosukee artisans. If it was carved by a Seminole or Miccosukee artisan, as I believe it likely was, the artisan was probably a male (Downs 1995:229).

25. Male: Cloth: Limbed: Big Shirt

a. No. of examples: 0

b. Discussion: This type was not observed in this study but is known to exist. I observed one for sale as part of a male/female pair at the Big Cypress Landing Convenience Store on February 14, 2022.

26. Male: Cloth: Limbed: Rancher

a. Discussion: This type was not observed in this study but is known to exist. I observed one, nicknamed "Willie the Journeyman," as part of a social media campaign by the Ah-Tah-Thi-Ki Museum beginning in 2021 (ATTK 2021).

Other Museums with Dolls

There are undoubtedly hundreds more Seminole dolls in museums around the world. A 2011 statewide museum collections survey of Florida that I conducted found dolls in the collections of the Dunedin Historical Society and Museum, Historical Society of Martin County, Lightner Museum, Museum of Seminole County History, and Polk County History Museum, as well as at least one anonymous museum (Bell 2011:24, Table1). As of 2016, the Marco Island Historical Society possessed two Type 1 Seminole dolls, one of which (2016-8-22) exhibits silverwork, eyebrows, a nose, and three rows of patchwork. A Type 2 male palmetto doll at the Field Museum in Chicago (343335) possesses two rows of patchwork, a turban, rickrack, and a unique palmetto-fiber rectangular base. Based on the typology

Figure 48. *An unidentified girl with two Type 1 dolls at the "Anderson Fruit Farm" in Fort Myers, Florida (December 26, 1933). Courtesy of the Ah-Tah-Thi-Ki Museum, ATTK2022.13.1.*

Figure 49. *The author with a Type 14 doll purchased at the Miccosukee Indian Village on the Tamiami Trail (August 20, 2017). Photo by Erin Wolfe Bell.*

and noteworthy characteristics outlined here, both dolls are relatively rare, the former likely dating to the 1930s and the latter to the 1950s or later.

Conclusion

Seminole and Miccosukee dolls are an undeniably charismatic and popular art form that has evolved over more than a century in South Florida (Figure 48). From child's plaything to commercial enterprise to "cultural attaché," the doll has also become a means of creating and sustaining traditions. For example, dolls are now often made explicitly for important tribal events such as the annual dollmaking contest at the Seminole Tribal Fair (Seminole Tribal Fair and Pow Wow 2021a). Dollmaking, a skill traditionally imparted orally and through demonstration between family members, is still being taught to younger generations. The Ah-Tah-Thi-Ki Museum, through its collections and programming, plays a vital role in facilitating this perpetuation of knowledge.

The doll, in its role as a symbol of Florida's Native American history and heritage, is an ambassador of sorts to the many non-Natives (including this author) interested in Seminole and Miccosukee culture (Figure 49). In 2004, a Type 2 doll was even pictured on a United States postage stamp (National Postal Museum 2022). In its more literal form, the doll continues to wear the "signs of the times," such as in a female Type 1 doll made for the (virtual) 2021 Seminole Tribal Fair and Pow Wow by artist Lorraine Posada, accessorized with a facemask during a global pandemic (Seminole Tribal Fair and Pow Wow 2021b). The doll continues to be incorporated into museum exhibitions (Lenz 2004:13-20, 135-38) and its general likeness adapted into new and innovative forms by contemporary tribal artists.

Acknowledgments. I acknowledge, with apologies, the likely many dozens of Seminole and Miccosukee dollmakers not mentioned by name in this article. That their names are not mentioned in this article is neither a statement on their worth nor their work, but simply a reflection of the way objects have traditionally been collected by museums (and of my own limited knowledge). I also wish to acknowledge the following individuals, without whom this article would not have been possible: Tara Backhouse, Matt Heenan, Robin Croskery Howard, Elise LeCompte, Michelle LeFebvre, William Marquardt, Heather Otis, Laura Dello Russo, and Nathan Sowry.

Appendix A. Seminole Artists Represented.

Name	No. of Dolls
Connie Frank Gowan	13
Minnie Doctor	11
Maggie Osceola	10
Shula Jones	6
Lucy J. Billie	4 to 6
Lucy Billie	2 to 6
Alice Osceola	5
Ida Cypress	4
Loretta Micco	3
Mabel Osceola	3
Sally Johns	3
"4 year old girl"	2
Bobby Henry	2
Carol Cypress	2
Effie Osceola	2
Mary Jane Storm	2
[Mary] Tiger	1
[Uknown] Tiger	1
Agnes Billie Cypress	1
Alice Huff	1
Annie C. Billie	1
Annie Cypress Tiger	1
Barbara Clay	1
Doctor Tiger	1
Dorothy Tucker	1
Elsie Roberts Jimmie	1
Ethel [Unknown]	1
Henry Osceola	1
Lena Billie	1
Lena Osceola Frank	1

Lizzie Buck	1
Lucy Johns	1
Mary B. Cypress	1
Mary Osceola	1
Mary R. Billie	1
Mary Tiger	1
Mina Osceola Micco	1
Mrs. Istimathli Ingraham	1
Mrs. John Osceola	1
Mrs. Tommie Tiger	1
Ruby Jumper Billie	1
Yolanda Ortero	1

Appendix B. Museums with Seminole Dolls Included in this Study.

Name	No. of Dolls
Florida Museum of Natural History[1]	275
Ah-Tah-Thi-Ki Museum	260
National Museum of the American Indian	92
National Museum of Natural History	35
American Museum of Natural History	21

1. All FLMNH dolls in this study are in the Florida Ethnographic Collection (FEC) within the Museum's Anthropology division.

Appendix C. Seminole Dolls Classified.

Catalog Number	Museum	Gender	Body Material	Body Type	Style
2012.9.2	ATTK	F	Cloth	Cylindrical	Traditional
2012.9.3	ATTK	F	Cloth	Cylindrical	Traditional
2018.32.1	ATTK	F	Cloth	Cylindrical	Traditional
2013-11-006	FLMNH	F	Cloth	Cylindrical	Traditional
2014.30.13	ATTK	F	Cloth	Head Only	Lapel Pin
2014.30.20	ATTK	F	Cloth	Head Only	Lapel Pin
2006-20-013	FLMNH	F	Cloth	Head Only	Lapel Pin
2006-20-014	FLMNH	F	Cloth	Head Only	Lapel Pin
2006-20-015	FLMNH	F	Cloth	Head Only	Lapel Pin
2006-20-016	FLMNH	F	Cloth	Head Only	Lapel Pin
2006-20-017	FLMNH	F	Cloth	Head Only	Lapel Pin
2006-20-018	FLMNH	F	Cloth	Head Only	Lapel Pin
248841	NMAI	F	Cloth	Head Only	Lapel Pin
2006-20-008	FLMNH	F	Cloth	Head Only	Other (Necklace)
2012-50-006	FLMNH	F	Cloth	Head Only	Rag
152872	NMAI	F	Cloth	Head Only	Rag
152873	NMAI	F	Cloth	Head Only	Rag
152874	NMAI	F	Cloth	Head Only	Rag
152875	NMAI	F	Cloth	Head Only	Rag
227722	NMAI	F	Cloth	Head Only	Rag
227723	NMAI	F	Cloth	Head Only	Rag
204359A	NMAI	F	Cloth	Head Only	Rag
204359B	NMAI	F	Cloth	Head Only	Rag
2007.28.7	ATTK	F	Palmetto	Cylindrical	All Palmetto
2018-10-001	FLMNH	F	Palmetto	Cylindrical	All Palmetto
E409750-0	NMNH	F	Palmetto	Cylindrical	All Palmetto
2007.9.128	ATTK	F	Palmetto	Cylindrical	Basket
2007.9.129	ATTK	F	Palmetto	Cylindrical	Basket
2017.33.2	ATTK	F	Palmetto	Cylindrical	Basket
50.2/ 6413	AMNH	F	Palmetto	Cylindrical	Pin Cushion
50.2/ 6404	AMNH	F	Palmetto	Cylindrical	Traditional
50.2/ 6405	AMNH	F	Palmetto	Cylindrical	Traditional
50.2/ 6406	AMNH	F	Palmetto	Cylindrical	Traditional
50.2/ 6407	AMNH	F	Palmetto	Cylindrical	Traditional
50.2/ 6408	AMNH	F	Palmetto	Cylindrical	Traditional
50.2/ 6417A	AMNH	F	Palmetto	Cylindrical	Traditional
50.2/ 6417B	AMNH	F	Palmetto	Cylindrical	Traditional
1995.36.1	ATTK	F	Palmetto	Cylindrical	Traditional
1996.45.1	ATTK	F	Palmetto	Cylindrical	Traditional
1996.45.2	ATTK	F	Palmetto	Cylindrical	Traditional
1996.46.2	ATTK	F	Palmetto	Cylindrical	Traditional
1996.46.4	ATTK	F	Palmetto	Cylindrical	Traditional
1998.49.1	ATTK	F	Palmetto	Cylindrical	Traditional
1998.50.1	ATTK	F	Palmetto	Cylindrical	Traditional
1999.55.1	ATTK	F	Palmetto	Cylindrical	Traditional
1999.55.2	ATTK	F	Palmetto	Cylindrical	Traditional
1999.57.2	ATTK	F	Palmetto	Cylindrical	Traditional
1999.61.1	ATTK	F	Palmetto	Cylindrical	Traditional
2000.60.1	ATTK	F	Palmetto	Cylindrical	Traditional
2000.63.1	ATTK	F	Palmetto	Cylindrical	Traditional
2000.63.2	ATTK	F	Palmetto	Cylindrical	Traditional
2001.118.1	ATTK	F	Palmetto	Cylindrical	Traditional
2001.119.1	ATTK	F	Palmetto	Cylindrical	Traditional
2001.120.1	ATTK	F	Palmetto	Cylindrical	Traditional
2001.122.1	ATTK	F	Palmetto	Cylindrical	Traditional
2001.124.1	ATTK	F	Palmetto	Cylindrical	Traditional
2001.124.2	ATTK	F	Palmetto	Cylindrical	Traditional
2001.126.1	ATTK	F	Palmetto	Cylindrical	Traditional
2001.127.1	ATTK	F	Palmetto	Cylindrical	Traditional
2001.128.1	ATTK	F	Palmetto	Cylindrical	Traditional
2001.129.1	ATTK	F	Palmetto	Cylindrical	Traditional
2001.130.1	ATTK	F	Palmetto	Cylindrical	Traditional
2002.146.1	ATTK	F	Palmetto	Cylindrical	Traditional
2002.148.1	ATTK	F	Palmetto	Cylindrical	Traditional

Appendix C. Seminole Dolls Classified. (continued)

2002.149.1	ATTK	F	Palmetto	Cylindrical	Traditional
2002.149.10	ATTK	F	Palmetto	Cylindrical	Traditional
2002.149.6	ATTK	F	Palmetto	Cylindrical	Traditional
2002.149.8	ATTK	F	Palmetto	Cylindrical	Traditional
2002.166.30	ATTK	F	Palmetto	Cylindrical	Traditional
2002.166.52	ATTK	F	Palmetto	Cylindrical	Traditional
2002.166.91	ATTK	F	Palmetto	Cylindrical	Traditional
2002.42.102	ATTK	F	Palmetto	Cylindrical	Traditional
2002.42.103	ATTK	F	Palmetto	Cylindrical	Traditional
2003.295.1	ATTK	F	Palmetto	Cylindrical	Traditional
2003.298.2	ATTK	F	Palmetto	Cylindrical	Traditional
2004.100.1	ATTK	F	Palmetto	Cylindrical	Traditional
2004.102.1	ATTK	F	Palmetto	Cylindrical	Traditional
2004.104.1	ATTK	F	Palmetto	Cylindrical	Traditional
2004.106.1	ATTK	F	Palmetto	Cylindrical	Traditional
2004.106.2	ATTK	F	Palmetto	Cylindrical	Traditional
2004.107.1	ATTK	F	Palmetto	Cylindrical	Traditional
2004.111.1	ATTK	F	Palmetto	Cylindrical	Traditional
2004.176.1	ATTK	F	Palmetto	Cylindrical	Traditional
2004.177.1	ATTK	F	Palmetto	Cylindrical	Traditional
2004.178.1	ATTK	F	Palmetto	Cylindrical	Traditional
2004.183.10	ATTK	F	Palmetto	Cylindrical	Traditional
2004.96.1	ATTK	F	Palmetto	Cylindrical	Traditional
2004.97.1	ATTK	F	Palmetto	Cylindrical	Traditional
2004.99.1	ATTK	F	Palmetto	Cylindrical	Traditional
2005.76.1	ATTK	F	Palmetto	Cylindrical	Traditional
2005.85.1	ATTK	F	Palmetto	Cylindrical	Traditional
2005.90.1	ATTK	F	Palmetto	Cylindrical	Traditional
2006.73.2	ATTK	F	Palmetto	Cylindrical	Traditional
2006.80.1	ATTK	F	Palmetto	Cylindrical	Traditional
2006.80.2	ATTK	F	Palmetto	Cylindrical	Traditional
2007.108.2	ATTK	F	Palmetto	Cylindrical	Traditional
2007.108.3	ATTK	F	Palmetto	Cylindrical	Traditional
2007.109.1	ATTK	F	Palmetto	Cylindrical	Traditional
2007.28.8	ATTK	F	Palmetto	Cylindrical	Traditional
2007.28.9	ATTK	F	Palmetto	Cylindrical	Traditional
2007.54.1	ATTK	F	Palmetto	Cylindrical	Traditional
2007.9.14	ATTK	F	Palmetto	Cylindrical	Traditional
2007.9.18	ATTK	F	Palmetto	Cylindrical	Traditional
2007.9.21	ATTK	F	Palmetto	Cylindrical	Traditional
2007.9.24	ATTK	F	Palmetto	Cylindrical	Traditional
2007.9.25	ATTK	F	Palmetto	Cylindrical	Traditional
2007.9.26	ATTK	F	Palmetto	Cylindrical	Traditional
2007.9.27	ATTK	F	Palmetto	Cylindrical	Traditional
2007.9.28	ATTK	F	Palmetto	Cylindrical	Traditional
2007.9.29	ATTK	F	Palmetto	Cylindrical	Traditional
2008.41.3	ATTK	F	Palmetto	Cylindrical	Traditional
2008.41.4	ATTK	F	Palmetto	Cylindrical	Traditional
2008.42.1	ATTK	F	Palmetto	Cylindrical	Traditional
2008.47.1	ATTK	F	Palmetto	Cylindrical	Traditional
2012.9.1	ATTK	F	Palmetto	Cylindrical	Traditional
2013.4.1	ATTK	F	Palmetto	Cylindrical	Traditional
2014.27.1	ATTK	F	Palmetto	Cylindrical	Traditional
2014.27.10	ATTK	F	Palmetto	Cylindrical	Traditional
2014.27.11	ATTK	F	Palmetto	Cylindrical	Traditional
2014.27.12	ATTK	F	Palmetto	Cylindrical	Traditional
2014.27.13	ATTK	F	Palmetto	Cylindrical	Traditional
2014.27.15	ATTK	F	Palmetto	Cylindrical	Traditional
2014.27.16	ATTK	F	Palmetto	Cylindrical	Traditional
2014.27.17	ATTK	F	Palmetto	Cylindrical	Traditional
2014.27.2	ATTK	F	Palmetto	Cylindrical	Traditional
2014.27.3	ATTK	F	Palmetto	Cylindrical	Traditional
2014.27.4	ATTK	F	Palmetto	Cylindrical	Traditional
2014.27.5	ATTK	F	Palmetto	Cylindrical	Traditional
2014.27.6	ATTK	F	Palmetto	Cylindrical	Traditional
2014.27.7	ATTK	F	Palmetto	Cylindrical	Traditional
2014.27.8	ATTK	F	Palmetto	Cylindrical	Traditional
2014.27.9	ATTK	F	Palmetto	Cylindrical	Traditional
2014.30.10	ATTK	F	Palmetto	Cylindrical	Traditional

2014.30.14	ATTK	F	Palmetto	Cylindrical	Traditional
2014.30.18	ATTK	F	Palmetto	Cylindrical	Traditional
2014.30.19	ATTK	F	Palmetto	Cylindrical	Traditional
2014.30.2	ATTK	F	Palmetto	Cylindrical	Traditional
2014.30.23	ATTK	F	Palmetto	Cylindrical	Traditional
2014.30.24	ATTK	F	Palmetto	Cylindrical	Traditional
2014.30.25	ATTK	F	Palmetto	Cylindrical	Traditional
2014.30.26	ATTK	F	Palmetto	Cylindrical	Traditional
2014.30.27	ATTK	F	Palmetto	Cylindrical	Traditional
2014.30.28	ATTK	F	Palmetto	Cylindrical	Traditional
2014.30.29	ATTK	F	Palmetto	Cylindrical	Traditional
2014.30.3	ATTK	F	Palmetto	Cylindrical	Traditional
2014.30.30	ATTK	F	Palmetto	Cylindrical	Traditional
2014.30.31	ATTK	F	Palmetto	Cylindrical	Traditional
2014.30.32	ATTK	F	Palmetto	Cylindrical	Traditional
2014.30.33	ATTK	F	Palmetto	Cylindrical	Traditional
2014.30.34	ATTK	F	Palmetto	Cylindrical	Traditional
2014.30.35	ATTK	F	Palmetto	Cylindrical	Traditional
2014.30.36	ATTK	F	Palmetto	Cylindrical	Traditional
2014.30.37	ATTK	F	Palmetto	Cylindrical	Traditional
2014.30.38	ATTK	F	Palmetto	Cylindrical	Traditional
2014.30.39	ATTK	F	Palmetto	Cylindrical	Traditional
2014.30.4	ATTK	F	Palmetto	Cylindrical	Traditional
2014.30.41	ATTK	F	Palmetto	Cylindrical	Traditional
2014.30.42	ATTK	F	Palmetto	Cylindrical	Traditional
2014.30.43	ATTK	F	Palmetto	Cylindrical	Traditional
2014.30.44	ATTK	F	Palmetto	Cylindrical	Traditional
2014.30.45	ATTK	F	Palmetto	Cylindrical	Traditional
2014.30.46	ATTK	F	Palmetto	Cylindrical	Traditional
2014.30.47	ATTK	F	Palmetto	Cylindrical	Traditional
2014.30.48	ATTK	F	Palmetto	Cylindrical	Traditional
2014.30.49	ATTK	F	Palmetto	Cylindrical	Traditional
2014.30.5	ATTK	F	Palmetto	Cylindrical	Traditional
2014.30.50	ATTK	F	Palmetto	Cylindrical	Traditional
2014.30.51	ATTK	F	Palmetto	Cylindrical	Traditional
2014.30.52	ATTK	F	Palmetto	Cylindrical	Traditional
2014.30.53	ATTK	F	Palmetto	Cylindrical	Traditional
2014.30.54	ATTK	F	Palmetto	Cylindrical	Traditional
2014.30.55	ATTK	F	Palmetto	Cylindrical	Traditional
2014.30.56	ATTK	F	Palmetto	Cylindrical	Traditional
2014.30.57	ATTK	F	Palmetto	Cylindrical	Traditional
2014.30.58	ATTK	F	Palmetto	Cylindrical	Traditional
2014.30.59	ATTK	F	Palmetto	Cylindrical	Traditional
2014.30.6	ATTK	F	Palmetto	Cylindrical	Traditional
2014.30.60	ATTK	F	Palmetto	Cylindrical	Traditional
2014.30.61	ATTK	F	Palmetto	Cylindrical	Traditional
2014.30.63	ATTK	F	Palmetto	Cylindrical	Traditional
2014.30.64	ATTK	F	Palmetto	Cylindrical	Traditional
2014.30.69	ATTK	F	Palmetto	Cylindrical	Traditional
2014.30.7	ATTK	F	Palmetto	Cylindrical	Traditional
2014.30.8	ATTK	F	Palmetto	Cylindrical	Traditional
2014.30.9	ATTK	F	Palmetto	Cylindrical	Traditional
2017.23.1	ATTK	F	Palmetto	Cylindrical	Traditional
2017.23.3	ATTK	F	Palmetto	Cylindrical	Traditional
2017.41.3	ATTK	F	Palmetto	Cylindrical	Traditional
2000-09-003	FLMNH	F	Palmetto	Cylindrical	Traditional
2004-204-003	FLMNH	F	Palmetto	Cylindrical	Traditional
2004-204-004	FLMNH	F	Palmetto	Cylindrical	Traditional
2004-204-005	FLMNH	F	Palmetto	Cylindrical	Traditional
2004-204-006	FLMNH	F	Palmetto	Cylindrical	Traditional
2006-19-001	FLMNH	F	Palmetto	Cylindrical	Traditional
2006-20-019	FLMNH	F	Palmetto	Cylindrical	Traditional
2006-20-020	FLMNH	F	Palmetto	Cylindrical	Traditional
2007-07-009	FLMNH	F	Palmetto	Cylindrical	Traditional
2007-07-010	FLMNH	F	Palmetto	Cylindrical	Traditional
2007-07-011	FLMNH	F	Palmetto	Cylindrical	Traditional
2007-07-012	FLMNH	F	Palmetto	Cylindrical	Traditional
2007-07-013	FLMNH	F	Palmetto	Cylindrical	Traditional
2009-07-001	FLMNH	F	Palmetto	Cylindrical	Traditional
2009-07-002	FLMNH	F	Palmetto	Cylindrical	Traditional

Appendix C. Seminole Dolls Classified. (continued)

2009-13-001	FLMNH	F	Palmetto	Cylindrical	Traditional
2009-13-002	FLMNH	F	Palmetto	Cylindrical	Traditional
2009-13-003	FLMNH	F	Palmetto	Cylindrical	Traditional
2009-13-004	FLMNH	F	Palmetto	Cylindrical	Traditional
2009-13-005	FLMNH	F	Palmetto	Cylindrical	Traditional
2009-13-006	FLMNH	F	Palmetto	Cylindrical	Traditional
2009-13-007	FLMNH	F	Palmetto	Cylindrical	Traditional
2009-13-008	FLMNH	F	Palmetto	Cylindrical	Traditional
2009-13-009	FLMNH	F	Palmetto	Cylindrical	Traditional
2009-13-010	FLMNH	F	Palmetto	Cylindrical	Traditional
2009-13-011	FLMNH	F	Palmetto	Cylindrical	Traditional
2011-11-003	FLMNH	F	Palmetto	Cylindrical	Traditional
2011-11-004	FLMNH	F	Palmetto	Cylindrical	Traditional
2011-11-005	FLMNH	F	Palmetto	Cylindrical	Traditional
2011-11-006	FLMNH	F	Palmetto	Cylindrical	Traditional
2011-11-007	FLMNH	F	Palmetto	Cylindrical	Traditional
2011-11-008	FLMNH	F	Palmetto	Cylindrical	Traditional
2012-46-003	FLMNH	F	Palmetto	Cylindrical	Traditional
2012-46-004	FLMNH	F	Palmetto	Cylindrical	Traditional
2012-46-005	FLMNH	F	Palmetto	Cylindrical	Traditional
2012-50-002	FLMNH	F	Palmetto	Cylindrical	Traditional
2012-50-003	FLMNH	F	Palmetto	Cylindrical	Traditional
2012-50-004	FLMNH	F	Palmetto	Cylindrical	Traditional
2012-50-007	FLMNH	F	Palmetto	Cylindrical	Traditional
2012-50-008	FLMNH	F	Palmetto	Cylindrical	Traditional
2012-50-009	FLMNH	F	Palmetto	Cylindrical	Traditional
2012-50-013	FLMNH	F	Palmetto	Cylindrical	Traditional
2012-50-014	FLMNH	F	Palmetto	Cylindrical	Traditional
2012-50-016	FLMNH	F	Palmetto	Cylindrical	Traditional
2012-50-018	FLMNH	F	Palmetto	Cylindrical	Traditional
2012-50-019	FLMNH	F	Palmetto	Cylindrical	Traditional
2012-50-021	FLMNH	F	Palmetto	Cylindrical	Traditional
2012-50-022	FLMNH	F	Palmetto	Cylindrical	Traditional
2012-50-023	FLMNH	F	Palmetto	Cylindrical	Traditional
2012-50-024	FLMNH	F	Palmetto	Cylindrical	Traditional
2012-50-025	FLMNH	F	Palmetto	Cylindrical	Traditional
2012-50-027	FLMNH	F	Palmetto	Cylindrical	Traditional
2012-50-003	FLMNH	F	Palmetto	Cylindrical	Traditional
2013-05-001	FLMNH	F	Palmetto	Cylindrical	Traditional
2013-07-001	FLMNH	F	Palmetto	Cylindrical	Traditional
2013-10-010	FLMNH	F	Palmetto	Cylindrical	Traditional
2013-10-011	FLMNH	F	Palmetto	Cylindrical	Traditional
2013-10-012	FLMNH	F	Palmetto	Cylindrical	Traditional
2013-10-013	FLMNH	F	Palmetto	Cylindrical	Traditional
2013-10-014	FLMNH	F	Palmetto	Cylindrical	Traditional
2013-10-015	FLMNH	F	Palmetto	Cylindrical	Traditional
2013-10-016	FLMNH	F	Palmetto	Cylindrical	Traditional
2013-10-017	FLMNH	F	Palmetto	Cylindrical	Traditional
2013-11-001	FLMNH	F	Palmetto	Cylindrical	Traditional
2013-11-002	FLMNH	F	Palmetto	Cylindrical	Traditional
2013-11-003	FLMNH	F	Palmetto	Cylindrical	Traditional
2013-11-004	FLMNH	F	Palmetto	Cylindrical	Traditional
2013-11-005	FLMNH	F	Palmetto	Cylindrical	Traditional
2013-30-003	FLMNH	F	Palmetto	Cylindrical	Traditional
2013-36-005	FLMNH	F	Palmetto	Cylindrical	Traditional
2013-36-006	FLMNH	F	Palmetto	Cylindrical	Traditional
2014-12-004	FLMNH	F	Palmetto	Cylindrical	Traditional
2014-12-005	FLMNH	F	Palmetto	Cylindrical	Traditional
2014-12-006	FLMNH	F	Palmetto	Cylindrical	Traditional
2014-12-007	FLMNH	F	Palmetto	Cylindrical	Traditional
2014-12-009	FLMNH	F	Palmetto	Cylindrical	Traditional
2014-12-012	FLMNH	F	Palmetto	Cylindrical	Traditional
2014-12-014	FLMNH	F	Palmetto	Cylindrical	Traditional
2014-12-015	FLMNH	F	Palmetto	Cylindrical	Traditional
2014-12-016	FLMNH	F	Palmetto	Cylindrical	Traditional
2014-17-003	FLMNH	F	Palmetto	Cylindrical	Traditional
2014-17-005	FLMNH	F	Palmetto	Cylindrical	Traditional
2014-17-007	FLMNH	F	Palmetto	Cylindrical	Traditional
2015-27-002	FLMNH	F	Palmetto	Cylindrical	Traditional

2015-27-003	FLMNH	F	Palmetto	Cylindrical	Traditional
2015-27-004	FLMNH	F	Palmetto	Cylindrical	Traditional
2015-27-008	FLMNH	F	Palmetto	Cylindrical	Traditional
2016-07-001	FLMNH	F	Palmetto	Cylindrical	Traditional
2016-07-044	FLMNH	F	Palmetto	Cylindrical	Traditional
2016-09-001	FLMNH	F	Palmetto	Cylindrical	Traditional
2016-17-002	FLMNH	F	Palmetto	Cylindrical	Traditional
2016-17-003	FLMNH	F	Palmetto	Cylindrical	Traditional
2016-17-004	FLMNH	F	Palmetto	Cylindrical	Traditional
2016-17-005	FLMNH	F	Palmetto	Cylindrical	Traditional
2016-17-006	FLMNH	F	Palmetto	Cylindrical	Traditional
2016-17-007	FLMNH	F	Palmetto	Cylindrical	Traditional
2016-17-009	FLMNH	F	Palmetto	Cylindrical	Traditional
2016-17-010	FLMNH	F	Palmetto	Cylindrical	Traditional
2016-17-011	FLMNH	F	Palmetto	Cylindrical	Traditional
2016-17-013	FLMNH	F	Palmetto	Cylindrical	Traditional
2016-17-014	FLMNH	F	Palmetto	Cylindrical	Traditional
2016-17-015	FLMNH	F	Palmetto	Cylindrical	Traditional
2016-17-016	FLMNH	F	Palmetto	Cylindrical	Traditional
2016-17-017	FLMNH	F	Palmetto	Cylindrical	Traditional
2016-17-018	FLMNH	F	Palmetto	Cylindrical	Traditional
2016-17-021	FLMNH	F	Palmetto	Cylindrical	Traditional
2016-17-022	FLMNH	F	Palmetto	Cylindrical	Traditional
2016-17-023	FLMNH	F	Palmetto	Cylindrical	Traditional
2016-17-025	FLMNH	F	Palmetto	Cylindrical	Traditional
2016-17-026	FLMNH	F	Palmetto	Cylindrical	Traditional
2016-17-027	FLMNH	F	Palmetto	Cylindrical	Traditional
2016-17-029	FLMNH	F	Palmetto	Cylindrical	Traditional
2016-17-030	FLMNH	F	Palmetto	Cylindrical	Traditional
2016-17-031	FLMNH	F	Palmetto	Cylindrical	Traditional
2016-17-032	FLMNH	F	Palmetto	Cylindrical	Traditional
2016-17-034	FLMNH	F	Palmetto	Cylindrical	Traditional
2016-17-035	FLMNH	F	Palmetto	Cylindrical	Traditional
2016-17-037	FLMNH	F	Palmetto	Cylindrical	Traditional
2016-17-038	FLMNH	F	Palmetto	Cylindrical	Traditional
2016-17-040	FLMNH	F	Palmetto	Cylindrical	Traditional
2016-17-041	FLMNH	F	Palmetto	Cylindrical	Traditional
2016-17-042	FLMNH	F	Palmetto	Cylindrical	Traditional
2016-17-043	FLMNH	F	Palmetto	Cylindrical	Traditional
2016-17-047	FLMNH	F	Palmetto	Cylindrical	Traditional
2016-17-048	FLMNH	F	Palmetto	Cylindrical	Traditional
2016-17-050	FLMNH	F	Palmetto	Cylindrical	Traditional
2016-17-052	FLMNH	F	Palmetto	Cylindrical	Traditional
2017-09-001	FLMNH	F	Palmetto	Cylindrical	Traditional
2017-09-002	FLMNH	F	Palmetto	Cylindrical	Traditional
2017-09-003	FLMNH	F	Palmetto	Cylindrical	Traditional
2017-09-004	FLMNH	F	Palmetto	Cylindrical	Traditional
2017-09-005	FLMNH	F	Palmetto	Cylindrical	Traditional
2017-09-006	FLMNH	F	Palmetto	Cylindrical	Traditional
2017-09-008	FLMNH	F	Palmetto	Cylindrical	Traditional
2017-09-009	FLMNH	F	Palmetto	Cylindrical	Traditional
2017-09-010	FLMNH	F	Palmetto	Cylindrical	Traditional
2017-41-001	FLMNH	F	Palmetto	Cylindrical	Traditional
2017-41-002	FLMNH	F	Palmetto	Cylindrical	Traditional
2018-15-002	FLMNH	F	Palmetto	Cylindrical	Traditional
2018-15-004	FLMNH	F	Palmetto	Cylindrical	Traditional
2019-09-001	FLMNH	F	Palmetto	Cylindrical	Traditional
2019-09-002	FLMNH	F	Palmetto	Cylindrical	Traditional
2019-09-003	FLMNH	F	Palmetto	Cylindrical	Traditional
2019-09-004	FLMNH	F	Palmetto	Cylindrical	Traditional
2019-09-005	FLMNH	F	Palmetto	Cylindrical	Traditional
2019-09-006	FLMNH	F	Palmetto	Cylindrical	Traditional
2019-09-007	FLMNH	F	Palmetto	Cylindrical	Traditional
2019-09-008	FLMNH	F	Palmetto	Cylindrical	Traditional
2019-09-009	FLMNH	F	Palmetto	Cylindrical	Traditional
2019-09-010	FLMNH	F	Palmetto	Cylindrical	Traditional
2019-09-011	FLMNH	F	Palmetto	Cylindrical	Traditional
2019-09-012	FLMNH	F	Palmetto	Cylindrical	Traditional
2019-09-013	FLMNH	F	Palmetto	Cylindrical	Traditional
2019-09-014	FLMNH	F	Palmetto	Cylindrical	Traditional

2019-09-015	FLMNH	F	Palmetto	Cylindrical	Traditional
2019-09-016	FLMNH	F	Palmetto	Cylindrical	Traditional
2019-09-017	FLMNH	F	Palmetto	Cylindrical	Traditional
2019-09-018	FLMNH	F	Palmetto	Cylindrical	Traditional
2019-09-019	FLMNH	F	Palmetto	Cylindrical	Traditional
2019-09-020	FLMNH	F	Palmetto	Cylindrical	Traditional
2019-09-021	FLMNH	F	Palmetto	Cylindrical	Traditional
2019-09-024	FLMNH	F	Palmetto	Cylindrical	Traditional
2019-09-025	FLMNH	F	Palmetto	Cylindrical	Traditional
2019-09-026	FLMNH	F	Palmetto	Cylindrical	Traditional
2019-09-027	FLMNH	F	Palmetto	Cylindrical	Traditional
2019-09-028	FLMNH	F	Palmetto	Cylindrical	Traditional
2019-09-031	FLMNH	F	Palmetto	Cylindrical	Traditional
2019-09-032	FLMNH	F	Palmetto	Cylindrical	Traditional
2019-09-034	FLMNH	F	Palmetto	Cylindrical	Traditional
2019-13-001	FLMNH	F	Palmetto	Cylindrical	Traditional
2020-25-002	FLMNH	F	Palmetto	Cylindrical	Traditional
2020-26-001	FLMNH	F	Palmetto	Cylindrical	Traditional
2020-26-002	FLMNH	F	Palmetto	Cylindrical	Traditional
88-06-004	FLMNH	F	Palmetto	Cylindrical	Traditional
88-06-006	FLMNH	F	Palmetto	Cylindrical	Traditional
E0663	FLMNH	F	Palmetto	Cylindrical	Traditional
E0806	FLMNH	F	Palmetto	Cylindrical	Traditional
201140	NMAI	F	Palmetto	Cylindrical	Traditional
221548	NMAI	F	Palmetto	Cylindrical	Traditional
223664	NMAI	F	Palmetto	Cylindrical	Traditional
224712	NMAI	F	Palmetto	Cylindrical	Traditional
228929	NMAI	F	Palmetto	Cylindrical	Traditional
241529	NMAI	F	Palmetto	Cylindrical	Traditional
241530	NMAI	F	Palmetto	Cylindrical	Traditional
248854	NMAI	F	Palmetto	Cylindrical	Traditional
251224	NMAI	F	Palmetto	Cylindrical	Traditional
255054	NMAI	F	Palmetto	Cylindrical	Traditional
255254	NMAI	F	Palmetto	Cylindrical	Traditional
255255	NMAI	F	Palmetto	Cylindrical	Traditional
255256	NMAI	F	Palmetto	Cylindrical	Traditional
255257	NMAI	F	Palmetto	Cylindrical	Traditional
255258	NMAI	F	Palmetto	Cylindrical	Traditional
255259	NMAI	F	Palmetto	Cylindrical	Traditional
255260	NMAI	F	Palmetto	Cylindrical	Traditional
255261	NMAI	F	Palmetto	Cylindrical	Traditional
255262	NMAI	F	Palmetto	Cylindrical	Traditional
255263	NMAI	F	Palmetto	Cylindrical	Traditional
255264	NMAI	F	Palmetto	Cylindrical	Traditional
255265	NMAI	F	Palmetto	Cylindrical	Traditional
255266	NMAI	F	Palmetto	Cylindrical	Traditional
255267	NMAI	F	Palmetto	Cylindrical	Traditional
255268	NMAI	F	Palmetto	Cylindrical	Traditional
255269	NMAI	F	Palmetto	Cylindrical	Traditional
255270	NMAI	F	Palmetto	Cylindrical	Traditional
255271	NMAI	F	Palmetto	Cylindrical	Traditional
255272	NMAI	F	Palmetto	Cylindrical	Traditional
255273	NMAI	F	Palmetto	Cylindrical	Traditional
255274	NMAI	F	Palmetto	Cylindrical	Traditional
255275	NMAI	F	Palmetto	Cylindrical	Traditional
255285	NMAI	F	Palmetto	Cylindrical	Traditional
255898	NMAI	F	Palmetto	Cylindrical	Traditional
258315	NMAI	F	Palmetto	Cylindrical	Traditional
258702	NMAI	F	Palmetto	Cylindrical	Traditional
260747	NMAI	F	Palmetto	Cylindrical	Traditional
260749	NMAI	F	Palmetto	Cylindrical	Traditional
262144	NMAI	F	Palmetto	Cylindrical	Traditional
265449	NMAI	F	Palmetto	Cylindrical	Traditional
265688	NMAI	F	Palmetto	Cylindrical	Traditional
224713A	NMAI	F	Palmetto	Cylindrical	Traditional
224713B	NMAI	F	Palmetto	Cylindrical	Traditional
241528A	NMAI	F	Palmetto	Cylindrical	Traditional
241528B	NMAI	F	Palmetto	Cylindrical	Traditional
244136B	NMAI	F	Palmetto	Cylindrical	Traditional

E351359-0	NMNH	F	Palmetto	Cylindrical	Traditional
E351360-0	NMNH	F	Palmetto	Cylindrical	Traditional
E363966-0	NMNH	F	Palmetto	Cylindrical	Traditional
E386798-0	NMNH	F	Palmetto	Cylindrical	Traditional
E403621-0	NMNH	F	Palmetto	Cylindrical	Traditional
E403622-0	NMNH	F	Palmetto	Cylindrical	Traditional
E403623-0	NMNH	F	Palmetto	Cylindrical	Traditional
E414232-0	NMNH	F	Palmetto	Cylindrical	Traditional
E418451-0	NMNH	F	Palmetto	Cylindrical	Traditional
E418452-0	NMNH	F	Palmetto	Cylindrical	Traditional
E418453-0	NMNH	F	Palmetto	Cylindrical	Traditional
E418454-0	NMNH	F	Palmetto	Cylindrical	Traditional
E418455-0	NMNH	F	Palmetto	Cylindrical	Traditional
E418457-0A	NMNH	F	Palmetto	Cylindrical	Traditional
E418457-0B	NMNH	F	Palmetto	Cylindrical	Traditional
E424872-0	NMNH	F	Palmetto	Cylindrical	Traditional
1995.34.6	ATTK	F	Palmetto	Head Only	Basket
2002.166.107	ATTK	F	Palmetto	Head Only	Basket
2002.166.53	ATTK	F	Palmetto	Head Only	Basket
2002.166.59	ATTK	F	Palmetto	Head Only	Basket
2002.166.61	ATTK	F	Palmetto	Head Only	Basket
2002.166.63	ATTK	F	Palmetto	Head Only	Basket
2002.166.75	ATTK	F	Palmetto	Head Only	Basket
2002.166.81	ATTK	F	Palmetto	Head Only	Basket
2002.166.90	ATTK	F	Palmetto	Head Only	Basket
2007.9.10	ATTK	F	Palmetto	Head Only	Basket
2007.9.2	ATTK	F	Palmetto	Head Only	Basket
2007.9.5	ATTK	F	Palmetto	Head Only	Basket
2017.35.2	ATTK	F	Palmetto	Head Only	Basket
2012-46-013	FLMNH	F	Palmetto	Head Only	Basket
2013-36-002	FLMNH	F	Palmetto	Head Only	Basket
2017-09-014	FLMNH	F	Palmetto	Head Only	Basket
97-008-001	FLMNH	F	Palmetto	Head Only	Basket
243096	NMAI	F	Palmetto	Head Only	Basket
255691	NMAI	F	Palmetto	Head Only	Basket
260112	NMAI	F	Palmetto	Head Only	Basket
50.2/ 6418	AMNH	F	Palmetto	Head Only	Lapel Pin
50.2/ 6419	AMNH	F	Palmetto	Head Only	Lapel Pin
1997.35.1	ATTK	F	Palmetto	Head Only	Lapel Pin
2001.123.2	ATTK	F	Palmetto	Head Only	Lapel Pin
2006.60.3	ATTK	F	Palmetto	Head Only	Lapel Pin
2008.42.2	ATTK	F	Palmetto	Head Only	Lapel Pin
2014.30.1	ATTK	F	Palmetto	Head Only	Lapel Pin
2014.30.15	ATTK	F	Palmetto	Head Only	Lapel Pin
2014.30.16	ATTK	F	Palmetto	Head Only	Lapel Pin
2014.30.17	ATTK	F	Palmetto	Head Only	Lapel Pin
2014.30.21	ATTK	F	Palmetto	Head Only	Lapel Pin
2014.30.22	ATTK	F	Palmetto	Head Only	Lapel Pin
2014.30.67	ATTK	F	Palmetto	Head Only	Lapel Pin
2014.30.68	ATTK	F	Palmetto	Head Only	Lapel Pin
2006-20-009	FLMNH	F	Palmetto	Head Only	Lapel Pin
2006-20-010	FLMNH	F	Palmetto	Head Only	Lapel Pin
2006-20-011	FLMNH	F	Palmetto	Head Only	Lapel Pin
2006-20-012	FLMNH	F	Palmetto	Head Only	Lapel Pin
2007-07-004	FLMNH	F	Palmetto	Head Only	Lapel Pin
2007-07-005	FLMNH	F	Palmetto	Head Only	Lapel Pin
2007-07-006	FLMNH	F	Palmetto	Head Only	Lapel Pin
2007-07-007	FLMNH	F	Palmetto	Head Only	Lapel Pin
2007-07-008	FLMNH	F	Palmetto	Head Only	Lapel Pin
2013-10-019	FLMNH	F	Palmetto	Head Only	Lapel Pin
2016-17-051	FLMNH	F	Palmetto	Head Only	Lapel Pin
2017-09-011	FLMNH	F	Palmetto	Head Only	Lapel Pin
2017-09-012	FLMNH	F	Palmetto	Head Only	Lapel Pin
2019-09-022	FLMNH	F	Palmetto	Head Only	Lapel Pin
2019-09-023	FLMNH	F	Palmetto	Head Only	Lapel Pin
2019-09-029	FLMNH	F	Palmetto	Head Only	Lapel Pin
2019-09-030	FLMNH	F	Palmetto	Head Only	Lapel Pin
2019-09-033	FLMNH	F	Palmetto	Head Only	Lapel Pin
2019-09-035	FLMNH	F	Palmetto	Head Only	Lapel Pin
E0998 (1)	FLMNH	F	Palmetto	Head Only	Lapel Pin

E0998 (2)	FLMNH	F	Palmetto	Head Only	Lapel Pin
E0998 (3)	FLMNH	F	Palmetto	Head Only	Lapel Pin
255277	NMAI	F	Palmetto	Head Only	Lapel Pin
255278	NMAI	F	Palmetto	Head Only	Lapel Pin
255279	NMAI	F	Palmetto	Head Only	Lapel Pin
255783	NMAI	F	Palmetto	Head Only	Lapel Pin
255784	NMAI	F	Palmetto	Head Only	Lapel Pin
258314	NMAI	F	Palmetto	Head Only	Lapel Pin
204358A	NMAI	F	Palmetto	Head Only	Lapel Pin
204358B	NMAI	F	Palmetto	Head Only	Lapel Pin
E418458-0A	NMNH	F	Palmetto	Head Only	Lapel Pin
E418458-0B	NMNH	F	Palmetto	Head Only	Lapel Pin
E418458-0C	NMNH	F	Palmetto	Head Only	Lapel Pin
E418458-0D	NMNH	F	Palmetto	Head Only	Lapel Pin
E418458-0E	NMNH	F	Palmetto	Head Only	Lapel Pin
E418458-0F	NMNH	F	Palmetto	Head Only	Lapel Pin
E418458-0G	NMNH	F	Palmetto	Head Only	Lapel Pin
E418458-0H	NMNH	F	Palmetto	Head Only	Lapel Pin
2006.90.4	ATTK	F	Palmetto	Head Only	Other (Bell)
2017-09-013	FLMNH	F	Palmetto	Head Only	Other (Bell)
255345	NMAI	F	Palmetto	Head Only	Other (Hair Tie)
255346	NMAI	F	Palmetto	Head Only	Other (Hair Tie)
E409714-0	NMNH	F	Palmetto	Head Only	Other (Hat)
2002.166.4	ATTK	F	Palmetto	Head Only	Other (Mannequin)
255450	NMAI	F	Palmetto	Head Only	Other (Sash)
2002.166.56	ATTK	F	Palmetto	Head Only	Pin Cushion
2017.23.2	ATTK	F	Palmetto	Head Only	Pin Cushion
2012-050-001	FLMNH	F	Palmetto	Head Only	Pin Cushion
E994	FLMNH	F	Palmetto	Head Only	Pin Cushion
255276	NMAI	F	Palmetto	Head Only	Pincushion
1999.54.2	ATTK	F	Palmetto	Horseback	Traditional
2014.7.2	ATTK	F	Palmetto	Limbed	Other
1995.32.1	ATTK	F	Palmetto	Limbed	Traditional
1997.36.1	ATTK	F	Palmetto	Limbed	Traditional
1997.36.2	ATTK	F	Palmetto	Limbed	Traditional
1999.53.1; 1999.53.3	ATTK	F	Palmetto	Limbed	Traditional
1999.53.2	ATTK	F	Palmetto	Limbed	Traditional
2013.28.1	ATTK	F	Palmetto	Limbed	Traditional
2012-50-017	FLMNH	F	Palmetto	Limbed	Traditional
2013-31-001	FLMNH	F	Palmetto	Limbed	Traditional
203612	NMAI	F	Palmetto	Limbed	Traditional
50.1/ 3850	AMNH	F	Wood	Cylindrical	Traditional
50.1/ 3851	AMNH	F	Wood	Cylindrical	Traditional
50.2/ 6402	AMNH	F	Wood	Cylindrical	Traditional
2001.113.5	ATTK	F	Wood	Cylindrical	Traditional
2006.74.1	ATTK	F	Wood	Cylindrical	Traditional
092885	FLMNH	F	Wood	Cylindrical	Traditional
2020-25-001	FLMNH	F	Wood	Cylindrical	Traditional
88-006-008	FLMNH	F	Wood	Cylindrical	Traditional
233136	NMAI	F	Wood	Cylindrical	Traditional
234606	NMAI	F	Wood	Cylindrical	Traditional
50.1/ 3852	AMNH	F	Wood	Limbed	Traditional
1995.29.1	ATTK	F	Wood	Limbed	Traditional
1995.30.1	ATTK	F	Wood	Limbed	Traditional
1995.31.1	ATTK	F	Wood	Limbed	Traditional
1995.38.1	ATTK	F	Wood	Limbed	Traditional
1998.51.1	ATTK	F	Wood	Limbed	Traditional
2002.166.73	ATTK	F	Wood	Limbed	Traditional
2004.156.1	ATTK	F	Wood	Limbed	Traditional
2004.192.1	ATTK	F	Wood	Limbed	Traditional
2005.10.1	ATTK	F	Wood	Limbed	Traditional
2005.10.2	ATTK	F	Wood	Limbed	Traditional
2005.74.1	ATTK	F	Wood	Limbed	Traditional
2008.23.2	ATTK	F	Wood	Limbed	Traditional
2008.23.3	ATTK	F	Wood	Limbed	Traditional

2008.46.1	ATTK	F	Wood	Limbed	Traditional
2011.36.1	ATTK	F	Wood	Limbed	Traditional
2017.17.1	ATTK	F	Wood	Limbed	Traditional
2017.24.1	ATTK	F	Wood	Limbed	Traditional
2012-50-035	FLMNH	F	Wood	Limbed	Traditional
2012-50-038	FLMNH	F	Wood	Limbed	Traditional
2014-17-006	FLMNH	F	Wood	Limbed	Traditional
E363811-0	NMNH	F	Wood	Limbed	Traditional
E363812-0	NMNH	F	Wood	Limbed	Traditional
E363813-0	NMNH	F	Wood	Limbed	Traditional
E363967-0	NMNH	F	Wood	Limbed	Traditional
50.2/ 6409	AMNH	M	Palmetto	Horseback	Big shirt
1999.54.1	ATTK	M	Palmetto	Horseback	Big shirt
2007.19.2	ATTK	M	Palmetto	Horseback	Big shirt
1996.46.1	ATTK	M	Palmetto	Horseback	Rancher
50.2/ 6403	AMNH	M	Palmetto	Limbed	Big shirt
50.2/ 6474	AMNH	M	Palmetto	Limbed	Big shirt
1996.44.1	ATTK	M	Palmetto	Limbed	Big shirt
1996.46.3	ATTK	M	Palmetto	Limbed	Big shirt
1996.46.5	ATTK	M	Palmetto	Limbed	Big shirt
1996.47.1	ATTK	M	Palmetto	Limbed	Big shirt
1996.47.2	ATTK	M	Palmetto	Limbed	Big shirt
2001.113.6	ATTK	M	Palmetto	Limbed	Big shirt
2001.118.2	ATTK	M	Palmetto	Limbed	Big shirt
2001.121.1	ATTK	M	Palmetto	Limbed	Big shirt
2002.149.5	ATTK	M	Palmetto	Limbed	Big shirt
2002.149.7	ATTK	M	Palmetto	Limbed	Big shirt
2002.149.9	ATTK	M	Palmetto	Limbed	Big shirt
2002.166.31	ATTK	M	Palmetto	Limbed	Big shirt
2002.166.51	ATTK	M	Palmetto	Limbed	Big shirt
2002.166.89	ATTK	M	Palmetto	Limbed	Big shirt
2002.42.104	ATTK	M	Palmetto	Limbed	Big shirt
2002.42.105	ATTK	M	Palmetto	Limbed	Big shirt
2003.298.1	ATTK	M	Palmetto	Limbed	Big shirt
2004.110.1	ATTK	M	Palmetto	Limbed	Big shirt
2004.178.2	ATTK	M	Palmetto	Limbed	Big shirt
2004.98.1	ATTK	M	Palmetto	Limbed	Big shirt
2005.76.2	ATTK	M	Palmetto	Limbed	Big shirt
2007.19.1	ATTK	M	Palmetto	Limbed	Big shirt
2007.54.2	ATTK	M	Palmetto	Limbed	Big shirt
2007.70.1	ATTK	M	Palmetto	Limbed	Big shirt
2007.9.17	ATTK	M	Palmetto	Limbed	Big shirt
2007.9.30	ATTK	M	Palmetto	Limbed	Big shirt
2011.5.1	ATTK	M	Palmetto	Limbed	Big shirt
2013.28.2	ATTK	M	Palmetto	Limbed	Big shirt
2013.4.2	ATTK	M	Palmetto	Limbed	Big shirt
2014.27.14	ATTK	M	Palmetto	Limbed	Big shirt
2014.30.11	ATTK	M	Palmetto	Limbed	Big shirt
2014.30.40	ATTK	M	Palmetto	Limbed	Big shirt
2014.30.65	ATTK	M	Palmetto	Limbed	Big shirt
2016.24.1	ATTK	M	Palmetto	Limbed	Big shirt
2000-09-002	FLMNH	M	Palmetto	Limbed	Big shirt
2007-07-014	FLMNH	M	Palmetto	Limbed	Big Shirt
2007-07-015	FLMNH	M	Palmetto	Limbed	Big Shirt
2011-11-002	FLMNH	M	Palmetto	Limbed	Big Shirt
2012-46-001	FLMNH	M	Palmetto	Limbed	Big Shirt
2012-46-002	FLMNH	M	Palmetto	Limbed	Big Shirt
2012-46-006	FLMNH	M	Palmetto	Limbed	Big Shirt
2012-50-012	FLMNH	M	Palmetto	Limbed	Big shirt
2012-50-026	FLMNH	M	Palmetto	Limbed	Big Shirt
2012-50-028	FLMNH	M	Palmetto	Limbed	Big Shirt
2012-50-029	FLMNH	M	Palmetto	Limbed	Big Shirt
2012-50-031	FLMNH	M	Palmetto	Limbed	Big Shirt
2012-50-032	FLMNH	M	Palmetto	Limbed	Big Shirt
2012-50-033	FLMNH	M	Palmetto	Limbed	Big Shirt
2012-50-034	FLMNH	M	Palmetto	Limbed	Big Shirt
2013-10-006	FLMNH	M	Palmetto	Limbed	Big Shirt
2013-10-009	FLMNH	M	Palmetto	Limbed	Big Shirt
2013-30-005	FLMNH	M	Palmetto	Limbed	Big Shirt
2014-12-001	FLMNH	M	Palmetto	Limbed	Big Shirt

2014-12-002	FLMNH	M	Palmetto	Limbed	Big Shirt
2014-12-003	FLMNH	M	Palmetto	Limbed	Big Shirt
2014-12-013	FLMNH	M	Palmetto	Limbed	Big Shirt
2014-17-002	FLMNH	M	Palmetto	Limbed	Big Shirt
2014-17-004	FLMNH	M	Palmetto	Limbed	Big Shirt
2015-27-009	FLMNH	M	Palmetto	Limbed	Big Shirt
2016-17-012	FLMNH	M	Palmetto	Limbed	Big Shirt
2016-17-020	FLMNH	M	Palmetto	Limbed	Big Shirt
2016-17-028	FLMNH	M	Palmetto	Limbed	Big Shirt
2016-17-033	FLMNH	M	Palmetto	Limbed	Big Shirt
2016-17-036	FLMNH	M	Palmetto	Limbed	Big Shirt
2016-17-039	FLMNH	M	Palmetto	Limbed	Big Shirt
201141	NMAI	M	Palmetto	Limbed	Big Shirt
203611	NMAI	M	Palmetto	Limbed	Big Shirt
203613	NMAI	M	Palmetto	Limbed	Big Shirt
203614	NMAI	M	Palmetto	Limbed	Big Shirt
221549	NMAI	M	Palmetto	Limbed	Big Shirt
224711	NMAI	M	Palmetto	Limbed	Big Shirt
241531	NMAI	M	Palmetto	Limbed	Big Shirt
251223	NMAI	M	Palmetto	Limbed	Big Shirt
255282	NMAI	M	Palmetto	Limbed	Big Shirt
255283	NMAI	M	Palmetto	Limbed	Big Shirt
255284	NMAI	M	Palmetto	Limbed	Big Shirt
255899	NMAI	M	Palmetto	Limbed	Big Shirt
265451	NMAI	M	Palmetto	Limbed	Big Shirt
265522	NMAI	M	Palmetto	Limbed	Big Shirt
244136A	NMAI	M	Palmetto	Limbed	Big Shirt
E363964-0	NMNH	M	Palmetto	Limbed	Big shirt
E363965-0	NMNH	M	Palmetto	Limbed	Big shirt
E403620-0	NMNH	M	Palmetto	Limbed	Big shirt
E418456-0	NMNH	M	Palmetto	Limbed	Big shirt
E424899-0	NMNH	M	Palmetto	Limbed	Big shirt
2012-50-030	FLMNH	M	Palmetto	Limbed	Big Shirt
2013-10-007	FLMNH	M	Palmetto	Limbed	Big Shirt
2014-12-008	FLMNH	M	Palmetto	Limbed	Big Shirt
2014-12-010	FLMNH	M	Palmetto	Limbed	Big Shirt
2014-12-011	FLMNH	M	Palmetto	Limbed	Big Shirt
2015-27-001	FLMNH	M	Palmetto	Limbed	Big Shirt
2016-07-045	FLMNH	M	Palmetto	Limbed	Big Shirt
2017-09-007	FLMNH	M	Palmetto	Limbed	Big Shirt
2018-15-003	FLMNH	M	Palmetto	Limbed	Big Shirt
2014.7.1	ATTK	M	Palmetto	Limbed	Other
50.2/ 6473	AMNH	M	Palmetto	Limbed	Rancher
1999.57.1	ATTK	M	Palmetto	Limbed	Rancher
2003.296.1	ATTK	M	Palmetto	Limbed	Rancher
2007.108.4	ATTK	M	Palmetto	Limbed	Rancher
2000-08-001	FLMNH	M	Palmetto	Limbed	Rancher
2012-50-010	FLMNH	M	Palmetto	Limbed	Rancher
2012-50-015	FLMNH	M	Palmetto	Limbed	Rancher
2012-50-020	FLMNH	M	Palmetto	Limbed	Rancher
2013-36-007	FLMNH	M	Palmetto	Limbed	Rancher
2016-17-046	FLMNH	M	Palmetto	Limbed	Rancher
241532	NMAI	M	Palmetto	Limbed	Rancher
50.2/ 6399	AMNH	M	Wood	Limbed	Big shirt
50.2/ 6400	AMNH	M	Wood	Limbed	Big shirt
50.2/ 6401	AMNH	M	Wood	Limbed	Big shirt
1997.37.1	ATTK	M	Wood	Limbed	Big shirt
2002.166.74	ATTK	M	Wood	Limbed	Big shirt
2004.105.1	ATTK	M	Wood	Limbed	Big shirt
092886	FLMNH	M	Wood	Limbed	Big Shirt
2013-10-008	FLMNH	M	Wood	Limbed	Big Shirt
2016-17-019	FLMNH	M	Wood	Limbed	Big Shirt
224710	NMAI	M	Wood	Limbed	Big Shirt
233135	NMAI	M	Wood	Limbed	Big Shirt
234605	NMAI	M	Wood	Limbed	Big Shirt
88-06-009	FLMNH	M	Wood	Limbed	Big Shirt
2012-50-039	FLMNH	M	Wood	Limbed	Rancher

References

ATTK (Ah-Tah-Thi-Ki Museum)
 2021 "Follow along with Willie on his canoe journey! He started at the Ah-Tah-Thi-Ki in his dugout canoe built by our Traditional Interpretation Coordinator, Daniel Tommie-" Twitter, November 30. Electronic document, https://twitter.com/ahtahthiki1/status/1465742452975976452, accessed February 16, 2022.

Archer, Layla R.
 2005 Seminole Dolls, Seminole Life: An Exploration of Tourism and Culture. Unpublished M.A. thesis, Department of Anthropology, Florida State University, Tallahassee.

Barbour, Thomas
 1944 *That Vanishing Eden: A Naturalist's Florida.* Little, Brown and Company, Boston.

Bell, Austin J.
 2011 Weaving a Community through a Common Thread: the Miccosukee and Seminole Tribes of Florida. Unpublished manuscript, University of Florida, Gainesville, electronic document, https://ufdc.ufl.edu/AA00012887/00001, accessed January 14, 2022.

Beloit College Digital Collections
 2022 Logan Museum of Anthropology, "Seminole Doll." Electronic document, https://dcms.beloit.edu/digital/collection/logan/search/searchterm/seminole%20doll, accessed January 10, 2022.

Bidney, Beverly
 2013 Maggie Osceola Celebrates 93rd Birthday among Family, Friends. *The Seminole Tribune* 26 November. Electronic document, https://seminoletribune.org/maggie-osceola-celebrates-93rd-birthday-among-family-friends/, accessed January 10, 2022.

Billie, Mary B.
 1980a "Interview with Mary B. Billie, Seminole Doll Maker." Audio recordings of Florida Folk Festival performances and other folk events, 1935-2001, Series S 1576, Transcription T-80-48, Florida Folklife Archive. Interview conducted on June 11, 1980. Interview on file, State Archives of Florida, electronic document, https://www.floridamemory.com/learn/classroom/learning-units/seminole-dolls/documents/interview/tape2.php, accessed February 12, 2021.

 1980b "Interview with Mary B. Billie, Seminole Doll Maker." Audio recordings of Florida Folk Festival performances and other folk events, 1935-2001, Series S 1576, Transcription T-80-47, Florida Folklife Archive. Interview conducted on June 11, 1980. Interview on file, State Archives of Florida, electronic document, https://www.floridamemory.com/learn/classroom/learning-units/seminole-dolls/documents/interview/, accessed February 12, 2021.

Billie, Ruby, and Betty Mae Jumper
 1982 "Ruby Billie interview for the Seminole Slide & Tape Project." Series S 1576, Container 8, C83-38. Seminole Slide & Tape Project. Interview conducted on January 27, 1982. Interview on file, State Archives of Florida, electronic document, https://www.floridamemory.com/items/show/238241, accessed March 8, 2021.

Blackard, David M.
 1990a *Patchwork & Palmettos: Seminole-Miccosukee Folk Art since 1820.* Catalog published in conjunction with the exhibition of the same name, Fort Lauderdale Historical Society, Fort Lauderdale, Florida, March 1 thru September 3, 1990.

 1990b Patchwork & Palmettos: Seminole-Miccosukee Folk Art since 1820. *American Indian Art* 15(2):66-83.

Blais-Billie, Dante
 2021 Decolonizing Gender and Language. *Ah-Tah-Thi-Ki Quarterly,* Fall 2021:7-8.

Close, Barbara
 2018 The Native Art of the Florida Seminole Indians. *Doll News* 67(2):108-111.

Cypress, Carol F.
 1999 Interview with Carol F. Cypress. Interview conducted on May 23, 1999. OH1999-8, on file at the Ah-Tah-Thi-Ki Museum, Big Cypress, Florida.

 2018 Interview with Carol F. Cypress. Interview conducted on September 20, 2018. OH2018-5, on file at the Ah-Tah-Thi-Ki Museum, Big Cypress, Florida.

Downs, Dorothy
 1995 *Art of the Florida Seminole and Miccosukee Indians.* University Press of Florida, Gainesville.

Dyen, Doris J.
 1980 Mary B. Billie and daughter Claudia C. John by a table under a partially built chickee - Big Cypress Reservation, Florida. State Archives of Florida, Florida Memory. Electronic document, https://www.floridamemory.com/items/show/120213, accessed January 7, 2022.

FLMNH (Florida Museum of Natural History)
 2021a "Seminole Doll Collection Overview." South Florida Archaeology and Ethnography. Electronic document, https://www.floridamuseum.ufl.edu/sflarch/collections/seminole-dolls/overview/, accessed March 8, 2021.

 2021b "Tourism." South Florida Archaeology and Ethnography. Electronic document, https://www.floridamuseum.ufl.edu/sflarch/collections/seminole-dolls/tourism/, accessed March 8, 2021.

 2021c "Dolls." South Florida Archaeology and Ethnography. Electronic document, https://www.floridamuseum.ufl.edu/sflarch/collections/seminole-dolls/dolls/, accessed March 8, 2021.

 2021d "Patchwork." South Florida Archaeology and Ethnography. Electronic document, https://www.floridamuseum.ufl.edu/sflarch/collections/seminole-dolls/patchwork/, accessed March 8, 2021.

 2021e "Features." South Florida Archaeology and Ethnography. Electronic document, https://www.floridamuseum.ufl.edu/sflarch/collections/seminole-dolls/features/, accessed March 8, 2021.

Garbarino, Merwyn S.
1989 *The Seminole*. Chelsea House Publishers, New York.

Johnson, Lynn
2008 *Native American Dolls of the Seminole and Miccosukees*. Douglas and Mary Lynn Johnson Publishing Company.

Jumper, Betty Mae
1988 Seminole Palmetto Dolls. *Seminole Tribune*, 11 January. Hollywood, Florida.

Kidwell, Clara Sue
2004 Introduction. In *Small Spirits: Native American Dolls from the Smithsonian National Museum of the American Indian*, pp. 13-21. Smithsonian National Museum of the American Indian in association with University of Washington Press: Washington, DC.

Lenz, Mary Jane
1986 *The Stuff of Dreams: Native American Dolls*. Museum of the American Indian, New York.

2004 *Small Spirits: Native American Dolls from the Smithsonian National Museum of the American Indian*. Smithsonian National Museum of the American Indian in association with University of Washington Press: Washington, DC.

Libhart, Myles
1989 To Dress with Great Care: Contemporary American Indian and Eskimo Doll Artists of the United States. *American Indian Art* 14(2):38-51.

Livingston, Stephenie
2014 "A living history." Florida Museum of Natural History, Research News. Electronic document, https://www.floridamuseum.ufl.edu/science/a-living-history/, accessed March 9, 2021.

MacCauley, Clay
1887 The Seminole Indians of Florida. In *Fifth Annual Report of the Bureau of Ethnology*, pp. 469-531. Washington, DC.

McQuiston, Don, and Debra McQuiston
1995 *Dolls and Toys of Native America: A Journey Through Childhood*. Chronicle Books, San Francisco.

Mechling, Jay
1996 Florida Seminoles and the Marketing of the Last Frontier. In *Dressing in Feathers: The Construction of the Indian in American Popular Culture*, edited by S. Elizabeth Bird, pp. 149-166. Westview Press, Boulder, Colorado.

Miccosukee Tribe of Indians of Florida
2021 "History," Miccosukee Tribe of Indians of Florida. Electronic document, https://tribe.miccosukee.com/, accessed March 9, 2021.

Moses, Mabel O.
1999 Interview with Mabel O. Moses. Interview conducted on June 17, 1999. OH1999-10, on file at the Ah-Tah-Thi-Ki Museum, Big Cypress, Florida.

National Postal Museum
2022 37c Seminole Doll single. Electronic document, https://postalmuseum.si.edu/object/npm_2005.2003.111.5, accessed January 11, 2022.

Oehlbeck, Barbara
1997 *The Sabal Palm: A Native Monarch*. Gulfshore Press, Naples.

Reeves, I. S. K. and Sara W.
2009 *The Seminole: Art of the Seminole 1820-1950*. Published in conjunction with the exhibit *The Seminole: Seminole Art 1820-1950*, Maitland Art Center, Maitland, Florida, March 13 thru April 26, 2009.

2018 *Enduring Beauty: Seminole Art and Culture*. Published in conjunction with the exhibition of the same name, Orlando Museum of Art, Orlando, Florida, March 22 thru July 8, 2018.

Repko, Marya
2009 *Angel of the Swamp: Deaconess Harriett Bedell in the Everglades*. ECity Publishing, Everglades City.

Roberts, Larry
2001 *Florida's Golden Age of Souvenirs: 1890-1930*. University Press of Florida, Gainesville.

Second-Jumper, Siegfried
2011 *Second Jumper: Searching for his Bloodline*. Lulu.com.

Seminole Tribal Fair and Pow Wow
2021a Adult/Youth Arts & Crafts Virtual Contests Results. Electronic document, https://semtribefair.com/virtualcontests/arts-crafts-virtual-contests-results/, accessed January 10, 2022.

2021b Adult/Youth Arts & Crafts Contest Gallery. Electronic document, https://semtribefair.com/virtualcontests/adult-youth-arts-crafts-virtual-contest-gallery/?cac=submission&ctx=page&sid=9003, accessed January 10, 2022.

Sieg, Jean
2018 Make a Seminole Costume for a 13 to 14-Inch Doll. *Doll News* 67(2):112-116.

Sturtevant, William C.
1971 "Creek into Seminole." In *North American Indians in Historical Perspective*, edited by Eleanore Burke Leacock and Nancy Oestreich Lurie, pp. 92-128. Random House, New York.

Thompson, Amanda
2021 "Doll," Ostego Institute for Native American Art History. Electronic document, www.otsegoinstitute.org/amanda-thompson.html, accessed February 9, 2021.

Tobias, Haji
2009 Seminole Moments Presentation Centers on History of Dolls. *Seminole Tribune* 30(12):2B.

West, Patsy
1998 *The Enduring Seminoles: From Alligator Wrestling to Casino Gambling*. University Press of Florida, Gainesville.

2002 *Images of America: The Seminole and Miccosukee Tribes of Southern Florida*. Arcadia Publishing, Charleston.

Zerkel, Sharon C.
2014 The Florida Seminoles and their Dolls. *Doll News* 63(4):52-63.

6

Epilogue: A Century of Collaboration and Consultation

William H. Marquardt

In 1923, Florida State Museum director Thomas Van Hyning purchased a Seminole man's long shirt from Tony Tommie, known as the first Native American from South Florida to attend school. The long shirt was displayed in the Museum's Seagle building exhibit space and later in the Object Gallery in Dickinson Hall. Florida Museum personnel have interacted with Florida Native Americans for at least 100 years.[1]

During visits to South Florida during his pioneering archaeological studies 1935-1953, John Goggin purchased Seminole objects at the Glade Cross Mission operated by Deaconess Bedell, although he engaged only infrequently with Native Americans (Weisman 2002:65-66). Many of the items Goggin obtained are now in the Museum's Florida Ethnographic Collection

(FEC) within its Anthropology Division. More intensive and focused interactions with Native Americans began in 1982 with curator Jerald Milanich's research in the Cove of the Withlacoochee and in 1994 during initial planning for the Hall of South Florida People and Environments under the leadership of Darcie MacMahon (Project Director) and William Marquardt (Curator). In this epilogue I summarize Florida Museum interactions with Florida Native Americans, focusing on the past 40 years.

Consultation on Research, Repatriation, and Reburial

Jerald T. Milanich served as Curator of Archaeology at the Florida Museum of Natural History

for 35 years. The author of numerous books and articles, he is probably the best known of all Florida archaeologists. In 1982-1983 when Milanich's team began the Cove of the Withlacoochee project, he initiated a discussion with Florida native people about a small Seminole-related site. At the time such communications were funneled informally through the director of the Governor's Council on Indian Affairs. The Council, located in Tallahassee, deals with Native American issues in Florida as a quasi-official state agency/foundation, which still exists today. In other words, to keep the Seminoles and other natives aware of archaeological projects, the archaeologists would sit down in Tallahassee with the Council's director. Then-graduate student Brent Weisman conducted the Seminole research phase of the project, which was the basis of his dissertation, later published by the University of Alabama Press (Weisman 1989). During his research, Weisman met and talked with Mike Osceola, who visited his excavation of a Seminole village site (Figure 1). Weisman was invited to Seminole Tribal headquarters in Hollywood by then-chairman James Billie, who showed great interest in the project (Brent Weisman, personal communication, January, 2021).

In 1991, in anticipation of excavations at the Fig Springs archaeological site, a seventeenth century Spanish mission, Milanich again consulted with both the Governor's Council and the State Historic Preservation Officer (SHPO). That was standard protocol whenever the likelihood of encountering human burials existed. In later years state laws and regulations were written to codify such protocols. All the mission-period human remains of Christian Timucua people were reinterred at the mission site during the field project, after additional consultations with the Governor's Council, the Florida State Historic Preservation Officer (SHPO), and the Catholic Church.

In 1991-1992 Milanich consulted with the new National Museum of the American Indian on the initial formulation of their collection policies, and in 1993-1994 he consulted with the National Park Service and representatives of the Miccosukee Tribe of Indians of Florida on the Everglades National Park and archaeological matters.

About 1991, Tina Marie Osceola invited Milanich to attend a conference in Naples, Florida, about the Columbian Quincentenary. Osceola had served on the board of the National Museum of the American Indian and was active nationally in indigenous affairs. Later, she helped Milanich to receive funding from the Seminole Tribe to publish *Hidden Seminoles—Julian Dimock's Historic Florida Photographs* (Milanich and Root 2011; Figure 2). She also wrote a foreword for the book. Later, the Seminole tribal museum (Ah-Tah-Thi-Ki) at the Big Cypress reservation asked if Milanich would work with their staff to curate an exhibit that used the photographs and information from the book. That exhibit ("Camera-Man: The Seminole through the Lens of Julian Dimock") was displayed in 2012 and 2013. At one point, Milanich led children from the Seminole school on a gallery tour. The Miccosukee liked the exhibit and asked Osceola to meet with Milanich to talk about their being able to access the photos, which Milanich arranged.

In 2010-2012 Milanich served as a Research Associate to the Seminole Tribal Historic Preservation Office on the Big Cypress reservation. During that time, he oversaw the preparation of a 74-page research design for the tribal archaeology staff.

Archeologist studying Seminoles returns to Citrus

By NORM SWETMAN
Staff Writer

Brent Weisman, archeologist from the University of Florida, who has been searching and making trial digs in Citrus County during the summer looking for Seminole artifacts, returned to talk to the Inverness Rotary on Wednesday.

With the major portion of grant funds coming from the Inverness club which donated $1,000 to the study Weisman brought them up to date on his findings.

"I am satisfied we have not yet located Osceola's village in the cove of the Withlacoochee," he said, and he added archeologists and technicians in other parts of the state are astounded at the various types of artifacts that have come to light in Citrus County.

"What this tells me is this area was once a crossroads of commerce and activity among prehistoric peoples dating back to before the time of Christ," he told Rotarians.

Don Shepard, who used old maps and diaries written by Lt. Henry Prince about the area shortly after the Second Seminole War, located the probable site of the main Seminole village. The information was passed along to the University who sent a search team under Dr. Jerald Milanich to make a trial dig. Results were interesting enough that Weisman, who is working toward his PhD, asked to make this his thesis project.

During the summer's search Shepard, Lyn DeLong, a teacher volunteer who videotaped the project, and other volunteers accompanied Weisman and helped dig and sift the diggings for artifacts.

"We have been overwhelmed with literally thousands of pieces of data from Citrus County," Shepard said, and he echoed Weisman's report that many of the potsherds pre-date Christ in their antiquity. "Scholars are perplexed by the number of cultures that have been uncovered here. There is no definite history written on any of these people and the startling finds."

Showing a slide show of their activities of the last three months Weisman said, "We have had tremendous local support in getting on people's property and the number of people coming forward to show us their finds that have been kept in their family for years."

The archeologist also said Citrus Countians have pinpointed a number of Indian mounds along the Withlacoochee River and inland. Mounds can tell them a great deal, he reported, some have been used for thousands of years and include refuse from their food supply such as snail, clam, fish, and animal bones.

"There were some tool artifacts displayed for us by local people who found them near the river. Some we identified with Indian tribes in Ohio, some from the Great Lakes thus showing the Indians traveled a great deal and a great distance to come to this area."

Weisman said his group was lucky enough to locate an old submerged dugout canoe and when the time comes they are going to claim it for research. "There were some others in this area but, unfortunately they disappeared and we haven't been able to locate them." He didn't know at this point how old the river craft were.

"I am continually amazed at the great amount of potsherds and artifacts there are in this area," he said, "We drove to Trails End Fish Camp that is built on top of an Indian mound, and we no sooner stepped out of the truck when we found a number of potsherds next to our vehicle."

During his slide presentation Weisman said they thought at one point they had come upon a wonderful discovery. On a lake island they found structures built of raw fieldstones, and it was only after investigation and inquiry they learned a young bachelor had planned to build a ranch house, some outhouses, and plant an orange grove.

For the time being, at least for six months, the field work is complete, he said. "The next big project is to wash and catalogue the artifacts. That's only the start. We want to also determine where to start the next main digs."

The climate for getting federal grants on this type of project is pretty grim, Weisman said. "It's the kind of program that needs time and some fantastic finds. I feel we have their interest but, we are going to have to prove to them we have what we know is here. It takes funding and that takes community support."

He said in order to carbon date the artifacts they already have would take about $2,500 and further funds to continue on with their research in Citrus County.

Weisman will be back in Citrus County on Sept. 28 to address the Citrus County Historical Society at 7:30 p.m. in the courthouse. The public is invited to attend and ask questions. Anyone wishing to contribute to the grant can call Joe

Fowler, president of the Historical Society at 726-1791 for further information.

DISCUSSING SEARCH FOR OSCEOLA'S CAMP that has remained hidden since the Second Seminole War are Brent Weisman (left), archeologist from University of Florida, and Chief Mike Osceola of Inverness, descendant of the famed war chief. Weisman addressed Rotarians at Ft. Cooper Station Restaurant on Wednesday.

Figure 1. *Brent Weisman appears with Mike Osceola (right) in a photograph published in the Citrus County Chronicle. Source: Citrus County Chronicle, Friday Sept. 2, 1983.*

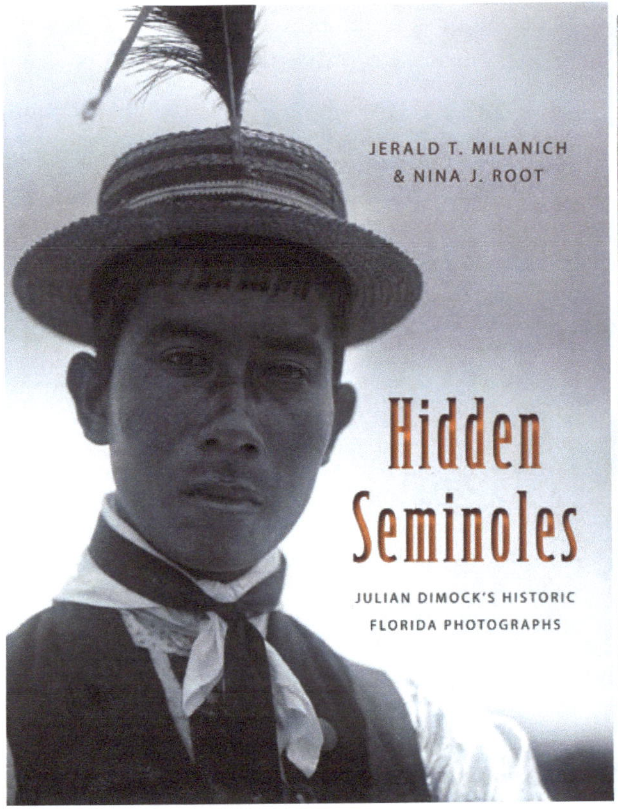

Figure 2. *Former curator Jerald Milanich collaborated with the Ah-Tah-Thi-Ki Museum in an exhibit and a teacher's guide featuring the photographs of Julian Dimock.*

Interactions concerning the reburial of human remains and burial goods in the Florida Museum's collections began about 1993. By mail, officials of the Seminole Tribe of Florida, Miccosukee Tribe of Indians of Florida, and the Seminole Nation of Oklahoma had been made aware of human skeletal remains and grave goods that likely were Seminole and/or Miccosukee people. These notifications were required by Federal laws and regulations. The skeletal remains, none of which had been excavated by Florida Museum staff, had been deposited at the Museum in the 1920s, 1957,

1959, and 1971. The Florida and Oklahoma Seminole people agreed to have the Miccosukee take the lead in the negotiations. As a result of amicable consultations, the human remains from South Florida were turned over to the Miccosukee while the remains from North Florida were reburied in Alachua County near where they had been excavated in 1949.

As Milanich neared retirement about 2006, the bioarchaeologist at the University of North Carolina announced that he had completed

analysis of the human remains from Tatham Mound in Citrus County, an early sixteenth-century burial mound that contained a relatively large number of Spanish artifacts believed to be from the Hernando de Soto expedition of 1539 and poorly preserved human remains, several of which exhibited cut wounds from metal weapons.

Before the project began about 1986, Milanich's team had made agreements with the landowners (the Boy Scouts of America), their Native American advisory committee, and the Florida SHPO to rebury the human remains at the conclusion of the analysis. In 2006 the book on the bioarchaeological research was in press and it was time to complete that task of reburial. However, between the time of the excavations and the present, the implementation of the Native American Graves Protection and Repatriation Act required consultation at the federal level. The Miccosukee entrusted the overseeing of the reburial of the human remains to the Seminole Tribe of Florida.

Twenty-two months, 292 emails, and much federal and state red tape later, the remains of nearly 370 people were reburied in the mound under the supervision of a representative of the Seminole Tribe of Florida (Milanich 2009). Milanich describes this process as "one of the most extraordinary events in my career. It could not have gone better and it gained trust from the Tribe. I suspect that trust was in large part responsible for my later working with the Tribe on matters of archaeology, historic preservation, book publication, and museum exhibition" (Jerald Milanich, personal communication, January, 2021).

Planning for the Hall of South Florida

In 1993, the Museum decided to feature South Florida in a permanent exhibit for the first time in its history. The exhibit was to be installed in the new exhibition center, Powell Hall, which was then in planning. This exhibit was to be in the largest of the permanent halls, a 6,050-square-foot space in the southwest corner of the permanent exhibition area. William Marquardt and an interdisciplinary research team had been undertaking research in Southwest Florida for a decade, so he assumed the role of Curator of the exhibit, while Dorr Dennis served as Chief Designer and Darcie MacMahon was overall Project Director. MacMahon, an archaeologist by training, held an advanced degree in Museum Studies from George Washington University and had interned at the National Museum of Natural History. She and Marquardt assembled a planning committee of artisans, educators, and specialists in exhibit evaluation.

Marquardt chaired the planning committee, which met 14 times between January and June 1994 (Marquardt 1994). Front-end evaluation took place in Gainesville with museum attendees. MacMahon and Marquardt held exploratory meetings with both Mikasuki-speaking and Creek-speaking Native Americans in South Florida. They paid courtesy calls on tribal leaders of the Seminole Tribe of Florida and the Miccosukee Tribe of Indians of Florida. The

six-month period culminated in a planning grant proposal to the National Endowment for the Humanities (NEH).

The NEH grant was received, leading to a year of intensive planning in 1995. This included trips to other museums, exhibit design, artist's conceptual drawings, a three-dimensional model, selection of objects, a conservation survey, script writing and formative evaluation, educational program planning, and both formal and informal meetings with a team of four Native American consultants to benefit from their perspectives and to discuss topics that might be culturally sensitive. Numerous interactions occurred at the museum and in South Florida at Seminole and Miccosukee reservations. Although many other Seminole and Miccosukee tribal members were consulted during the project, we had four core consultants and spent countless hours with them in person, in Gainesville and

Figure 3. *Native American Consultants on the Hall of South Florida People and Environments exhibit. Standing: Madelaine Tongkeamha, Joe Quetone, William Marquardt, Mary Frances Johns; kneeling: Billy Cypress, Darcie MacMahon.*

South Florida, and via correspondence while the exhibit was in development, forming deep relationships that were sustained long after the exhibition opened (Figure 3). These consultants were:

- Billy L. Cypress, executive director of the Seminole Tribal Museum authority, a Mikasuki-speaking Seminole

- Mary Frances Johns, educator and artisan, a Mikasuki-speaking Seminole

- Madelaine Tongkeamha, educator and artisan, a Creek-speaking Seminole

- Joe Quetone, Chair of the Florida Governor's Council on Indian Affairs, a Kiowa tribal member.

In addition to formal group meetings that were recorded and transcribed (Marquardt ed. 1995), the group traveled together to the Pineland archaeological site and had several informal meetings over meals in Southwest Florida and in Marquardt's and MacMahon's homes in Gainesville.

MacMahon and I took advantage of times when tribal members were in Gainesville to ask their opinions on directions our exhibits were taking (Figures 4a, 4b). We also gained insights into material culture and tradition by spending time with tribal members on the reservations (Figures 4c, 4d) and attending tribal festivals (e.g., the Speckled Perch festival in Okeechobee, the tribal rodeo in Immokalee). We interviewed and photographed patchwork and bead artists such as Martha

Figure 4. *(a) Seminole tribal chairman James Billie offers his opinion on artwork proposed for the Legacy Gallery, South Florida Hall. Left to right: William Marquardt, Chairman Billie, Darcie MacMahon. (b) Mary Frances Johns and Jay McGirt consult with artist/designer Merald Clark about the Calusa leader's gallery, as Darcie MacMahon looks on. (c) William Marquardt and Darcie MacMahon talk with Ronnie Billie as he works on a playground shade cover. (d) Darcie MacMahon and Dorr Dennis talk with Henry John Billie (right), at the time the only active maker of traditional Seminole dugout canoes.*

Jones, basket makers such as Connie Frank Gowan and Mary Frances Johns, and canoe-maker Henry John Billie. We attended the Miccosukee tribal holiday festival and children's musical play at the invitation of the tribal chairman and met renowned former Miccosukee tribal chairman Buffalo Tiger and his two sons, Stephen and Lee.

On trips to Billie Swamp Safari on the Big Cypress reservation, we listened to story tellers and visited with craft workers and other tribal members there.

We spent considerable time at Okalee Museum in Hollywood, Ah-Tah-Thi-Ki museum in Big Cypress, and the Miccosukee Village Museum on the Tamiami Trail. We had the honor of witnessing Chairman James Billie's interview with Susie Jim Billie (then about 103 years old), which took place in her chickee with four generations of her offspring present (Figure 5). On another occasion, Marquardt visited with Miccosukee tribal member Ronnie Jimmie at his home and interviewed him about how traditional tribal medicine was taught.

Figure 5. *(a) Filmmaker Leslie Gaines and his crew film Chairman James Billie's oral history interview with Panther clan matriarch Susie Jim Billie; William Marquardt (far left) records the interview, with permission, on a camcorder. (b) Five generations of Panther clan women gather in the chickee of Susie Jim Billie (center), then about 103 years old.*

Figure 6. *(a and b). Seminole tribal elders were invited to view the collections.*

At the time, he and Mohawk tribal member Jerome Rockwell were studying with tribal maker-of-medicine Sonny Billie.

In March 1997, Seminole tribal elders were invited to visit Gainesville as a group, and were shown objects from our extensive collections, stimulating much discussion (Figures 6a, 6b). The visiting elders were hosted for dinner in the then-empty South Florida hall, accompanied by selected members of Florida Museum staff and UF dignitaries (Figure 7a). After-dinner musical entertainment was provided by the Museum, which was reciprocated when a group of elders sang songs for the staff (Figure 7b). As an expression of gratitude for the visit, the elders gifted a splendid sweetgrass basket for our collection, made by Agnes

Figure 7. *(a) The tribal elders were hosted for dinner in the then-empty Hall of South Florida People and Environments. (b) After musical entertainment provided by the Museum, some of the elders responded by offering some songs of their own.*

142

Figure 8. *As a thank-you gift, the Seminole elders donated a magnificent sweetgrass basket to our collection (FLMNH cat. no. 97-8-1).*

[a]

[b]

Figure 9. *(a) William Marquardt (right) introduces Seminole medicine man Sonny Billie in the Powell Hall classroom. (b) At the grand opening of the South Florida hall, Darcie MacMahon converses with Sonny Billie and Pat Francescini as Edith Marquardt looks on.*

Billie Cypress (basket) and Lucy Johns (lid). The basket (FLMNH cat. no. 97-8-1; Figure 8) was included in the "Native Americans in Florida Today" gallery of the South Florida hall.

Prior to the public opening of the Florida Museum's new exhibition and education building, Powell Hall, Marquardt asked renowned Seminole medicine man Sonny Billie to bless the building and he graciously agreed. At the time, he served as the principal maker of medicine for both the Seminole and Miccosukee tribes. On February 1, 1998, Marquardt and MacMahon met Mr. Billie before dawn in front of Powell Hall. Accompanied by his two assistants, Ronnie Jimmie and Jerome Rockwell, with Marquardt and MacMahon walking behind, Mr. Billie made a circuit around the building, beginning at the east and moving counter-clockwise, ending once more in the east. He spoke in the Mikasuki language throughout the circuit, distributing sacred water from a container he had brought with him from the Everglades. When the circuit was completed, he explained in English that his intent had not been to bless the earth, because it is already sacred, but instead he had asked the Creator to bless those who would enter the building, that they might learn, and that their visits might lead to understanding.

On another occasion, Sonny Billie gave a talk to an enraptured group of children and adults, and toured the then-completed North Florida hall, commenting favorably on the trading scene

represented in that hall. Mr. Billie and his partner Pat Francescini, as well as several Seminole tribal members, later returned for the grand opening of the South Florida hall in October, 2002 (Figure 9). Native Americans demonstrated traditional crafts during opening week, including Jay McGirt, a member of the Seminole Nation of Oklahoma, who demonstrated the Creek/Seminole art of fingerweaving. A shoulder bag as well as the finger-woven sash that he made are now in the Florida Museum's collections (FLMNH cat. nos. 2003-67-1 and 2003-67-2; Figures 10a, 10b). Madelaine Tongkeamha (Figure 10c) demonstrated patchwork, Martha Jones demonstrated beadwork (Figure 10d), and Mary Billie demonstrated basket making (Figure 10e).

Epilogue

Preparing the Interactives

Film footage was used extensively in both interactive and passive presentations within the South Florida hall. For the Natural Habitats Study Center, a re-enactment was staged by filmmaker Leslie Gaines at Emerson Point, featuring Seminole people acting as Calusa natives (Figure 11). The actors included William Cypress, Daniel Tommie, Samuel Tommie, and Samuel's daughter Jerica Sanders. Among the topical touch-screen interactives in the Seminole/Miccosukee gallery are Samuel Tommie playing the flute, Mary Frances Johns making a basket, Madelaine Tongkeamha talking about the importance of cultural identity, Seminole Tribal Chairman James Billie speaking about the special roles of clans, and Jerica Sanders explaining Mikasuki language pronunciation.

South Florida native people posed for three of our mannequins in the South Florida hall. Sylvester Jimmie, Ronnie Jimmie's son, posed for the boy carrying the shark in the teaser opening gallery (Figure 12a), Ronnie Jimmie's daughter Frankie Billie posed for the dip-net girl, and Martha Jones posed for the elder making patchwork using a hand-cranked Singer sewing machine (Figure 12b).

[a]

[b]

[c]

Figure 10. *Native American crafts are demonstrated at the public opening of the South Florida hall, October, 2002. (a) Jay McGirt, a member of the Seminole Nation of Oklahoma, demonstrates finger weaving during public opening week of the South Florida hall. (b) Jay McGirt's finger-woven sash (FLMNH cat. no. 2003-67-2). (c) Madelaine Tongkeamha (left) discusses patchwork with a museum visitor. (d) Martha Jones makes a beaded bracelet. (e) Mary Billie makes a sweetgrass basket.*

[d]

[e]

144

Figure 11. *William Cypress (a, b), Daniel Tommie (c), and Samuel Tommie and Jerica Sanders (d, e) acted as Calusa people in the re-enactment filmed for the South Florida hall.*

Ms. Jones also made the patchwork outfit in medicine colors and the beadwork that her mannequin is wearing and instructed us on how to design the scene and on the making of patchwork in general. She also joined us at the museum to help us assemble the display. Marquardt and MacMahon spent considerable time with all participants at their homes and workplaces on the various South Florida reservations.

Other Interactions

Florida Museum interactions with tribal members have not been restricted to matters of cultural sensitivity, repatriation, and exhibit planning. To mention a few others:

- Tribal members and museum staff have visited the Florida Museum's FEC to view and study objects (Figure 13).

- Seminole tribal member Brian Zepeda served on the advisory board of the Florida Museum's Randell Research Center.

- Marquardt consulted with tribal member Willie Johns on education and public archaeology.

- During the exhibit planning, MacMahon and Marquardt visited with staff and consulted on collections at the Ah-Tah-Thi-Ki Seminole tribal museum on the Big Cypress reservation.

- Marquardt invited Ah-Tah-Thi-Ki Museum executive director Paul Backhouse, Museum director Kate Macuen, collections manager Tara Backhouse, and tribal member Willie

Figure 12. (a) Ronnie Jimmie (background) holds an artist's sketch of the proposed "shark boy" mannequin as his son, Sylvester, poses for photographs while holding a 20-pound bag of rice. (b) Martha Jones sits with the finished mannequin of a patchwork artist. She posed for the mannequin and also made the patchwork skirt, cape, and beads.

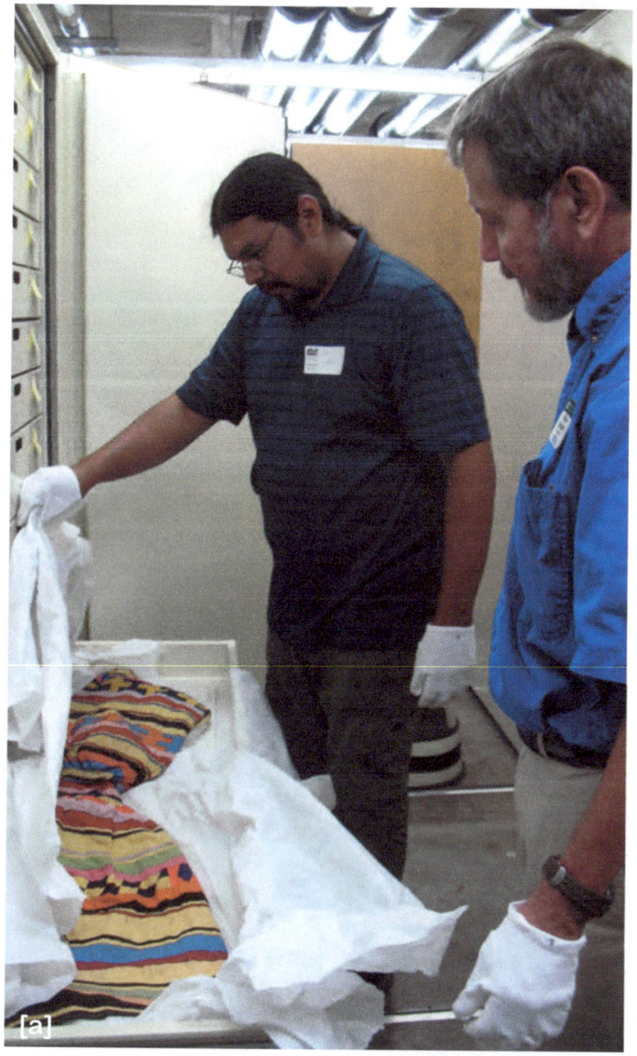

Figure 13. (a) Seminole tribal member and artisan Pedro Zepeda views long shirt with then-curator William Marquardt, 2013. (b) Then-curator William Marquardt discusses dolls with Seminole tribal member Rita Youngman. (c) Paul Backhouse and Kate Macuen of Ah-Tah-Thi-Ki Museum discuss bandolier bag designs in the Florida Ethnographic Collection, hosted by William Marquardt.

Johns to Gainesville to meet with him and Stacey Huber, Karen Walker, and Keith Reeves to examine the early nineteenth-century Mantrone-Cardinal long coat, then on loan to the Florida Museum, when it was not clear where the coat would be donated (Figure 14).

- Museum Studies graduate student Shawna Pies arranged for photographs by Eric Zamora of a selection of FEC objects, consulted with Ah-Tah-Thi-Ki Museum staff and tribal members, then for her thesis project created a Wiki web site that attracted numerous Native comments.

- Museum Studies graduate student Austin Bell consulted with Seminole tribal genealogist Geneva Shore on his M.A. thesis project, examined collections at Ah-Tah-Thi-Ki, and published an article in the *Ah-Tah-Thi-Ki Museum Quarterly*.

- Stacey Huber went to the Ah-Tah-Thi-Ki Museum to research her thesis exhibit,

Figure 14. *Stacey Huber (left) shows the Mantrone-Cardinal longcoat to Keith Reeves, Kate Macuen, Tara Backhouse, and Seminole tribal member Willie Johns. Mr. Reeves subsequently purchased the object and donated it to the Florida Museum (FLMNH cat. no. 2019-22-1).*

#Nativemade: Seminole and Miccosukee Patchwork, for her master's degree from the University of Nebraska-Lincoln. Huber formed relationships through social media (Instagram), with Vennessa Osceola (Seminole), Alley Cypress (Miccosukee), and Althea Frye (Miccosukee) to help create the exhibit. Huber also worked as a curatorial assistant in the FEC at the Florida Museum.

- Aaron Ellrich wrote a history of the Ah-Tah-Thi-Ki tribal museum for his M.A. thesis in Museum Studies, consulting with staff and Native Americans at the Big Cypress reservation. Ellrich also contributed a section on Seminole/Miccosukee basketry for the FEC web site and worked as a curatorial assistant at the Florida Museum.

- Museum Studies graduate student and curatorial assistant Katie Matthews authored a section on Seminole/Miccosukee dolls for the FEC web site.

- Marquardt and Walker attended the funeral of Billy L. Cypress and MacMahon attended the funeral of Mary Frances Johns.

- Florida Museum staff members Douglas Jones, Darcie MacMahon, Karen Walker, and William Marquardt attended the grand opening of the Ah-Tah-Thi-Ki Museum facility on Big Cypress reservation in August, 1997. Marquardt and Walker attended its twentieth anniversary celebration in 2017.

Epilogue

Collections Improvements

One of my top priorities after becoming curator of the South Florida collections in 1988 was to improve the conditions of the Florida Ethnographic Collection (FEC), composed mostly of objects made or used by Seminole/Miccosukee people. A conservation assessment led to the Museum's setting goals in 1991 for improving curation conditions throughout the institution. However, due to space limitations, all of the ethnographic collections, including those from South Florida, were moved to a former classroom where the collections were secure, but conditions were crowded.

In 2010, Museum administrators authorized funds to renovate the Special Collections Room (SCR) to provide 250 square feet of space for the FEC. This solution was an improvement but not ideal because the FEC was obliged to share space with several other collections. It did, however, allow us to bring Seminole/Miccosukee materials together into one space for the first time, ensure that all items were stabilized and protected in archival containers, create a database, and provide a place where tribal members, students, and other scholars could once again visit the collections. Upon my retirement in 2018, the FEC was well curated but still housed in a room with other collections. I hope my successors will continue to advocate for a dedicated space for the FEC so that tribal members and others can learn from them in a comfortable and appropriate setting.

Summary

Cordial and mutually beneficial relationships between the South Florida Archaeology and Ethnography program and Florida Native Americans have been ongoing for some 25 years. Similarly, former curator Jerald Milanich consulted often with Florida Native Americans while undertaking archaeological and historical research during 1982-2006.

As curatorial, collections, and exhibits personnel reach retirement age, new relationships will need to be forged with younger tribal members and with changing tribal museum personnel. These will be important as museums and Native American tribes commit to mutually respectful discourses concerning tribal patrimony and institutional responsibility. Such discourses have characterized interactions in the past, and there is no reason why they cannot be continued in the future.

This book holds tangible evidence that museum collections are bountiful sources of research and continued learning. Some professional anthropologists fail to appreciate this aspect of ethnographic collections, imagining that Seminole and Miccosukee objects are of value only for exhibition – art objects to be displayed to please the public. Certainly, many objects in the Florida Museum's collection and in the collections of other museums *are* beautiful and can entertain and inspire us. But they are more than they may first appear to be. They are touchstones – reference points – with stories to tell us if we only take them seriously and take the time to listen.

Acknowledgments. I thank Darcie MacMahon, Jerald Milanich, Karen Walker, and Brent Weisman for assistance with this summary.

Note

1. In 1988, the name of the institution was changed from Florida State Museum to Florida Museum of Natural History.

References

Marquardt, William H.
  1994 The Domain of the Calusa: Report of the Calusa/Southwest Florida Exhibit Planning Committee, June 30, 1994. 26 pp. On file, Anthropology Division, Florida Museum of Natural History.

Marquardt, William H. (editor)
  1995 Discussions with Native American Consultants Concerning the Planning of the Hall of South Florida People and Environments. Transcripts on file, Anthropology Division, Florida Museum of Natural History.

Milanich, Jerald T.
  2009 The Realities of Reburial. *Archaeology* 62(2):18, 56-61.

Milanich, Jerald T., and Nina J. Root
  2011 *Hidden Seminoles: Julian Dimock's Historic Florida Photographs.* University Press of Florida, Gainesville.

Weisman, Brent R.
  1989 *Like Beads on a String: A Cultural History of the Seminole Indians in North Peninsular Florida.* University of Alabama Press, Tuscaloosa.

Weisman, Brent R.
  2002 *Pioneer in Space and Time: John Mann Goggin and the Development of Florida Archaeology.* University Press of Florida, Gainesville.

Index